Darling Alicia

The Love Letters of
Alicia Kaner and Stephen Merrett

Edited by
Vernee Samuel

Matador
5 Weir Road
Kibworth Beauchamp
Leicester LE8 0LQ, UK
Tel: (+44) 116 279 2299
Email: books@troubador.co.uk
Web: www.troubador.co.uk/matador

ISBN 978 1848761 643

British Library Cataloguing in Publication Data.
A catalogue record for this book is available from the British Library.

Cover design by Janet McCallum: quilted wallhanging by Alicia Merrett

www.darlingalicia.co.uk

Typeset in 11.5pt Garamond by Troubador Publishing Ltd, Leicester, UK
Printed in the UK by TJ International, Padstow, Cornwall

Matador is an imprint of Troubador Publishing Ltd

For Gill, who makes connections.

Sir, more than kisses, letters mingle souls.
John Donne
to Sir Henry Wotton, 1597

Dear Steve,

Along with so many others, I loved the Afternoon Play of your letters and am delighted that a book is to be published.

My memories of our schooldays are still vivid and heartwarming, particularly the school plays and play-readings. Our progress through those years and forms was truly one of the happiest times of my life. I know "Darling Alicia" will be a great success, so full of love, truth and wit and I wish you and it every possible success!

Ever, Derek

INTRODUCTION

This book contains an edited selection of the 165 love letters written by Alicia Kaner and Stephen Merrett during 1966-67. Their long distance courtship could only be accomplished by letter as Alicia was in Argentina while Steve was thousands of miles away, initially working in India and then returning home to England. This introduction is intended to give the reader some background to the touching and highly charged love story contained in the letters.

Stephen Richard Merrett was born in Hackney, London, in 1939, into an extended, working class, East End family. Passing the eleven plus exam in 1950, he attended Leyton County High School for Boys where his best friend was Derek Jacobi. After two years in the Royal Air Force, he became the first person in his family to go to university, studying philosophy and economics at Bristol before taking a higher degree at Oxford University. In the autumn of 1964, Steve accepted an invitation to work as an economic researcher at the Di Tella Institute in Buenos Aires, a key centre for social science research in Argentina. Steve's research topic was the economics of education and, in particular, students' economic struggles to graduate from the University of Buenos Aires.

Alicia Noemí Kaner was born in Buenos Aires, Argentina, in 1942, into a close-knit, middle class Jewish family, originally from Eastern Europe. She went to school during the presidency of Juan Domingo Perón – whom she actually met. When Alicia was 16, her mother died of cancer and a year later her father married Perla, a widow with two grown-up sons. It was a happy marriage and Alicia and her younger sister Ester got on well with their stepmother and two stepbrothers. Alicia continued to live at home while studying sociology at the University of Buenos Aires. In 1965, in order to become more financially independent, she took up a position as a secretary in the Di Tella Institute.

On her first day at work, Alicia was sitting at her desk, when she noticed a handsome young man standing at the other end of the row of secretaries. Alicia bent towards Joan, the girl on her right, and asked: "*Who* is that man?" Joan replied that his name was Steve, he was an Englishman, and had been working as a research fellow for nearly a year.

Later the same day, Steve was standing on the second floor of the Institute when he saw a stunningly beautiful girl coming up the spiral staircase. He turned to his friend Donald McNab, who taught English to the researchers, and said "*Who* is that woman?" Don replied that her name was Alicia and that she had just started work at the Institute.

At the time, Steve was seeing an Argentine girl, Mariella, also a secretary at the Institute, and Alicia was engaged to be married to an engineering student. Steve soon realized how much he was attracted to Alicia, but he was due to leave Argentina within a couple of months, and fought off his desire to get closer to her. Alicia too was aware of how attractive she found Steve and how much she enjoyed their conversations about politics and ideas, but she was conscious of his relationship with Mariella and held back from getting closer to him.

In the winter of 1965, Steve returned alone to England, via Cuba, and became a researcher at the London School of Economics. He began a study of education and work in the Indian fertiliser industry and in January 1966 he flew to New Delhi, where he was to remain for the next year.

Alicia was particularly interested in Steve's trip to Cuba as she had used her left wing connections to advise him on how to travel there. In 1965, travel from Argentina to Cuba was officially illegal but Alicia knew that a few planes a week took off from Mexico and recommended this route to Steve. On his arrival back in England Steve wrote a letter about his adventures in Cuba, which Mariella read aloud to everyone in the office. Alicia was delighted to hear that the journey had been a success, and wrote a short reply, which she gave to Mariella to enclose in her next letter to Steve.

A short time afterwards, Alicia gave up her job at the Di Tella Institute and then broke off her engagement. She returned to studying full time with the aim of completing her sociology degree. She occasionally visited the Institute to use their well-stocked library and on one of her visits she heard that Steve's relationship with Mariella had ended, although they remained friends and still corresponded.

However, Steve and Alicia still had no way of writing directly to each other as they did not have each other's addresses. Eventually, Steve decided to enclose a note to Alicia within a longer letter to Mariella about his early impressions of India. But as by then Alicia had left Di Tella, Mariella placed the note quietly in her desk-drawer.

Some days later, Alicia popped in to use the library and was tipped off that Mariella had a letter for her. Alicia asked Mariella outright for the letter – and got it – together with Steve's address in Delhi. This serendipitous event was to change both their lives forever.

A short note about the letters

In 1966, letters took about three weeks to cross the globe. Quite early in their correspondence, Steve and Alicia agreed that they could not bear to wait for a reply before writing another letter. Thus, each might write two or three times to the other before receiving a reply. A further complication was that, every so often, letters were delivered out of sequence but were, quite naturally, answered as they arrived.

In compiling this book, we found that the smoothest narrative was achieved by arranging the letters in the sequence that they were written. In consequence, the reader will find that sometimes questions are answered out of order and, at other times, there is a long gap between a particular letter and the answer to its contents. If this causes the reader the occasional moment of confusion, rest assured that the vagaries of the postal service were far more provoking for Steve and Alicia all those years ago.

All Alicia's letters, whether written in English or in Spanish, have been left in her own style, to catch the flavour of the original correspondence.

Vernee Samuel

Buenos Aires
15 May 1966

Dear Steve,

Just a few lines to tell you that I have read your letter
to Mariella about Cuba, and it seems that you had a fascinating experience. How is your work in India going?
What's your research subject? Have you managed to teach
Indian women to use the contraceptive pill? Not an easy
task I expect! I am studying statistics at the moment, a
hard subject for me, and plan to continue with my
University studies. Thank you for your regards.

    Cordially,
      Alicia

India International Centre
40, Lodi Estate
New Delhi – 3
May 1966

Dear Alicia,

It was even more interesting actually being there. I am
thinking seriously of returning to the University of
Havana in 1968 if they will have me.

Not only is it impossible for me to teach Indian women
contraception, I seem unable to persuade them to run the
original risk! Their celibacy seems to be absolutely
complete – but then I haven't really tried.

I have now read Beattie's 'Other Cultures', am halfway through Frazer's 'Golden Bough' and Malinowski and Evans-Pritchard are lined up next.

Lots of luck with statistics, I began to enjoy it most when I actually used some of the techniques in my own research. Perhaps you'll find it the same?

Lots of love,
    Steve

———ᴡᴡ———

Chilecito, La Rioja
11 June 1966

Dear Steve,
    Here I am, in the province of La Rioja, which is a very beautiful place – I am part of a field trip researching rural-urban migration, together with other sociologists and psychologists, and other students (like myself) from the University of Buenos Aires – I presume you've heard from Mariella that I am not working at the Di Tella Institute any longer – I decided to have a go at finishing my University degree by the end of next year if at all possible – after that, perhaps I'll try to get a scholarship to Oxford, to study Social Anthropology with Evans-Pritchard. When I get back to Buenos Aires I'll write a longer letter.

Affectionately,
    Alicia

———ᴡᴡ———

New Delhi
5 July 1966

Dear Alicia,

How funny that you should send me a card at the very time I was trying to get hold of your address! You remember when I was in Buenos Aires, we discussed, just before I returned to England, my hypotheses on the "economic activity of the Argentine engineering student?" Well, the most interesting section of my work has now been published by the Bulletin of the Oxford University Institute of Economics and Statistics, and I wanted to send you a copy of the article. I will do so as soon as I receive the offprints.

I am very glad to hear that you are thinking of coming to England. It would give me great pleasure to see you again. Though if it's anthropological field-work that fascinates you then the Indian villages are ripe for it, and of course much has already been written on the caste system.

After finishing Beattie, and Fraser I am about to start Malinowski's "Argonauts of the Western Pacific", which I believe combines scholarship with a lust for life – how rare and how admirable.

I have just finished a long tour of India's nitrogenous fertiliser industry, and managed to visit the states of West Bengal, Bihar, Punjab, Maharashtra, Kerala and Madras all in the space of a couple of months. Very tiring, but fascinating. I have met very few Indians I have really liked and admired – they seem to be terribly dull, unpoliticized people. You know how I like talking politics!

What a pity I shall not see you for such a long time ($1\frac{1}{2}$ years if you come to Oxford in October 1967); it would be great fun to have a tête-á-têtc and hear your views on the recent revolution.

My warmest regards,
  Steve

—*/w*—

Buenos Aires
23 July 1966

Dear Steve,
  What a wonderful tour of India! Much more exotic than my trip to the Argentine provinces of Catamarca and La Rioja.
  It will be good to receive the reprint of your article about the engineering students of the University of Buenos Aires, and I'll be delighted to send you my comments. I'm afraid I'm not in touch with engineering students any more, as I have broken my engagement with that particular engineering student.
  In fact, this last month of March has been quite revolutionary in my life: I broke a marriage engagement, left my job at the Di Tella Institute (and therefore stopped earning money) and decided to get on with my studies, which I had almost abandoned eight months ago. A month later I began my teaching career at the University with an appointment as 'practical workshop assistant' in 'Introduction to Sociology'. And two months after that I began to work on a research project on rural-urban migrations, a really interesting subject and a very important one to understand some aspects of the economic life of Argentina. And as I told you,

after graduation I am hoping to get a scholarship to study Social Anthropology in England, USA or a European country. But it won't happen in 1967, because I won't be able to complete my degree until the end of 1967 or even March 1968.

And what are your plans for next year? Are you going to stay in India, go back to England or work in another country? Do you plan to come to Buenos Aires again?

I look forward to having news from you again soon.

Warmest regards,
    Alicia

—ᗡᐯᗡ—

British Hospital
New Delhi
29 August 1966

Dear Alicia,

I am writing to you from the British Hospital in New Delhi where I am under observation for acute appendicitis. The doctor will let me know the results this afternoon, but I feel pretty sure that it's a mild case of indigestion as a result of eating some rather weary prawns in a curry last night. If I do have appendicitis I'll write to let you know tomorrow, if not, I'll write a letter from the Himalayas which I anticipate visiting sometime in mid-September.

I was very glad to see that you have broken off your engagement, what a shame you didn't do so earlier whilst I was in Buenos Aires – I might still have been there today!

The project is going smoothly, if rather slowly, and in the next few weeks we expect to be writing the first draft of a monograph on the fertilizer industry. I have had to read a little chemical engineering in order to get the change of technology clear in my own mind and this was very fascinating. It's strange but intellectually I so often find the grass is greener on the other side of the hedge (do you know that English expression?). A propos, the other day I met M.N. Srinivas, India's foremost anthropologist, who is Professor of Sociology at the Delhi School of Economics. India's anthropology is still mainly physical, rather than cultural anthropology so the latter comes under Sociology which in India, with its 550,000 villages and subsistence agriculture makes good sense. He is a wonderful man and I have promised to go to the University soon and talk to him about the impact of industrialization on caste relationships and vice versa.

Do you know, Alicia, a straight fact? I have made a list of all the occupation titles in use in just the fertilizer industry. There are over 1,000! This is largely because they so often append to a title 'junior' or 'senior' or 'chief' or 'sub' etc. I counted and found that 60% of the titles had at least one word indicating status rather than function in it. To me this seems a direct result of the hierarchical nature of caste relationships. I would like to see a study showing whether it affects industrial relations – I'm sure it must do.

Please in your next letter tell me your views on the new political situation*, especially with reference to the University. I noted with pleasure that the Science Faculty

*In June 1966 there was a right-wing military coup in Argentina.

had been at the forefront of opposition. Is this correct and do you think the Jewish faculty members have played an important role? (The Doctor has just come in to say my temperature is rising which is not a good sign.) When are you coming to England?

Write soon, my fondest regards,
    Steve

—◈—

British Hospital
New Delhi
2 September 1966

Dear Alicia,

As you can see the doctor's worst intuitions proved correct. As the pains subsided in my stomach, my temperature rose and the Indian surgeon diagnosed acute appendicitis. That was about 2pm. Within an hour I had been scrubbed like a new-born babe, shaved, and laid out on the operating table. They said it took an intra-venal injection 50% greater than normal to put me to sleep and even that didn't work so they administered some gas and that did the trick. (I was very pleased about that – must be my great lust for life!). The operation, I believe, lasted about 20 minutes, and there were no complications although the appendix itself was very much inflamed.

Since then I have been recovering steadily. The first two nights they gave me pain-killing injections so I could sleep well, but tonight I feel so much better that I won't even take sleeping tablets. In three days' time they will remove the stitches and I'll probably leave hospital on Tuesday next.

Today I went for a walk round the garden for about 20 minutes, and felt pretty good. This afternoon the off-prints came from my article on the Argentine engineering student and I'll send you a copy next week when I'm out of hospital. It's a bit more complicated than I remembered, and I suppose the most 'professional' piece of writing I've produced. But the present work on India is far more interesting, because its scope is so much wider.

Sorry my writing is so bad, I'm a bit giddy. Why don't you come to England for a holiday next spring? (European-type).

Yours,
    Steve

———

Buenos Aires
15 September 1966

Dear Steve,

Your first letter arrived when I was in Mar del Plata, attending the 37th International Congress of Americanists; and the second one arrived today, before I had begun to write the answer for the first letter.

I am very sorry for your poor appendix, ripped from your body so violently. I hope you have recovered now, and are working again, or, even better, climbing the Himalayas. How had you felt, alone in a foreign country, with nobody of your family caring for you when you were ill?

You asked me to tell you my views on the new political situation, especially with reference to the University. That is a big subject and it may well take several letters, not just one. Briefly: things are very bad for students, and for the country too. The slogan of the new government is: put the principle of authority above all. Botet, the new Rector of the University said in an interview published in *Primera Plana*: "I am sorry if research work is interrupted, or if researchers abandon their work, or even if they leave the country; we do not care for particular research projects or particular researchers; nobody is irreplaceable; what we care for is the greatness of our country, and we will be greater only if everybody accepts and follows the principle of authority" (that is, military law). Doesn't it sound absurd? Everything is like this, we can hardly believe our ears. But the people must get used to this new state of things, or leave the country. I don't think a revolt could have any results here and now. But students continue fighting. Here in Buenos Aires they are rather divided and therefore weak, but in Córdoba they are really strong. There was a strike at the University of Córdoba which lasted almost two weeks; a student was shot by the police and died yesterday, and the Rector closed the University 'for an indefinite period of time'.

In the Science Faculty, opposition to the military regime has been greater because both students and professors were badly beaten on the day the University was 'intervened' (placed under military rule) in July. Some of them were badly hurt, and 200 people were sent to jail. Next day almost the whole body of Science professors presented their resignations. Most professors in the Philosophy and Literature Faculty did too. The government, through the new Rector, has been unable to re-open these two faculties. It is said that they will transfer Psychology to the Faculty of Medicine, and Sociology to the Faculty of Law – which sounds very bad.

Re-your question about the role played by Jewish Faculty members – I think it is not especially relevant. There are lots of Jews in the University, but I think they are the most 'assimilated' section of the Jewish community, so it can't be said that their religion made any difference. What I do think is that perhaps their condition of Jews may imply some special character traits or cultural tradition that might have some influence in their predisposition to fight and rebel.

As the mail takes about two weeks to get from India to Argentina and vice-versa, I suppose I will have to wait a month to get an answer to this letter. So I won't wait for your reply, instead I will write again in a few days with the latest news about the political situation, and other things that might interest you. Please do the same, if you feel like it.

I didn't know that English expression, 'to find the grass is greener on the other side of the hedge', but I can guess what it means.

May I ask you some personal questions? You don't have to answer them. Are you really a globetrotter? Why have you come to Argentina, and then go to India, and then go who knows where? Do you plan to return to England at any time to stay there, or just for a visit? Are you still in contact with Donald, Chacho and other Argentine people?

About my own future as a student in the University of Buenos Aires, I rather doubt that I will be able to finish my degree course as soon as I hoped. I am really 'en el aire', as we say in Spanish, i.e., not knowing what to do. I'll have to wait until the faculty re-opens, and see what happens then.

Congratulations on your new article on the Argentine engineering student, and I hope to receive the promised copy soon.

I would be delighted to go to England for next European Spring and have some tête-à-tête talks with you as you suggest, but it is not easy (oh, money, yours is the kingdom of this earth!), but I will think about it. Steve, why don't you come to Argentina instead for a little while? Hope you are completely recovered from your operation by now.

Fondly,
    Alicia

—⁓—

New Delhi
20 September 1966

Dear Alicia,

What a fascinating letter! I feel impelled to reply immediately.

You ask me, am I really a globetrotter? My first reaction is to say: My greatest interest in all the fields of economics is the economics of the low-income countries – development economics – and I'm convinced the only real way to understand growth processes is to live in a low-income country. So when I graduated from Oxford I took the first opportunity offered to me to work in such a country – Argentina. I left after only 14 months because I don't like porteños*. They are not Latin American at all but embittered Europeans. My dismay at the growing interest in the "rate of return approach" to the economics of education led me to look for the opportunity of working on its chief rival, "the manpower forecasting approach", and LSE offered me just such a chance in India. I shall not stay in India more than a year because once again I feel alienated. I cannot identify myself with the Indian people, and abhor Hinduism even more than that other great barbaric religion, Roman Catholicism. Therefore my work can give me pleasure only qua economist, qua professional and not as a social being. And this is not enough.

So my vague plans for the future are: to return to England in February, and carry on with work on this project in the LSE for about one year. After that to move on and my present inclinations are either some research fellowship on an aspect of Latin American economics (a very phoney 'materia' *(subject)*), or a job in Geneva with the International Labour Organisation, or a job with the government of Cuba. The last is the one that interests me most, and I shall begin negotiations with the Cuban embassy next spring.

My second reaction is "Yes, all that is true. However in the past few years this young man has been to almost every West European country – and certainly not for "professional" reasons. On graduation he takes the first opportunity to cross the Antipodes to the other side of the world.

Porteños are the people who live in Buenos Aires, which has a large port area.

Stays a little more than a year then flies to the Indian sub-continent, which again he is itching to leave. These are merely symptoms of a pathological desire to escape from himself, which he hides from himself by the rationalization (a rather subtle one admittedly, but he has a devious mind) of "professional interest." The desire to "identify" with a people provides confirmation of this hypothesis; it is a form of self-immolation. However, since it is always <u>he</u> who disembarks from ship or plane, whether in Argentina, or India or in the future Cuba, he is condemned to lifelong disappointment since no man can escape himself."

There, I have laid my heart bare. Polonius said:

"'Tis true 'tis pity,
And pity 'tis, 'tis true."

Since we are asking searching questions, I ask: "Why are you writing to me?"

I still have not despaired of seeing you in England next April. I'll try to find out if there is a cheaper way than those horribly expensive VC-10's of British United Airways. The local Argentine embassy might know. You also asked if I still write to my Argentine friends. The answer is I write only to you and to Oscar Braun*, who is in Oxford. Donald and Chacho both owe me letters, and Mariella and I have stopped writing to each other.

I have grown a beard, started during my stay in hospital, and recently had a really handsome suit, styled in

---

* Steve first met Oscar Braun in Buenos Aires, having learnt that he had been accepted as a post-graduate at Steve's Oxford University college. Steve and Oscar soon became best friends.

the Indian fashion with high button-up collar, made for myself in grey raw silk from Benares.

I promise you I'll buy you a sari if you visit me next year. How's that for bribery and corruption?

Yours,
    Steve

PS. Please send me a photo.

———

Buenos Aires
30 September 1966

Dear Steve,

I received the copy of your article on Argentine engineering students while I was struck down with a bad case of laryngitis – I spent a week in bed. I read the article straightaway and liked it a lot. I had already read some of it in draft at the Di Tella Institute, but it really seems much more 'professional' so neatly in print. And today I received your letter of September 22nd, in reply to mine.

I liked your response to my questions. It's set out exactly in the tone I was expecting – and the one I prefer. I was asking about your 'globetrotter soul' precisely because (you once told me) that even before graduating and starting to work outside England, you had made a trip around Europe, with a tent and a rucksack – is that right? Did you go by yourself or with friends?

I fully agree that to study anything related to man as a social being, one of the best methods is what we anthropologists call 'participatory observation', that's to say to live with, and share the life experiences of the people studied. It seems that it is the same in economics, or can be in some cases. Although it seems to be a magnificent method, I personally am a bit reticent to put it into practice – maybe I'm a bit too shy for that kind of intense interaction. But one can get over it I suppose.

The state of the University in Argentina is really bad – and in my Faculty, appalling. It seems that next term there will be no courses at all run in either Sociology or Psychology, because almost all the teaching staff have resigned. So it is impossible for me to get on with my studies for the time being. To make up for the absence of University life, and not to give up studying, I get together regularly with a group of friends, and a Faculty teaching assistant, in order to continue studying on our own. One of the main themes we'll look at will be the Industrial Revolution in England. If you have a good bibliography on the agricultural revolution that preceded the industrial one, I'd be really pleased if you could send it to me.

The current regime in the Faculties is really militaristic. To be allowed to enter the Faculty of Philosophy and Letters you have to hand in your University card at the entrance, and collect it when you leave. You can enter the building only to go to the library or to sort out any admin in the Students' Office. You're not allowed to talk while you are queuing. You can't stand in the hall doing nothing in particular, you can't form groups of more than three persons, you can't walk up to classrooms on the next floor because the stairs are obstructed by furniture. The Students' Centre was broken into, and the office where they sell the publications we need for our studies is closed.

An anecdote: a girl is standing in the hall of the Faculty, doing nothing special. A policeman comes up to here and says: 'Miss, what are you doing?' 'Thinking' says the girl. His reply: 'Just listen, move along and don't challenge me or I'll take you to the police station.'

What do you think of that? What a way to study – at one's ease, eh?

At the moment my parents are in London. They will return in three or four days' time, after travelling through various European countries, including the Soviet Union and Czechoslovakia. We'll see what they have to say after three months sightseeing. They are the kind of tourists that go into everything in depth. I asked them to look at England with special care, and report back in detail. I've been to Europe once (but only to Israel to visit my stepbrother who lives there, and to France and Italy) in January-March 1964. I suppose that a cheaper way of travelling than by VC-10 is by boat; but the cost of living has to be taken into account as well. Perhaps I could get a scholarship to study in London, it could be Sociology, or to follow a language course to improve my English, which leaves much to be desired. As well as my 18 completed Faculty subject courses, I have a 'Certificate of Proficiency in English of the University of Cambridge' – is that of any use?

Now's the time to answer your question: why am I writing to you? Reply No. 1: because I like getting letters from people in other countries, so they can tell me how life is in places quite different from my own country, and to exchange views. Reply No. 2: uy! That's much more difficult. When you were here, last year, you seemed to me what in the Buenos Aires slang they call 'un tipo muy macanudo', 'a really great guy', and in some of the brief chats we had, I had the impression that we could communicate well with each other, have a good 'rapport', because in a number of things our interests and opinions coincide. I could not prove this fully because suddenly you had gone, and it was left in the air. Reply No. 3: I've known for some time that you and Mariella are not writing to each other any more; perhaps that's had some influence.

I'm sending you a photo, as you requested; it's a little old (my hair is longer now) but it's the only print I have at the moment. I'll send you a better one when I can. Do send me a photo of you with your beard, to compare your old face with the new one.

Now it's my turn to ask: why are you writing to me? Why are you interested in me visiting you in England? Even bribing me with a sari! Well, I'd love to have one, but not as a bribe, only as a present. Invitations apart, bribery and corruption – nice! But not with saris, such trivial and mundane things! Let's talk about intellectual matters and psychoanalysis.

How is your ex-appendix? As you make no reference to it, I suppose you've forgotten all about it.

You did not respond to my suggestion that you make a short trip to Argentina. Don't you think that's a good idea? And it's easier, isn't it, for a globetrotter to travel than for a penniless student? If I was still working as a secretary, money matters may not be so complicated. I hope I haven't bored you with such a long letter. I'll expect your bearded photo with great interest.

Affectionately,
Alicia

—◊◊—

Almora
The Lower Himalayas
30 September 1966

Dear Alicia,

I spoke with the Lama Govinda at 4.45pm. I remember the time distinctly, for on my way to his small house I passed two notices. One said "Visitors received strictly between 4pm and sunset." The second said: "Visitors are requested not to harm the inmates." I felt that I had arrived in Pooh-land. [Winnie the Pooh is a small bear, the protagonist in a series of small books by A.A.Milne. His forest land is studded with quaint inconsequential notices.] I rapped on the window of his bungalow, and after some murmuring a woman with a striking, gypsy-like face appeared at the pane and asked me to sit outside and wait for a short while. Sitting down in a deck-chair I noticed another facing me as if set out for a tête-à-tête. The Lama is a strange man, I had heard, living as he does six thousand feet up in the Himalayas with Nanda Devi and the invisible frontiers of China clearly to be seen on a day without mist and haze. Perhaps he knew I was coming and accordingly had set out the chairs. But I had decided to do so only two hours previously...

But then so many of the local population are uncanny. The first I met was Kaku, who has a long, bony face and a thin goatee, large dark eyes and a prominent fleshy nose. He lives with Zeet, a Dutch woman who three years ago came up here with her husband, the Cultural Attaché to India of Her Royal Majesty's Government of Holland, and had thereafter returned only once to Delhi; sufficient time for her to divorce her husband and kiss her children good-bye. We discussed Chaudhuri's "Continent of Circe," the seasons and the Pindari Glacier, ate Indian toffee and drank South Indian coffee. (Delicious!) I seem to remember that she always said "we" and he always "I."

Three golden eagles circled in the valley far below the house of the Lama Govinda and I could see with what care the valley-sides had been terraced for rice and other food-grains. Now they glowed green with the ripening crop. The lady re-appeared and invited me inside. (So much for the chairs!)

The Lama Govinda must be sixty or seventy years old, with a white and wispy beard very much like that of Ho Chi Minh. His eyes sparkle blue and he is dressed in a full length red robe and after greeting me, hands placed flat together on his chest, with the word "namaste" he sits down cross-legged on a fine carpet and leans back against a cushion. The audience lasted over an hour and we flitted like butterflies from subject to subject, as new acquaintances tend to do; from "Oh! What a Lovely War," to South Vietnam, to Teilhard de Chardin and finally to an account of his first and most powerful religious experience. He is a mystic. I believe his books are widely known, in fact he described to me in some bewilderment a review of his latest work by our infamous Malcolm Muggeridge. I drank orange squash and ate cold, roasted chestnuts from his estate.

Before sunset I said I had to return to Almora. He and his wife, who is a Parsee from Bombay and went to a finishing school at Harrow-on-the-Hill, asked me to visit them again when I return from my trek to the Pindari Glacier. As I set out for the distant town dark storm-clouds "like a scab on the horizon" rolled down the valley.

Purple globes of light pulsated on all sides, and the thunder crackled continually. The first perfidious rain-drops were light, but my journey lasted almost two hours and the last half-hour was in pitch darkness with only the lightning to guide me. The rain streamed down, the lightning flashed, the thunder roared all about me and it seemed to be the end of the world. Now I strip the clothes from my body in my dry and silent room and know I was not dreaming for here I find – a pocketful of wet chestnuts.

Yours,
    Steve

—◦◦◦—

New Delhi
13 October 1966

Dear Alicia,

This morning I received your letter, and will reply to it at length very soon, but before I do let me give you some news and describe my trip after leaving Almora.

When I was at the Centro de Investigaciones Económicas I wrote a longish paper entitled "Student Finance in Higher Education," which had a high political content. Two journals turned it down – the editors of both are known reactionaries. Now it has been accepted by the "Economic Journal," which is, I suppose, the major journal of economics in the world. I was enormously pleased – what a pity you're not here to celebrate with me.

For these last six days I have been walking in what must

be the loveliest hill country in the world, a natural paradise. I am in the Lower Himalayas, in the very North of the State of Uttar Pradesh, Kumaon district, the unique claim to fame of which is its man-eating tigers. During the last six days I and my Head Guide-cum-Chief Cook-cum Leading Coolie, Lackshman Singh, have walked the 35 miles from Kapkot, the last point on the motor road running from Almora hill station, to the Pindari Glacier, and back again, in the course of which we ascended from 3,500 feet at Kapkot to 13,000 feet at the Pindari Glacier. The Glacier lies, it is said, about 10 miles from the Chinese border. The names of the villages through which we passed are pretty: Kapkot, Loharket, Dhakuri, Dwali, Khati and Phurkia.

Here man forms part of the landscape without dominating it. The air is clear and colours seem to sparkle. At night the stars glitter with an incredible intensity as if Sirius and Venus had multiplied a thousand times and one senses with a physical impact how the universe dwarfs our planet, inducing in me nostalgia, sadness, and terror like a clenched fist. It is a land for mystics. I have seen golden eagles methodically sweeping the air in arcs or hopping in an ungainly fashion from rock to rock at the side of a river. A marten slipping quickly into the bamboo. A score of monkeys, a circus of monkeys, trapezing through the trees as I startle them, then lining up on the crest of a hill to inspect the intruder, their thick white fur encircling black, snub-nosed faces like a Byzantine halo. Buffalo, sheep, goats and cattle thread their way along the mountain tracks tended by a scruffy nine-year old boy in thread-bare sacking. A gorgeous bird with deep blue wings and body, russet-breasted, with a creamy white capped head and a tail of flashing scarlet, flits in a series of short loops across the river, finally shooting up to catch from the air a butterfly. A golden-breasted bird flutters away trailing its long, blue-barred tail and uttering cries of alarm to all who care to listen. Quails pigeon-toe across the narrow track in single file.

Fingers of light are interlocked with the tall firs as the sun's rays stream down the hill. A torrent falls sheer over black rock into the snow-white, snow-fed, ice-cold stream. Paddy glows with an intense green, finally ripe, and a woman scythes her way through the fine crop. Wild strawberries can be found and blackberries too. Nanda Kote, 23,000 feet high gleams at the head of the valley. A fern trembles in the rising wind, a cloud drifts over the sun, hail patters through the leaves and the glorious riot of colour grows sombre. It is autumn and fresh snowfalls on the near peaks augur winter.

"Affectionately" and more than affectionately,
Yours,
    Steve

—◦◦◦—

Buenos Aires
16 October 1966

Dear Steve,
The Faculty of Social Sciences reopened two days ago, and I began to follow courses on three subjects: Argentine Sociology, Industrial Sociology, and Elements of Methodology and Social Research Techniques. This opening is better than nothing, now at least we can keep

in contact with other fellow students. But I do not expect to learn much in an Argentine University now, I will only try to sit as many examinations as I will be able to, and try to get my degree – although we can't actually say if we will still have a degree in Sociology next year.

My parents arrived from Europe about two weeks ago. They flew directly from London to Buenos Aires. In spite of their pleading of having very little money for the voyage, they brought some very nice English cashmere jumpers for my sister and me. They also brought me some beautiful tourist guides to Prague and London. One of the prettiest is about Oxford. What a nice place! Which college did you study in?

I was also trying to understand a map of the centre of London. It's almost impossible! It seems to be a very complicated city. It is frustrating, because I can find my way round perfectly well in Rome and Paris (with a map in my hand, of course), but London is much worse. Of course I have already been in Rome and Paris, but not in London. My parents were staying in a hotel near Marble Arch. Where do you live in London? (when you are there for short periods, between journeys). It is doubly frustrating because I am known as 'the girl with the map' in my circles, or 'the girl who never loses herself in an unknown district'. This is because I can always find an address and how to get there; this was a very useful skill in my research project when I had to do some surveys in an area of the city I hadn't been to before.

So – and what do you feel about contemporary England? Strange phenomena seem to be taking place there now, with beatniks on the loose – or maybe they are just normal boys and girls who dress and act in an absolutely different way than their classic predecessors. My father liked London very much – its architecture and its majesty, but my stepmother on the other hand says that it is a grey city with serious people, not kind, always raining. They visited a couple of friends of my stepbrother who live there and they told her that it is impossible to make friends with English people; they are very stiff, they are not affection-ate, not like we Latins are. They have only made friends with foreigners like themselves, who have scholarships to study in the same place. And this is not the first time I am told that foreign students in England, no matter how nice people they might be, are absolutely unable to establish a real friendship with English people. Do you think it is true? If it is really so, why does it happen?

As you can imagine, lots of students (most of them graduates) are now leaving Argentina to find better posi-tions in other countries. Most of the people of the Faculty of Sciences are going to work in Chile, Peru, Venezuela, U.S.A., etc. Lots of professors have left too. My step-brother will be getting married at the end of the year and plans to leave for the USA next May. He got a Guggenheim scholarship and will go to Cincinnati first, and then to Houston, Texas, for three years, to study and work in the field of Neurology and Neurosurgery. Yesterday a couple of friends of mine (both of them geol-ogists) left for Paris to study one year there.

At this point I realize that you may feel confused about my complicated family. I'll explain: In the beginning there was my mother, my father, my sister Ester, who is five years younger than me, and myself. My mother died seven years ago, and my father married again, to a widow that had two sons from a previous marriage. The elder, Carlos, who is now 30, is married and has two little wonderful girls, he is a physician and lives in Jerusalem. Then comes Horacio, who is 26 (two years older than me), who is also a physician and is the one going to USA next year. I hope it is clear now. And what about your family? Please tell me, I'd like to know.

Have you listened to the latest Beatles' number, 'Yellow Submarine'? I love it. Have you got a chance of going to dancing parties in India? I hope you do, otherwise it would be very boring, to be always studying or working – or travelling. Do you like Latin people? What is the difference you find between 'porteños' and other Latin American people – like people of the provinces of Argentina, or the Cubans?

Things are going badly in Uruguay too – have you heard about it? And there are also students' strikes in Brazil. Here, the students' strike in Córdoba continues. The Faculty of Architecture has been closed for the rest of the year, many professors have been expelled from the University, and five women from a Commission of University Students' Mothers have been put in jail. What do you think of this?

I know my English is not that good at the moment, through lack of practice, so please do point out any glaring errors.*

Hope you received my last letter with the photo.

Yours truly,
Alicia

*Alicia's first eight letters were written in English, the rest have been translated from the original Spanish.

New Delhi
18 October 1966

Dear Alicia,

What a lot of questions you've asked me. I'll try to deal with them one by one. Why don't I write about my appendix? Because all I have to remind me of the operation is a thin red line on my navel, no pain, no complications, no interest!

With respect to publications on the British Agricultural Revolution, all I can do is suggest you look up any bibliographical references in Clapham's economic history of the UK. Will I come to Argentina? Not in the foreseeable future, it's too European, and the people I met were, in general, too embittered and harsh for me to wish to work there again. Do I have a photo of me in a beard? Yes, but unfortunately it's on an 'Agfa' film, which cannot be developed in India, so we'll have to wait till next Spring and I'll give you a nice, technicolour copy. I like the photo you have sent me very much; it's almost exactly as I remember you, save that I had forgotten what sensual lips you have. Does this reveal a passionate nature masked by your usual diffidence?

Why am I writing to you and why do I want you to come to England? No rationalizations here. First, and for me very very important I find you sexually attractive. Second, I liked very much to talk to you about anything in the very few occasions that we chatted together in Buenos Aires and would have tried to come closer to you but for the fact that I was to stay so little time and it would have wounded Mariella deeply. Third, I enjoy reading your runaway typewriter very much, and would like to see if the intimacy we maintain on paper could be matched when we look into each other's eyes. If I can fall in love with the "paper Alicia"...

So let me make some definite proposals. First, that next spring – April – you sail to England in the cheapest passage you can find (without having to share your bed with chickens or meat carcasses) – some kind of cargo boat. I'll pay half your return fare. It may be that we shall grow so fond of each other in grimy old London that we'll not want to buy the return ticket. That we'll just have to find out together.

Second, the problem of expenses whilst you are in England. There seem to be two alternatives, a scholarship or work. I have already written off to the LSE to get the names of the professors in charge of the Department of Anthropology and the man who deals with student scholarships. (Am I right in thinking that it is Social Anthropology that you wish to study?) I'll write to them when I get their addresses and find out what can be done.

The possibility of you getting employment I suggest we try if these other attempts fail. A scholarship of about £12 per week should be enough to live on. If all goes well we can travel to the Continent next summer together. Personally, I would like to spend a few weeks in one of the East European countries.

I have no more news so I'll stop here. Are you a girl who finds it easy to make important decisions? I should think not – in that we are probably very similar. Still, I have made mine.

One last question: what is your date of birth?

Yours,
    Steve

—◁w▷—

Buenos Aires
20 October 1966

Dear Steve,

I was deeply shocked by the two letters I received this morning. I thought all day long about the Lama Govinda and your trip through the Lower Himalayas. I wish I could have been there, too! Have you been to see him again? Your description of the region is so vivid that I can feel the mystical spirit that presides it...and that seems to have permeated you too. How can you write so well as to transmit the very soul of things? I envy you for having such an ability.

Now, hurrah! for the publication of your paper in the 'Economic Journal' and what it implies. I celebrate the event with you from here, and send you a congratulatory kiss.

Winnie the Pooh sounds a familiar story – I remember a book I used to read when I was a child (and afterwards too), called 'El osito Pu'. I can't remember the name of the author, and I can't find my copy. Perhaps they have something in common?

I told you a while ago that I attended the 37th Congress of Americanists, held in Mar del Plata in the first week of September, but I didn't speak to you about my experiences there. It was a different world to what I'm used to – the atmosphere of an international meeting, for one not accustomed to travel continually (as you are) is something completely new. I met different people, with different ideas and different ways of doing things. I met people who had been among the Indians of Brazil, or among the semi-civilized natives of Peru, Mexico, or in Africa. I learnt about the way of life in the favelas – the shanty towns of Rio de Janeiro, about the ancient semi-pagan and semi-Christian myths in the forests of Peru, about the relations between language and culture, and much more.

I will always remember a talk we had with John Murra, a Rumanian-born anthropologist, who studied in the USA but spent most of his fieldwork time in Peru. He is a man of about 50 years old, with grey hair that reminds me of the typical mane of an orchestra director – especially when he shakes his head while speaking. The main subject discussed by the group was 'acculturation'. He said something very brief – but it was an absolutely different approach to all the others. He asked why it seemed necessary to 'acculturate' the Indians to our Occidental-Christian Society – if we really think it is not a very good one, with its wars and neuroses and economic instability and so on and so forth. Why don't we respect their ancient cultures and help them to maintain and protect them, instead of trying to make them abandon their old culture and acquire a new one? It is a question of model of identification – western culture, in spite of its apparent benefits, offers very few positive things to Indians. They lose a world in which they felt secure, and acquire none to replace it, because western society always marginalises them. So they have no reference background to lean on – and fall into different forms of rebellion or escape; besides, they have real economic problems to survive.

My brother is getting married on November 25 – and my house is in upheaval. His bride is a delicious girl, English teacher and translator, especially on psychological subjects. She spent a year in USA, studying, and also travelled through Europe. I told you they are going to Cincinnati next year with a scholarship. First they will be touring Europe for a month. My parents are organising a big party, for a hundred people. My stepbrother and his intended have met only four months ago – before that my brother had been a Don Juan who swore that he would never marry in his life. The family can hardly believe it.

Please tell me more about your talk with the Lama Govinda, and especially about what he told you about his religious experiences. Do you know something? One of my fantasies, when I was a little girl, was to meet a real living Lama. My father used to tell me stories every night, about a little girl that travelled the world with her dog. One of my favourite stories was one about her trip to Tibet, where she visited the Lamas in Lhasa.

I expect your reply to my last two letters.
Fondly yours,
    Alicia

New Delhi
25 October 1966

Dear Alicia,

I was deeply shocked to hear of the death of your great-aunt's poodle. I was even more deeply shocked to hear you were deeply shocked by my two letters from the Himalayas, and pray to the Lord that this shocking reaction will not recur. You remember you asked me to comment on your English? Well, "deeply shocked" means, sort of horrified, wounded and saddened. I never imagined my letters were so powerful! Another one is to call someone "delicious." When I say "Alicia is an absolutely delicious little piece" this is an accurate, but rather eccentric, risqué compliment. You meant to say "delightful." Delicious refers to the pleasurable sensation of eating a chocolate éclair, Kaiserschmarren or a banana split.

I was indeed getting rather nonplussed about the composition of your family. I would like to describe mine to you, but it's so fantastically complicated, I have decided to draw a family tree:

Dad   Mum
      Steve

An interesting fact is that I, my father, my paternal grandfather and my paternal great-grandfather (and perhaps beyond this) are all called Stephen Richard Merrett. So to maintain the tradition I have to call my first son by the same name. Do you approve?

Another interesting quasi-fact is that my paternal grandmother is a Romany – a Central European gypsy.

This is supposed to account for my emaciated features, a certain facility with language, and my devout worship of the Goddess Aphrodite.

Do I go to parties and dances here? No, I'm afraid not. But that doesn't make life dull. Any foreigner living in India who finds life dull would have to be extraordinarily insensitive or a diplomat. A propos, do you <u>promise</u> to teach me the tango when you come to London? I still feel guilty that I never learnt in Buenos Aires, but no-one could teach me, and I didn't find any booklets on the subject.

Where do I live in London? My parents live in Leytonstone on the fringes of the infamous "East End" which has got some great pubs, Chinese restaurants and the worst slums in town. I am looking forward to flat-hunting when I get back. I'd like to get a place on the edge of one of our beautiful parks, perhaps in Richmond or Hampstead.

At Oxford, I was a student of Nuffield College, which is restricted to post-graduates in the Social Sciences. It is really very ugly and has an ill-proportioned tower like a witch's hat, black as pitch. (Have you read "The Tin Drum" by Günter Grass. It's absolutely magnificent). But if one knows Oxford very well it is really gloriously pretty, especially in the interior of colleges like Merton, Magdalene and St. John's, and down by the river Cherwell (pronounced Charwell) and the Isis (really the Thames). We'll go there for a few days next April and I'll have you meet Oscar and Sonia Braun. Oscar is at Nuffield himself. Do you or your family know him? The full surname is Braun-Menendez – they seem mostly to be fat capitalists. Oscar is a Socialist.

Are the English unfriendly? I suppose they are when one meets them initially. I don't know, it's difficult to say never having experienced them as foreigners. But one great quality they have, relative to other peoples I know such as porteños and middle-class Indians, is an enthusiasm for theatre, politics and un-material things. It is also a very free country, which is nice.

Before I forget Alicia, will you give me a brief description of your academic experience so that when I write to LSE (I now have the addresses of the man who deals with scholarships and the Professor of Anthropology) I can give them your background. Do you want to study Sociology or Anthropology?

In about a week's time I should receive your reply to my 'definite proposals' about your coming to England. I have felt, I don't know why, a bit down in the mouth just lately, and I would have liked to have you here so we could have gone dancing or for a drive on my scooter into the countryside.

Yours,
    Steve

—⁓—

Buenos Aires
27 October 1966

Dear Steve,

I don't know if I will be able to put in words what I felt after reading your letter [18 Oct] one hour ago. It was seeing, written in a piece of paper, all the things I have been thinking about during the last weeks. I began to shake – and I still do now, after reading your letter for the fourth or fifth time. I feel like touching heaven – a dream came true.

What my feelings are – what I think about your proposals – that needs no explanations, because I feel the same as you do. Reading your letter was almost like reading my own thoughts. But you are right in thinking it is not easy for me to make important decisions; I must confess that I'm afraid – afraid of waking up one day and see that everything was a dream – and have other fears too. I'll find out shortly which are my concrete possibilities of travelling in April – money, ships, scholarships, work, and so on – and will give you a definite answer. Anyhow, I think you know that I <u>do</u> want to go and see you again and talk to you and be near you and see if you are still the same young man I liked so much last year, plus the wonders I have felt through your letters.

Answering your questions: First, I was born on February 5, 1942. And you? Second: leaving aside my lips – I do have a passionate nature, I think.

Last week, while rummaging in a bookshop, I found two Walt Disney versions of Winnie-the-Pooh. It is exactly the same 'Osito Pu' I used to read! I am happy to find that my old friend is loved by so many English children.

Last Saturday I saw one of the best films I have ever seen: 'A man and a woman', directed by Claude Lelouch, with Anouk Aimée and Jean-Louis Trintignant. If you have the chance to see it, do so. The film was awarded first prize at the Cannes Festival – but that is not as important as the images in the film, the colours, the gestures, the cinematographic language that transmit sensations and feelings without words – they are wonderful. The story is a simple one, but with psychological depth. I think it is the first time I see in the screen an erotic situation in which something is not going well, and they make you feel it and understand it.

I am fond of sounds and music as much as I am of images. Yesterday I was recording in my small tape-recorder some of Joan Baez's songs (volume 5 – not available in Argentina – a friend got it from USA and lent it to me for a few days). It has such sweet songs as the Brazilian 'O Cangaceiro', the old ballads 'The unquiet grave' and 'The death of Queen Jane', the modern ballad 'I still miss someone', and a song from Richard Dyer-Bennet to a poem of Lord Byron: 'So we'll go no more a'roving'. It says, more or less:

'For the night was made for loving,
and the day returns too soon,
still we'll go no more a-roving
by the light of the moon'.

I am very sorry to have been unable to record the songs Donald and you sang at the party we had at home last year, a week before your departure. Do you remember how much I liked one of them? I asked you to sing it again for me.

As today I was out all day, I found your letter when returning very late at night – and now it is about 3.30 am, near dawn! But I felt compelled to answer you immediately. You know something? All day long I felt I must return home – but as I was too busy to do so, I phoned two or three times and asked if there were any news for me. The answer was always 'No news', but they said nothing about your letter! But when I arrived back I was almost sure that I should find a letter – and I did! And what a letter!

Dear Steve, I would very much like you to give me more details about your work in India, and about your travels – Europe, Cuba, and so on. After reading your descriptions of what you have seen at the Lower Himalayas, now I understand why you like travelling so much.

Write to me soon. I'll do the same.
Lots of love.
    Alicia

PS. Don't you need an expert, nice-looking secretary and research assistant for your year's work in London? I can fulfil the duties pretty well.

I thought of the cheapest way of travelling across the ocean. I'll follow Winnie-the-Pooh's method of getting the honey from the top of the tree, and I'll use a balloon – red or blue – to go from here to the place you are.

—⁓—

Agra
29 October 1966

Dear Alicia,

This morning at 7 am. I set off from New Delhi for Agra which is 124 miles due South. My companion is Roger Catchpole, a young Englishman, graduate of Cambridge, and friend of Paul Matthews, as I may have mentioned before, who is working with me on this manpower-planning project. Roger recently came down from Pokhra in Nepal where he is in charge of a resettlement camp for Tibetan refugees. He's very enthusiastic about his work and likes nothing better than to talk about winter wheat, their new Israeli stud goat, Tibetan burial customs etc. Neither of us had seen Agra so we've come down together.

The Emperor Shahjahan, son of Jahangir, grandson of Akbar the Great, had many wives one of whom, so it is told, he loved most dearly. She was called Arjuman Banu, who later in life because of his great love for her and her beauty, became known as Mumtaz Mahal Mumtazul-Zamani, the Exalted of the Palace, Wonder of the Age. They were married in 1612, and when she died eighteen years later she had borne him fourteen children. After her death he vowed to build her the most magnificent tomb the world had ever seen, and this is known as – the Taj Mahal.

I saw it this afternoon. It is situated on the bank of the River Yamuna which flows from Delhi and is one of the three sacred rivers which meet at Allahabad. It is made of white marble, into which is carved the entire scriptures of the Koran. Shahjahan, of course, was Muslim. The walls have a bas-relief of orchids and roses, and the two tombs themselves are inlaid with great delicacy by lapis lazuli, black marble, cornelian, jade, bloodstone and agate in the form of small flowers. One's voice echoes and re-echoes at the centre of the mausoleum, and I began to wonder how magnificently one of the great classical Indian singers could moan a lament here. Through the marble lattice work one can see the great walled Red Fort built by Akbar.

From a distance, even with a thick stream of Indian and foreign tourists, the Taj Mahal is just breathtakingly beautiful, shimmering white, symmetric against the cloudless blue sky. Tonight I shall see it by the light of the full moon. What a pity you're not here to share the experience.

1 November 1966

This morning I arrived back in Delhi and can continue my letter. The Taj in the full moon floats like an ice palace, a fantastic ship, a magic mosque. However, in India, no sensation is unalloyed, for I watched it with about 45,000 other people. Pickpockets were there, and loutish college students some of whom plied my friend Roger with obscene questions, and others who jeered and catcalled at the two of us as we walked past them. I met a Bulgarian friend the following day, a big-boned girl of great poise and enthusiasm who said her evening had been completely spoiled as she was constantly molested. All of the European and American friends I meet are convinced that xenophobia has increased within the past year. I was myself stoned, but not hurt, by a gang of young men a few weeks ago in the lovely park adjoining my hotel.

Anyway, to resume the thread of my journey, on Sunday night I travelled to the capital of Rajasthan – Jaipur. My impressions are very disjointed: of an old beggar whose hair was yellow and silver, his skin coal-black with a crust of dirt curled up sleeping, or dead, completely naked save for a tattered shirt, lying on the pavement of one of the main streets; of a haggard woman in her brilliant red and yellow Rajasthani skirt suckling her filthy child on a bus in a small village near the palace of the Maharaja of Jaipur, the child so ill-fed that the skin on its buttocks and arms lay in loose, arid folds like parchment; of children shitting into the open water-conduits of the backstreets of Jaipur, of a man urinating in the gutter outside the Hawa Mahal – the Palace of Winds; of the stench of human urine and pigs rooting for human faeces;

of the temple of Kali Devi, with her eighteen arms riding the night like a Valkyrie, the skulls of the dead make up her necklace; of the Amber Palace, Tiger Fort, Moghul paintings, ancient armour, sun warming the pink-plastered sandstone, the slap of clothes beaten against a rock and Czechoslovak pantomime.

In Delhi we hear that the Union Minister for Home Affairs, in this secular State, is to ask the individual states not already doing so to ban cow slaughter, and a nine year old girl in Andhra Pradesh is fasting for the location of the 5th steel plant at Vishakapatnam.

At times like this I feel the whole bloody country will go up in flames.

Yours,
    Steve

—◦◦◦—

Buenos Aires
3 November 1966

Dear Steve,

Last weekend I stayed in Mar del Plata for three days, a town that delights me in autumn, winter and spring but which I detest in summer – so full of people! The sun was shining, the sea was green, and I was lying on the sand trying to get a suntan, in spite of the cold air freezing my bones, reading a book, listening to the tumbling of the waves, and lamenting that you were not here with me. At the Mar del Plata Naval Base the Puma was anchored, an English warship that had come from South Africa to sort out the issue of the Malvinas [Falklands] Islands. In the evening the Casino was full of English officers and sailors. As I do not gamble (I went because all my friends go, and leave behind enormous sums on the tables – I was thinking how many books could be bought with that money) I chatted with some of them. I tried to get a job as Ship's Captain, to travel to England free of charge – but the only vacancy they had was in the kitchens, washing dishes! I didn't really fancy that, so I dropped the idea...

How's your beard? Still growing, or have you shaved it off? Will it last till Spring? Can't you get the film developed soon? I'd love to have an up-to-date photo of you. And talking of photography, about three weeks ago we were burgled, and among other things they stole my camera, therefore I'm about to buy a new one (with the insurance money) and I'm as happy as a child with a new toy.

I'd like you to tell me about the current disturbances in India, the violent events in the state of Andhra Pradesh. The Argentine newspapers say that the crowd was led by leftist students – is that true? It seems that there were many killed – but I imagine that is nothing in comparison with the number of people who die of hunger every day...

About dancing...I am not very good at tango, but I promise to teach you the little I know. For my part, I hope you'll teach me exotic dances such as 'surf', 'shake', etc. It seems the latest fashion in London for dancing is 'looping' but I've no idea what it is.

The Braun-Menendez family name is very well known in Buenos Aires, because they were the owners of half of Patagonia, fascists and aristocrats. I do not know your friend Oscar Braun, but if he is a socialist

I'll be reconciled to the family. He must be the black sheep!

What I wish to study is really the interdisciplinary area between Sociology and Social Anthropology. Here in Buenos Aires I am committed to Sociology because the degree in Anthropology is predominantly oriented towards archaeology and pre-history. But I like the English school of Social Anthropology, I enjoy the writings of Radcliffe-Brown, Evans-Pritchard, Leenhardt, etc., so I lean in that direction, given that I do not know much about British Sociology. I am particularly attracted to the study and development of communities, and also the study of urban sub-cultures (neighbourhoods, collective organizations etc....).

I'm so buried under papers, leaflets, prospectuses and other stuff about how to travel to England on a low budget, that I haven't had time to read everything yet. But here is what I have gleaned so far:

1. The cheapest way to travel to England seems to be with the steamer Arlanza of the Royal Mail Lines, which leaves from Buenos Aires on April 7th and arrives at Southampton on April 26th. Tourist Class, one way, costs $280, which in Argentine pesos is 60,000-65,000 at the current exchange rate. One way or another, without robbing a bank, I'll get the money.
2. What seems more complicated is the question of having enough money to support myself in England; and then there is the visa problem.

3. To enter England as a tourist, you do not need a visa, but you can only stay for three months; and in order for Immigration to let you in, you have to show that you have enough funds to support yourself because of

course tourists are not allowed to work. And if you do not have a return ticket, you have to leave a deposit as a guarantee – I don't know how much.

4. To come in as a student, you have to show on arrival proof of your admission to a University, and whether you have a scholarship, or funds to support yourself.

5. If you intend to work, you must have a contract with an employer, and above all a permit of the Ministry of Labour (a yellow form), and these papers and permits are provided only in exceptional cases, i.e. given only for 'certain limited classes of work for which British workers are not available'.

6. If you wish to reside in the UK, you have to make special enquiries. 'Admission to the UK for residence is at present normally restricted to certain limited classes of persons. These comprise in the main the wives, minor dependent children, elderly parents and distressed relatives of persons who are already resident in the UK and are able and willing to provide adequate accommodation and maintenance.'

7. To sum up: the most logical thing is for me to enter England as a tourist. But: tourists cannot work or study, therefore, how can I survive? I can probably rely on having a little money with me (I've not yet spoken to my parents about my planned journey) but it wouldn't last long.

8. Ideally I'd need to get a scholarship from the University of London – although courses do not start

until September. I cannot apply from here, so I rely on you to check what can be done.

9. Seriously – what about me working for a few months for you – as a secretary and research assistant? Would it be possible to get that kind of job, financed by the LSE? I could work as a specialist in underdeveloped countries (?), a 'class of work for which British workers are not available'!

10. If you come in with one type of visa (for example, tourist) and then you want to change it (for another such as student, worker etc.) you have to leave the country and come back in again (even if it is from France).

I'll wait for your suggestions: perhaps you can find out more from India. The vital thing is to solve my maintenance problem for a few months – and also whether we'll go in the summer to the Continent. The rest we'll see through later when I am in London – we'll have to explore that together.

If the English are, as you tell me, great enthusiasts of the theatre, politics and immaterial things, and live in a free country, I'm sure I'll like them, and I'll try to get over their initial unfriendliness.

A silly question: what do the initials LSE mean?

About your projects for the near future – are you still thinking of working for a year in England and then getting work somewhere else, maybe with the Cuban government, or with the ILO? Or have your plans changed?

Another question: did you find it difficult to adapt to life in Argentina? Or in India? Didn't you miss your family, your friends? Don't you feel lonely sometimes? I may be projecting my own concerns – but you have to take into account my Latin character, very different from the British one, so – among other things – I do not control my emotions as well as you all do.

A final question (that may not elicit an immediate answer): where do you think I shall live in London?

Well, this time my pen – or rather typewriter – really did run away with me – four pages, and it's 2.30 am! But I had lots of things to tell you, and I'm not as brief, concise and synthetic as you are – you'll have to teach me.

Regards from my great-aunt (the owner of the dead poodle) to your gypsy ancestors.

Yours,
    Alicia

PS. What I meant to say with 'I was deeply shocked' was 'it struck me with great force'.

PS2. I haven't read "The Tin Drum", but I'll try to get it.

PS3. My mother was called Dora, and following the custom of the family, I should call my first daughter by that name. Good idea?

New Delhi
6 November 1966

Dear Alicia,
    This letter is a rag-bag, a collection of bits and pieces,

odds and ends, replies to questions, new questions.

I was born on June 7th 1939, a very very hot summer's day in Hackney Hospital in London's East End, within the sound of Bow Bells when they were ringing loud and the wind was in the right direction; so, you see, I am a true Cockney, although I have lost or erased my accent. 3 months later, as my mother never ceases to remind me, with a rueful shake of her head and a glint in her eye, the Second World War broke out.

What do your parents think about your enquiries into coming to England, to see a man you've not seen for 11 months and with whom you have never been alone? They must think you're crazy!

As soon as I receive your curriculum vitae I'll start writing to my LSE contacts. Perhaps work as a research assistant in one of the London colleges may be found, we'll see.

Now, my sweet, a most intimate question… What are your measurements? I want to have a salwar and kameez made for you, it's a North Indian costume for women and the best description I can provide is that it is similar to a cheong-sam over skin-tight ruffled jeans. Unlike the sari, it is made to measure, so you'll have to provide me with some hard facts. Centimetres will do, I've got some log tables.

I've enclosed two cuttings: the matrimonial column shows how caste, colour, education and income predominate as criteria for choice of a spouse. The second, today's front page, shows that I'm not hysterical when I tell you that the whole bloody country may go up in flames. The beginning of the famine in Bihar and Uttar Pradesh could lead to a major national tragedy during the coming months, with its dreadful climax next May-August.

Since you pop into the Di Tella Institute from time to time, let me know the latest gossip. Is Alba married? Has Graciela left for Mexico? Do you still see Donald and Chacho? Is Mario a good Super-Jefe? – I'm sure he is. Does anyone know how Joan is?

I have had a dose of bacillary dysentery for the past three days, which left me so exhausted and misanthropic I couldn't write to anybody, not even you, but today sees me coming out of the wood.

So accept my love,
Yours,
    Steve

———

Buenos Aires
8 November 1966

Dear Steve,

In my last letter I asked you to tell me what's happening in India, what are your impressions, what was going on in Andhra Pradesh, etc. Today I received your reply, that is to say your letter from Agra, which also includes the beautiful account of your visit to the Taj Mahal. What an extraordinary experience! Although I was not there, your description helped me be part of it.

You had never mentioned your friend Paul Matthews before this letter. And please write something about your work in the 'manpower-planning project', it sounds really interesting.

I am working really hard at the moment, because by

the day after tomorrow we must have completed a report on the research on 'Internal Migration' in which I am involved, and I am typing up the final version (very neatly, not all rambling like these letters!) and it's quite long and full of statistical tables. I am also regularly attending classes in the Faculty – when circumstances permit, because there are recurring strikes, meetings, discussions, etc. The prospects in the country are pretty dire. Last night President Onganía read a long-awaited speech in which he announced the economic measures that the military junta is taking to halt inflation. Tami, Petrecolla, and Zalduendo (all former researchers at the Di Tella Institute) and others in the Christian Democrat team, who held high positions in the Central Bank, resigned a few days ago, because they were in disagreement with the measures that the president was going to announce, and they considered that their advice was being ignored. Alsogaray's hard economic line, which is a defence of the agricultural oligarchy, takes precedence. Those hardest hit by these measures will be the middle class, small industry and trade, which were already under attack from the very beginning of this military government, when they dismantled their credit sources, the Cooperatives. It is a triumph too of the monetarist line over the structuralists, a government thumbs-down to rational planning of the economy – a liberal victory with a rightist tendency, free trade, free play for market forces – will we end up again at laissez faire, laissez passer?

Dear Steve, I've got thousands of things to tell you, but once again it's very late – almost 2 in the morning – and I'm very tired from typing all day! So I'll say goodnight.

Yours,
Alicia

New Delhi,
14 November 1966

Darling Alicia,

Oh! what an age it seemed for your letter of November 3rd to come; it arrived at last this afternoon. I have been in a very irritable mood these last three or four days waiting for it, and not eating properly, so it was a great joy to read this long manuscript I've just received. Tomorrow I shall be my usual charming and affable self (?)

A few preliminary questions before I forget

(i)   do you smoke?
(ii) can you cook?
(iii) do you play any musical instrument?

A few days ago a wizened old Muslim arrived in town from Kashmir. His name is Jaffa Ali, he is a merchant and his specializations are papier-mâché, stoles and shawls. I bought some papier-mâché decorated pieces from him, really very lovely and have bought you for a birthday present a pretty, heart-shaped trinket box which I'm sure you'll like very much. I'll give it to you at Southampton! I also bought for myself an antique brass begging bowl with a charming floral design and a papier-mâché lamp stand for my mother. By the way, what are your favourite colours and colour combinations? so I can get you a sari and salwar kameez that you'll like.

I shaved off my beard a couple of weeks ago, though in

fact it looked quite nice when properly trimmed. Perhaps I'll grow another next year.

I managed to get some friends returning to England to take my Agfa film with them, they'll post it in London to the local processors who will send the slides to my parents. I have already written to them asking for a colour print of the one shot in 48 with my portrait (who says I'm egocentric?) & if it's not too unflattering (who said I'm vain) I'll send it to you. And I'm eager to have a photo with you & your long hair – I'm very fond of long hair in girls.

I thought I would phone you at Christmas or on your birthday. Good idea?

LSE = London School of Economics and Political Science. It's funny, here people often say "Ah, yes! Laski's institute." Harold Laski lectured at LSE until the early fifties I believe, and seems to have had a spellbinding personality. Unfortunately the still-enduring left-wing reputation he gave to the place is not justified by the academic staff, who include some of the most reactionary economists in Britain.

The money guarantee or deposit to a person entering the UK with only a single ticket presents no difficulty at all; I'll put up the money.

As far as what type of visa you should enter on, I think it best to discover first what the chances are of you securing a scholarship, and if that falls through, an occupation. I shall write off tonight to the Professor of Anthropology at LSE to see how the ground lies, and let you know in about 14 days.

I don't think it would be a good idea for you to work for me; I don't want to confuse my roles. I might start chasing you all round the office at 10 am and then ask you to take dictation at 10 pm. I want to meet you on equal ground, with no element of hierarchical relation. Steve & Alicia, not Mr. Merrett & Miss Kaner. But if it proves impossible to get you a scholarship – and I believe it <u>will</u> be impossible – then the chances of your securing a job in some secretarial capacity, or as a translator, or as a research assistant should be very good. But I don't want you to have to interrupt your studies yet again, so we'll see if we can get a scholarship, keeping our fingers crossed.

When I come home in February I shall live with my parents until I find myself a flat, which will probably take 3 or 4 weeks. It seemed to me to be a good idea for you, with my mother's agreement, to turn our "front room" (a kind of unused living room) into a bed-sitter when you arrive and to live there until you had found a flat of your own, or found a girl friend with whom you wanted to share. Then again, we could live together, but aside from any moral objections you may have – I have none – I think that would be something of a psychological mistake, to prejudge the whole issue. To put the matter of living together, or working together, as clearly as I can, I think it would be a mistake since we would not retain our personal autonomy and not be able to make a free choice in deciding whether we wish to get married. Do you agree? This is out of my head, my blood murmurs other-wise, but I'm more Anglo-Saxon than Latin in spite of my gypsy grandmother. (Oscar always says that I'm not English at all.)

In my next letter I'll write about cows and my initial reaction to Argentina and India. For now let me tell you once more that I have fallen in love with you through your letters and only wish I could embrace, caress and kiss the Alicia of flesh and blood so far from me,

Steve

———〜〜〜———

New Delhi
15 November 1966

Darling Alicia,
Cows. It is estimated that in India there are between 200 and 280 million cattle, excluding buffaloes. In Hindu Mythology the cow is a sacred animal, and symbolizes mothers and motherhood – Mata Ghai, Mother Cow. Why it is sacred is not known precisely; it may be that its worship is a carry-over from animist cults, it may be that to the Aryans as they made their slow way down the valley of the River Indus (thus Hindu) the cow and the bullock played such a key part in their lives, supplying both milk and acting as a draught animal, that it became a principle not to kill it. Whatever the case it is now Holy.

Unfortunately the cattle population is now increasing at about 6% per annum and the disadvantages of the enormous cattle population are very great. First, the number is so great that milk yields per cow and *total* milk yields would increase with a fall in the total number of cows. This is because so much fodder goes to barely keeping them alive that only what little is left goes to producing milk. Second, culling is necessary for improved breeds. Third, overgrazing is leading to soil erosion in places like Gujarat. Fourth, the animals themselves suffer from slow starvation. [The Hindu attitude is entirely negative: the cow must not be killed, but to mistreat it and to let it starve is no sin.] Fifth, the international price of cattle carcases is said to be $100. If one-half of the cattle population was slaughtered during the next 5 years, the foreign exchange earnings would equal $12 billion! That is, twice the aid requirements for the Fourth Five Year plan.

The government has allowed in a rather underhand way some 'rendering' plants to be set up in different parts of the country during the past few years, e.g. in Goa and Madras. Now the reactionary, right wing, communal Hindu party – Jana Sangh – is using these as sticks to beat the government and increase their own strength in the forthcoming elections next February. There has been widespread agitation throughout the country, and as is often the case in India, violence has succeeded. The Home Minister, or rather ex-Home Minister, Gulzarilal Nanda, who is opposed to cow slaughter himself, recently directed the State governments which allow slaughter to ban it. On Monday November 7th as you probably saw in your newspaper, the agitation was climaxed in Delhi by a march led by "sadhus", Hindu holy men, on Parliament itself, the day ended with eight dead, 56 cars gutted, and many banks, cinemas & restaurants attacked.

You didn't say whether you approved of "Stephen Richard"; I am happy that you maintain your family tradition but I've never yet met a girl who would willingly accept the name "Dora". Why not make Dora the second name, eg Alicia Dora X? Is that consistent with tradition? Still, since you're not yet in the family way, there's no urgency is there!

Paul has just been phoning his attractive Sikh girlfriend Rani, and she has given me all the measurements I shall need to get your salwar-kameez. They are: length, collar bone to knee; shoulder width; waist; bust; hips; length, waist to ankles. O.K?

Paul is tall, fair-haired and blue-eyed. Really quite handsome, I guess. He is very friendly, fascinated by India, a bit lazy, very sensitive to social privilege and ostentation, rather prudish, a mild disciple of the Bishop of Woolwich, has a certain sartorial elegance and dances well.

I'm half-way through Bottomore's Sociology, which is fast convincing me that you sociologists are great frauds, armchair empiricists, banal, circumlocutous, arid. Do you agree, Miss Kaner? In the post within the past week have arrived from Blackwell's in Oxford: Levi-Strauss, "Structural Anthropology". E.E.Evans-Pritchard, "The Nuer", and the three volumes of Deutscher's biography of Trotsky. The last I am saving to read till I get back to England so that I can discuss them with Oscar and my other friends. It seems such an inviting prospect, England, its pubs, theatres and cinemas in 3 months, and the pleasure of your company in 5.

How are you honey? I miss you very much and wish you were with me. Your postal "kiss of congratulations" has only whetted my appetite and I feel very hungry.

All my love,
Steve

Buenos Aires
16 November 1966

Dear Steve,

People in the Di Tella Institute: I saw Donald last May, on a bus; I don't think he works at the Institute any more, because of their budget cuts. I saw Chacho recently, when I went to the library; he too was passing through, because as you know he now works in the Federal Investment Council, and we only exchanged a few words. Mario really seems to be a good Super Chief. I saw Joan once, we travelled together on the tube, she was as pretty as ever; it is said that she wants to leave her new job, because they make her work too hard and she's not used to that (you treated her too well!). In the passageway the secretaries don't make up the famous 'team' of the Institute any more, the new ones are quite plain. Those who tell me the latest news are Mariella and Teresa, but I don't tell them all my news, which makes me feel guilty.

I finished my research report at last, and felt absolutely exhausted after a week of intensive work, so to recover I went away for the weekend with some friends, staying at the country house of a friend who has wheat and cattle, near Tandil in the province of Buenos Aires. It was great, eleven people lazing around, living with gas-lamps in the mud, eating grilled meat, drinking mate, or me and two other girls cooking (while the boys washed the plates and dried them or chased the cattle away). If you had been there...

If you have any influence with the Great Knight Commander and Perfect Regulatory Mandarin of Weather in London, tell him to make London less cold, wet and snowy. My parents complained a lot about the

English weather, and an aunt who came back from London a few days ago caught pneumonia. I really prefer the sun and a warm breeze to cold and rain.

Poor Steve, after your bacillary dysentery you must be pale and thin. I hope you are better now.

You ask me what my parents think about my enquiries about the possibility of travelling to London to see you. I must confess that so far I have received no official news in that respect. Things are in separate compartments. On the one hand, they've known for some time that I would like to go to England to study, and that recently I've been checking out the possibilities more intensively; but they expect that it will happen after I graduate – whereas if things move forward at the normal pace in the University of Buenos Aires (!) I wouldn't finish until December 1967. On the other hand, they know you through the letters you send me, because I've read out to them a translation of some parts of your stories about Jaipur, the Pindari, and the Lama. Perla (my father's wife) was very enthusiastic about that one, and that predisposed her in your favour; on several occasions she asked me about your work, your plans, if you'll stay long in India and whether you are thinking of coming back to Argentina soon.

I have told my stepbrother (the one who is getting married next week) and he said I was completely crazy. The main problem is that when I tell my parents that I want to go to London to see you, at the same time I'll have to ask them for money for the journey. And money is a difficult old question between my father and me, which explains in part the fact that although I am the daughter of a bourgeois industrialist who could perfectly easily pay for my University studies, I have been working since I was

18. I don't regret this, because I believe that work has been a good experience for me. The situation hit crisis point just at the time that I joined the Di Tella Institute; that crisis made it necessary for me to earn more money, so as not to have to ask for any cash at all from him, and that was complicated with a crisis about my studies. (But the positive side of all this was that it led to us meeting.)

Those reasons, plus others, such as some fears, and certain objective, external conditions like the uncertainty of how I'll be able to live in England (although my savings are not exhausted yet), the money problems, and the fact that sometimes I also think that maybe I am a bit crazy, thinking of leaving my home, my work, my degree course, a certain security and stability, and a life that's more or less well ordered, to cross the ocean, travel to an unknown country (I don't have a globetrotter soul like you), all this for a vision, that opens for me marvellous panoramas – but that for now is not more than that, an imagined idea, lacking the all-important confrontation with reality. If they were not to match, the shock could be very destructive for me; the risk is enormous.

For those reasons I'd like to make to you a counter-proposal: that you come to Argentina, on a visit. The invitation includes living in my house (that is, board and lodging), and the possibility of making a journey together to somewhere in Argentina or South America. This would replace your planned holidays in Europe; you could come in February or March, directly from India, and stay here a couple of months (or more, if you can), or otherwise during the European summer holidays (June-July-August). Or whenever you want to and can do – as soon as possible. If the vision matches the reality, and everything goes well, I can go to England with you afterwards. That way the objective difficulties will be more easily resolved.

I hope you'll understand my point of view; through our letters, and from our brief acquaintance, we both feel we'd very much like to meet again, to match the vision with the reality, and to establish a closer relationship between us. And we have to find the best way to achieve this, and seek a solution that offers fewer risks and sacrifices for both of us.

That leaves my study plans in England in place, as well as our travelling to Europe together. I'm delighted by the idea of travelling with a Steve of flesh and bone, if he is like the paper Steve – and I believe he is.

My stepbrother's birthday is on the same day as yours, June 7th, and next year he will be in London on that date, on the last stage of his journey through Europe before starting a spell of 3 years' work in Cincinnati on June 15th. He was born in 1940. In spite of the fact that he upset me badly when he said I was crazy, he is a great guy. And my father, in spite of his defects, is a terrific, funny old man. (Oedipus Complex – I mean, Electra).

I ask you a question on Perla's behalf: in what language did you speak with the Lama? English?

Goodnight now – tomorrow I have to get up early to study and also to help in the house, as Perla does not feel too well these days and tries not to overdo things, so she'll feel well for the party next week, her son's marriage.

I hope you are well, healed and that you reply soon to my counter-proposal.

I accept your love, and I send my own,
Yours,
    Alicia

Buenos Aires
20 November 1966

Dear Steve,

I've just come back from walking along the streets of my neighbourhood. It is the most beautiful night, the sky star-studded and shimmering, and the rustling of the leaves in the high foliage of the trees accompanied me like a lullaby. It is not cold but the heat of summer has not yet arrived and the breeze is smooth and caressing. I stopped for a short while at the rail crossing in the square of Juramento and Freyre to see the trains passing with their lights and their rattling rhythm. It was an enormous contrast with the bustle of Corrientes Street, where I'd come from, full of cars and open-backed vans stuffed with people shouting and celebrating the triumph of Racing Club in the Football Championship. There are few people in the streets of Belgrano although it isn't very late, so in this silence one hears the sounds of cats and footsteps on the pavement. I was looking at the sky and remembered a phrase from an old song: 'Catch a falling star and put it in your pocket, save it for a rainy day.' I was walking slowly, thinking of my four-times-a-day strolls to the Di Tella Institute, and remembering one afternoon when I walked back home with you, and now wishing you were here with me, that you could feel the sounds and scents that I was enjoying.

After a careful search I found Leytonstone, Hampstead and Richmond in London's tube map, but of course that tells me nothing about what these places are like. Do tell me about them.

I read your article in the *Review of Economic Development*. I very much liked the angle you take on the subject. And I was very enthusiastic about the final phrase referring to myth, as the theme of myth and language is a great favourite of mine.

Yesterday I went to a friend's birthday party, Graciela No. 2 (I have at least five girlfriends called Graciela), which was great, we danced, we sang and listened to friends playing the guitar up to 4.30 am. I wished so much that you could have come with me! I met a friend there who has just come back from Europe (he was in Spain for a year on a scholarship) and he told me that the English in general seem to him the greatest bunch of people that he met in Europe, very human, and interested in many things at the intellectual level. Furthermore, he enjoyed several sunny days in London! It has very much improved my image of London and the English. I thought your character was an exception, but it seems that's not so, and that makes me happy. But I believe that you retain your specialness perhaps because of your unusual Gypsy grandmother.

How do you feel in India? In one letter you told me that you wanted to leave straightaway. Why? Because of an anxiety to escape from yourself, by escaping from your immediate environment? To a great degree one constructs one's surrounding world, one chooses it to be one way or another, and then must accept it or try to reject it. I believe that it is one's own attitudes that condition the attitude of others, and that it is not so much a matter of changing other people, but of modifying your own attitude to them. But that is not easy to do – I must confess I find it difficult, not to say impossible (for example, my relationship with my father). But when I have succeeded, the results have been fascinating.

The wind is bottled up in the garden of my house, and what in the street is a mere breeze, from my home and through the closed window sounds like a hurricane.

I don't quite follow your description of the Indian dress that you want to buy for me. You'll have to do a sketch so that I have an idea of what measurements you need. But, wouldn't it be easier to buy me a sari?

Goodnight Steve, until my next letter,
With Love,
    Alicia

——

Buenos Aires
24 November 1966

Darling Steve,

I don't want you to grow thin and irritable, please eat properly so as to look handsome and charming (as you usually are). I will write you as often as possible, to avoid long waits.

I loved your letter of the 14th and I read it again and again. I liked it particularly because it seems we think alike on many subjects, especially about how to build a good relationship with each other. It would be great for me to live at your parents' when I first arrive, to allow time to adapt and begin to study or work. Later I can live by myself or with a girlfriend. About us living together, any possible objections on my part would not be on 'moral' grounds – respect for certain laws imposed by society –

but just as you say, of a psychological character, to retain at the beginning a certain liberty and autonomy in our relationship. Now I'll reply to your questions:

I smoke very little. Sometimes I smoke one or two cigarettes a day, after meals or with a coffee, and some times I don't smoke at all. And you?

I can cook a bit. I usually stick to Argentine food: steak and chips, omelettes, fried eggs, etc., and some desserts, like chocolate cakes and éclairs. But my specialities are enormous sandwiches (Dagwood style), canapés and cold dishes, not to speak of the marvels I can perform with tinned food. But I like cooking, and I manage to cook new dishes from time to time. What I don't like is washing up, do you?

Unfortunately, the only 'musical instruments' that I know how to play are the tape-recorder and the record player. And you?

My speciality is to make dolls of different types, made of cloth, felt, string, wire, etc., and at one time I sold them to earn money. My sister too is very arty-crafty, currently she's making mobiles in plastic, and earns quite a lot from selling them. This is a skill inherited from my mother, who was very crafty, she sewed and knitted very well, made toys, etc.

I look forward to receiving your colour photo. What a shame you shaved off your beard! It must have suited you very well. I'm taking lots of photos at the moment, because I am trying out my new camera and I have to take photos of my stepbrother and his bride, at the wedding party (which is tomorrow), etc., in black and white and in colour. I've already seen the first negatives, they came out very well and the prints will be ready next week. As soon as I have them, I'll select a few that show me at my best (who said that you are the only vain one?) and I'll send them to you.

I'm delighted with the idea of your ringing me! My number is 73-9838. It would be ideal if you could phone me on New Year's Eve or on Christmas Day. I want to hear your voice *soon*! I may not be in Buenos Aires on my birthday. Could you let me know beforehand? I believe that in 'person-to-person' calls, you can send a warning the day before, or a few hours before, so that the person receiving the call is at home at the time of the call. It had crossed my mind to call you, but I did not say anything because it seemed so expensive. But what worries me most is that I won't know what to say to you, because when there are so many things to say, and you've got only three minutes on the phone, one feels tongue-tied. Please speak slowly, otherwise I may not understand you.

Thank you in advance for the birthday present you bought for me, and thank you too for your proposal to deposit the necessary money with the British Office of Immigration; I hope it won't be necessary.

Could you give me the LSE address, so I can ask directly for information on how the courses are organized? If I didn't get a scholarship and had to work instead, would it be possible to sit in as an observer on some of the courses, so as not to lose complete connection with the University?

Will it be difficult for me to find a job? I read in the newspaper that unemployment in England was on the increase. It would be nice if I could find a job at the University.

I also got your letter about cows, with the newspaper

clipping. What a complicated problem! Religion and the economy are too mixed up, and I can see in India tradition is very strong.

I'm in agreement with 'Stephen Richard'. According to my family's tradition, it would not be correct to give a daughter of mine my own name, but there would be no problem in using Dora, as a second name. Moreover, I am not too respectful of tradition, so when the time comes for choosing a name (which I suppose is still quite far off) I may change my mind, and not follow tradition at all.

Here are the measurements that you need for my salwar-kameez. They are (in metres): length, collar bone to knee: 1 m.; shoulder width: 0.37; waist, 0.65; bust: 0.88 m.; hips, 1.02 m; waist to ankles: 0.90 m. My favourite colours are turquoise, emerald green, and shocking pink; I also like blues (not too dark), and bright reds; the combinations of shocking pink and turquoise are very pretty; yellow is also a lovely colour, but I find it more difficult to wear. I like brilliant greens (not dark) and clear. You can mix and match white with any of these colours.

Mr. Merrett, I feel offended by the manner in which you, sir, refer to sociologists, but I must confess that I somewhat agree. That's why I like the interdisciplinary area between Sociology and Anthropology: to use some sociological techniques (statistics), and part of your action plan (urban societies), but to work with anthropological techniques (participant observation) as well, to avoid the main shortcomings of both disciplines: Sociology's excessive theorization (to say a great deal and end up saying nothing worthwhile or useful) and the excessive empiricism of Anthropology from the ethnographic point of view.

My sweet Steve, I've decided to make you a list of

things I like, things I don't like, shortcomings, virtues and other things that can be interpreted in various ways depending on the point of view of the beholder. I hope you will do the same:

I like the theatre, the cinema and talking over a coffee.
I like to listen to discussions of politics, although I tend to be a bit shy about giving my own opinion.
I don't like practical jokes.
I love to drive cars.
I tend to get depressed when I feel lonely and without support.
I love to listen to music.
I love men with brown hair.
I have a slight tendency to be a bit lazy and idle, from time to time.
I'm a bit jealous.
I like to travel, to get to know new places and people.
I like brown-haired Englishmen.
I am mimosa. (I think that this word, in the sense I give it, does not match the dictionary translations).
I am sensitive to cold.
I have possessive tendencies.
I have a tendency to stay up late and get up late if I can.
I think I write better than I talk (at least until I feel at ease).
I tend to miss my family and friends when I am far away and do not see them for a long time.
I have a tendency to adapt well to external circumstances.
I am affectionate.
I like very much a brown-haired Englishman called Steve.

I have a tendency to copy the accent, intonation and the way of speaking of the people who are close to me (which could be very useful in improving my English).

Enough for today!

Dear Steve, your letter of the 14th has cleared up some of my doubts and fears, and made me happy. But I await your response about the chances of your coming to Argentina. When the excitement over my stepbrother's wedding is over, I'll find an appropriate time to talk to my parents about the possibility of going to England. I hope they will not say I am crazy.

I send you a kiss and a hug with all my love.
Alicia

———

New Delhi
25 November 1966

Darling Alicia,

This afternoon I'm setting off on a short trip to Chandigarh and Nangal in the Punjab, partly business, partly pleasure, so I thought I'd write to you before I leave, although I haven't had a letter from you for about 10 days now.

At the moment I still have not received any colour prints from England, so I'm sending you a photo I found in my drawer the other day, taken while I was at Bhopal in Madhya Pradesh collecting data on the employees in the Heavy Electricals plant there. Everybody compliments me on what a pretty girlfriend I have when I show them your picture. I also read out a passage from your letter after the Congress of Americanists – you remember, a contrary view on acculturation. Sir Robert Rae, a wonderful old Scot who is out here doing a study for UNESCO said that you were much too intellectual for me.

The night before last I and Paul Matthews held a cocktail party which went off very well, lasting from 7 pm to about 11.30 pm. The guests included Sir Robert Rae; David Rubin, an American novelist; Kusum Nair, the author of "Blossoms in the Dust"; Ottome Klein, a Dutch anthropologist with wonderful taste in interior decoration; Rani Singh, Paul's girlfriend; O.P. Agarwal, Chief Manpower and Training Officer of the Fertiliser Corporation of India; Salwar Latif, a young Indian journalist with the Hindustan Times; Eileen Mazumdar of All-India Radio, etc. etc. A very mixed bunch you see, and quite a swinging evening. For the first time in ages I got very "plastered" and spent most of the night vomiting and the morning taking Aspros.

Yes, my plans about the future have changed a little. I have heard that working with the international organizations can be very frustrating, since for political reasons, office is often held by mediocrities, and one is constantly trying to avoid stepping on the toes of this or that country. My ideas now centre on Cuba as always, and alternatively getting a job in the UK. in one of our nationalised industries as an economist. In my year in India I have spent a good deal of time in large fertiliser plants and find it fascinating to analyse how they are changing, the importance of foreign capital, pricing policies, technological change. I'd be quite happy to get out of the academic world for a while, with its two dimensional graphs and smooth curves, and neat mathematical formulae and "constant returns to scale", all the facile, fake assumptions of textbook economics.

While I remember, when you come to England will you bring me

i.   some yerba mate,
ii. the sketches by Juan Carlos Castagnino accompanying Sabato's "Tango: canción de Buenos Aires." I had all the sketches, but the two best ones were stolen a few weeks ago.

From your last couple of letters it seems clear that you are rather anxious about what life will be like in England when you first arrive, and ask me how I felt when I came to Argentina and India. Well, to the last question I'll tell you when I see you – my strongest memory is of terrible loneliness and isolation. However, I do not think my experience will be the same as yours since I had no one to meet me on arrival, and you will have me standing on the dockside with my arms open wide waiting to give you a long, long kiss of welcome.

I imagine that your reactions will be to think how bloody cold England is, to remark how pasty-faced and ill the people look, how quickly they seem to move, what a great treasure of art, theatre and cinema and history London has to offer, to begin to long to talk Spanish with a fellow Argentine combined with frustration at not being able to express all the subtleties of your thoughts clearly in English, and to miss, at the beginning rather desperately, your parents, siblings and friends. But I'll be there and I'll introduce you to all my friends, and show you our great capital city and beautiful countryside so that at the end perhaps you'll feel the advantages make up for all the things you miss or dislike. One thing I must tell you, which I have not said before, is to say how much I admire your courage in coming all this way alone, to be with me, and I'll do my best not to disappoint you. Your courage in this contrasts oddly with the picture I have of you sometimes of the diffident, fawn-like Alicia.

Recently I bought a slide rule from a friend of mine who's a Dutch irrigation expert who returned to Europe, it's been most useful, just like a new toy for me. I am constantly pleased and surprised that it gives the right answer to all the divisions, percentages and multiplications I ask of it.

Finally, I have often wondered what your father's profession is, and whether your parents emigrated to Argentina or were born there; additionally, what is perhaps a silly question, do they mind that I am not Jewish?

Well, that's about all for now. I keep meaning to tell you about the project, but never quite get round to it, do I? Perhaps I'll tell you in my next letter. I hope soon to get a reply to at least *one* of the four letters I have sent you in the past couple of weeks. You must have a heart of ice to leave me languishing for so long without a reply.

All my love,
Steve

Buenos Aires
27 November 1966

My very dear Steve,

It is half past four in the afternoon on a very sunny Sunday with the most marvellous clear blue sky, and I'd love to be lying on a beach, face towards the sun, with nothing to do but listen to the murmur of the sea. So as an alternative I spent an hour in my garden after breakfast, enjoying the sun and reading. Then I went back to studying, sitting at my desk which stands by a window leading to the garden, so it allows me to see the sun, the sky, the green of the trees and flowers of every colour. Now I am having a break, to write to you. Later on two or three friends are coming, to chat and listen to music. One of them will bring a record that came out recently of some Brazilian songs, composed, played and sung by the famous Dorival Caymmi and Vinicius de Moraes. The main topics of conversation will be, for sure, the University's problems (ever present), the latest Argentine literary vanguard works published by Editorial Jorge Alvarez, today's elections in Uruguay, the activities of the Red Guards in China, the events in Vietnam, the dock-workers' strike, the recent screening of 'The Gospel According to Matthew' by Pier Paolo Pasolini (I have not seen it yet, but some friends say it's excellent), and our visit to the theatre recently – three short plays, in the Teatro Los Independientes: 'The Bear' by Anton Chekhov, 'Cecé' by Luigi Pirandello, and 'The Anger of Phillip Hotz', by Max Frisch. So here you have a description of one of my Sunday afternoons, which I so much wish you could share with me.

My brother's wedding, which was yesterday, was really lovely. There was a family lunch at home with Haydée's parents (the bride), and a party for friends, in the evening, in my house. The party was great fun (I think that it is the first time in my life that I've enjoyed a wedding; usually they are very boring) and we danced till three in the morning, non-stop. I was chatting with a friend of Haydée, called Alicia Ballsells, who returned three months ago from London, where she was studying Linguistics for two years, at University College, with a scholarship from the British Council. She's an English teacher. I asked her about the LSE, and she said it is one of the most wonderful places in the world to study and where students are very much like Argentine students, in the sense of being committed. 'Of course' she said, 'after Laski...'

I really like your idea of my working as a translator, but although I could translate reasonably well into Spanish, to translate into English is not really feasible for me.

What is the rate of exchange of the dollar to the rupee? President Onganía began a so-called 'exchange freedom' on the Argentine foreign exchange markets, but all they managed to achieve is to raise the price of the official dollar, from 218 Argentine pesos to 250 – and the 'parallel' market, where the dollar costs around 270 pesos, continues to exist.

One of the nicest presents given to my stepbrother was a key ring of Indian silver, a 'lucky key ring', which was given to him by Doctor Marie Langer, one of the most distinguished psychoanalysts in Argentina – it is lovely: it is like two semi-circles of wrought silver, from which hang a number of small silver balls, close together, and they tinkle with a smooth sound as you move the key ring. I particularly like silver ornaments, but I dislike gold ones.

To the list I sent you the other day, please add as well: I love wearing men's sweaters. (What are yours like?)

Dearest Steve, the thought that you are going to telephone me is making me very nervous and I am waiting for the moment (still some way off!) with much anxiety, joy and fear at the same time.

Each day I miss you more and wish you were here with me to share so many things, talk, and embrace each other. Write again soon.

With all my love,
Alicia

PS. (1 am, on 28.11.66) In the late Sunday afternoon we went for a drive through Palermo and the Costanera, and we sat on some steps by the river – the river was calm, there was a full moon, and the lights of the city formed a semi-circle – it was almost perfect: the only thing missing was you.

—⁓—

New Delhi
1 December 1966

Darling Alicia,

You suggest that I come to Argentina. This is impossible for two reasons: first, I cannot afford the return air fare, London–Buenos Aires, second, even if I could, I don't have the time necessary to make the trip. You see I get only six weeks holiday a year, one week to take in Easter, one at Christmas. But I feel that I would like to be close to you for 3-4 months in order to know whether to ask you to be my wife. A flying visit of 4 weeks is just not sufficient.

If we are to meet, to collide or to coalesce, it must be in London, next April, when the skies are blue, the air cool, and the sun yellow on the walls of tower and column.

Your material difficulties and anxieties fall, it seems, in two groups. First, you must ask your father, Agamemnon, for the fare. But I've already told you I'll pay half your return fare, which will equal the single one-way fare. So I can buy your ticket for the outward journey.

Second, your living expenses in London. At the beginning they will be minimal, since you will be living with my parents at no charge of course. If you wish to move out to a flat, and in any case when we go to Eastern Europe and Moscow, you will need some money of course. I now begin to feel that the chances of you getting any kind of scholarship are zero. If you agree I will start making enquiries now about the possibilities of secretarial – cum – translation – cum – research assistant work in London. That could well solve the short-term money problem. If you do eventually decide to stay in England with me, then we shall have to decide whether you should carry on working, or get a place (i.e. as a student) at London University in the Department of Sociology or Social Anthropology. I am writing tomorrow to the Professor in the latter Department (Lucy Mair) for information – I believe it would be relatively easy for you to get a place (though, as I say, without a scholarship).

Third, you will have to give up, temporarily or, I hope, permanently, your family, career, etc. etc. That is perfectly correct.

Fourthly, after coming to know each other better, we may decide it's all a mistake, and our love is parchment love, that whilst the ink flows in the pen, the blood does not through the veins. Perfectly correct, and we shall if it proves to turn out that way, both be unutterably miserable.

What a logical bastard I am. I just say this: risk it. Risk it. Please come to me, I want you very much.

Yours, with all my love,
    Steve

———

Buenos Aires
2 December 1966

My Dearest Steve,
    Your letter of the 25th arrived today, when I was feeling a bit low: on the one hand, I had no letters from you for nine days; and on the other hand, the idea of going alone to England, leaving so much behind, is really scary. I am less courageous than you imagine!

My father was born in Odessa, Russia, in 1903. The son of a wealthy bourgeois, he spent his childhood in great comfort, and after school he went to University to study engineering. But the Russian Revolution put a stop to that, so when he was 18 he left Russia, spent a year wandering through Europe (a hard year, suffering hunger, war and hiding), and then took a boat bound for South America.

He arrived in Buenos Aires with just two dollars in his pocket; but he already had there a cousin who had arrived before him, and he helped him settle in, look for work, learn the language, etc. He did many things in his life, in the fields of trade and industry, and he is currently the manager and Chairman of the Board of a textile factory. He has been a great reader all his life and is very knowledgeable. When I was a child he taught me geography and history well before I had to study them at school. His political position is *sui generis*: he approves communism in the USSR, but in Argentina he is a bourgeois who wishes to see no social revolutions. His middle-class friends consider him a communist sympathizer, but my left-wing friends say he is nothing more than a bourgeois who's a little less rigid and more sympathetic than others.

My late mother was born in one of the agricultural colonies in the Argentine province of Entre Rios, set up by Jews brought over from Russia by Baron Hirsch. My grandfather was from a small village in Russia, and here he was 'Inspector of Colonies'. He was a wonderful person, and I loved him dearly. Perla, my father's present wife, has a similar background: born in Argentina, daughter of Russians. She's a philosophy graduate.

On your question on whether your not being Jewish matters to them, I think that yes, it probably matters a bit, but by now they're getting used to mixed marriages in the family. My stepbrother, Horacio Breyter, has just married Haydée Fernández (daughter of Catholic Spaniards) and my sister's fiancé is Hector Fernández Barrios (unrelated to Haydée). So they have to accept it, due to force majeure! By the way, what are you, Protestant or Catholic?

I was delighted to receive your photo, but I'm awaiting

another in which I see you better, in this I hardly recognize you! From the technical point of view, I'm sorry to have to be critical of it: your face has too great a contrast between light and shadow. But don't worry: you'll see what lovely photos I'll take of you next year.

I'll soon get a copy of a photo of me taken two weeks ago at my friend Graciela's birthday party and I'll send it to you. I think I look quite pretty in it, although usually I am not especially photogenic. Talking of parties, how different are party hours here and there! You talked about a cocktail party lasting from 7 pm till 11.30 pm, while parties here usually start at 10.30 pm and finish at 3 or 4 am – we are a nocturnal people! But I think that in most of Europe, except for Paris, after 11 pm there is nothing much to do. Especially in London, from what I am told. I shall miss our Latin ways, because I am a night owl and can never get to bed before one a.m. But what worries me most about London is that it is cold. I am devilishly prone to the cold!

My hair has now grown down to my shoulders; but although I water it everyday, I can't get it to grow more quickly. This being your speciality field – do you know of a good fertilizer to help hair growth?

I bought 'The Tin Drum' of Günter Grass, but I have not yet started reading it because: first, I lent it to Perla, who is in bed and bored – it seems she will have to have an operation next week, she has a some kind of growth in her womb, and for the past month has had heavy bleeding. Second, I have two exams in the coming week and I have little time and a lot to study. So I'll start it in about ten days time. Perla likes it a lot.

Please tell me what's your father's job, and what he and your mother are like. What do they think of your constant travelling? Don't they miss you a lot? At home, the fact that one of my stepbrothers lives in Israel, and the other is soon going to the States, is almost a tragedy for Perla, who is very close to her children. With this background, you can imagine how they'll respond to the idea that I want to go to England, and under such peculiar circumstances. What does your mother think about me going to live with her for a time?

Do I really give the impression of being an intellectual? Don't trust appearances, I'm not really. It depends on the point of view you are taking: if you are thinking of girls who only talk about clothes, parties and boys, then 'yes', I must be an intellectual, but if your reference point is real intellectuals, according to the sociological definition, then I am far from that.

But I am more concerned about your image of me being very shy. I probably am a bit shy but not so much. Perhaps you have this image because at the Di Tella Institute, especially at the beginning, I felt very different from the other secretaries, I didn't share their world. Although maybe the reason was that I felt shy when I was with you – possibly because I liked you too much. You turned my life upside down – I was engaged to be married, and meeting you evidently shook my relationship – you cost me quite a few psychoanalytic sessions! When you left Argentina, I tried to forget you; you were geographically out of reach, but, above all, for me you were 'another's property'. There were also other reasons which eventually led to my breaking my engagement.

The late part of the Buenos Aires theatre season seems quite promising. Today I saw 'Help, Valentino', a series of sketches on the 'porteño' fashions of this year, quite entertaining. In the next day or two I will attend a recital of 'Songs of Protest: Traditional and Modern' by Carlos Waxemberg, the Pete Seeger of Argentina. Next week I have tickets to see Sir John Gielgud and Irene Worth in 'Men and Women of Shakespeare', in the Theatre San Martín.

The London you are portraying – cold and with pale faces – and your forecast that I shall miss my family and friends, and that I won't be able to express myself well in English for a while – well! that is not very encouraging on a day when I feel low! Two things comfort me: one, on the days when I want to speak Spanish I can go to see Mara and Enrico Stefani, friends of my stepbrother who have been living in London for two years (he's a doctor and a super guy), and second, and most important, you'll be there to help me overcome problems, and prevent me feeling lonely and abandoned.

Steve, how much I want to see you. I hope that you have by now received my letter in which I invite you to come to Argentina, to see what happens between us – if things go well – before I undertake the long voyage to England. I think that your experience in travelling makes it much easier for you to come here than for me to go there. When you leave India, why don't you make a little trip through Africa and then spend your holidays in Buenos Aires? I explained clearly my reasons in the other letter. I am eager to hear what you think about it.

I hope then that you'll be able to phone me – something that delights me and scares me at the same time.

Let's hope the postal service improves. I do not have a heart of ice, but the complete opposite, it is full of love, and I don't want you languishing for lack of replies – I hope that on your part you don't leave me feeling low!

    With all my love,
        Alicia

———ww———

New Delhi
2 December 1966

Darling Alicia,

How are you, honey? How nice it would be to have you here next to me to tell you how pretty your new hairstyle is, and bite the lobe of your ear.

Music. Music? Music! My favourite singer is Bhimsen Joshi, my two chosen instrumentalists Janos Starker and Uhstad Ali Akbar Khan, my favourite whisky-time listening the Art of the Fugue by – his name slips my mind, but I think the initials are J.S. My only goddess, Miss Billie Holiday.

I spoke to the Lama in English. He speaks only English, German, French, Spanish, Hindi, Bengali and Tibetan.

My touch of the bacillaries has gone, which is just as well since otherwise I would not be able to sit at my writing desk long enough to complete even a sentence. (Did I ever tell you I'm an inveterate liar?) (Don't believe that last proposition.) I think I caught it from the food or water. The American Peace Corps physician on welcoming a new batch of volunteers to India said that they were to assume that the entire sub-continent is covered by a thin layer of faeces. Everybody gets dysentery, it's locally known as "Delhi belly."

The lines you recite from an old song were plagiarized from a poem by one of England's greatest literary figures. The first verse is:

"Go, and catch a falling star,
Get with child a mandrake root,
Tell me, where all past years are,
Or who cleft the Devil's foot,
Teach me to hear mermaids singing,
Or to keep off envy's stinging,
And find
What wind
Serves to advance an honest mind."

No good student riots lately, Chavan got tough and threw all the ringleaders into prison. The best outside views on India, I think, are the reports of the correspondent of the London "Times". You'll find them in the British Council Library.

I recently heard a very very funny dirty joke about an Irish landlady who was walking past her lodger's room late one evening, and to her surprise, on peeping through the half-opened door…

But it needs to be *told* not written, with an Irish accent which I imitate quite well, so I'll leave it for the telling.

Farewell,
All my love,
    Steve

New Delhi
5 December 1966

Darling, darling Alicia,

Two warm wonderful letters to show me your heart is not of ice but of fire.

Do I smoke? No, never.

Can I cook? No, and have no real desire to learn. But I love washing up plates when there's plenty of hot water and some liquid soap to make everything smooth and gleaming with soap bubbles. So you see we are perfectly compatible.

The address of the person you should contact at the LSE is (& she's female):

Professor Mair, Department of Anthropology, London School of Economics, Houghton Street, London. W.C.2, England.

If you mention my name in the letter, which you might as well do, I am officially a "Research Officer" in the "Unit for Economic and Statistical Studies on Higher Education."

My mother has written to say that most of my photos of the Himalayas and the Taj Mahal trip have come out very well, and I am expecting my colleague David Ovens to bring them out in a few days. However I believe the one of me bearded is very dark, so I may have to leave you guessing about my physical appearance a little longer. I'll see how the slides have come out.

I've just been informed by Mr Daniel, the telephonist at the Centre, that the phone call will cost 63 rupees for 3 minutes. 21 rupees = £1. He also said that the line should be perfectly clear – which I don't believe. I am going to phone you on 1st January 1967, since this year is going to be crucial in our personal relations, and I want it to start beautifully.

Finally let me describe to you the intimate virtues of my personality and the few trivial (and attractive) defects.

I like theatre, cinema, football on television and long discussions over beer.

I hate talking over breakfast and before I've finished reading the paper.

I like talking politics

I am very frank.

I love telling and listening to obscene stories.

I love driving my scooter, except in Old Delhi, which is full of buffaloes.

I very much like to be alone for a day or two from time to time.

I like listening to almost any kind of music.

I like dark-haired women.

I loathe criticism and am easily discouraged by it.

I am very jealous, but unfortunately not in a very virile way. I just sulk.

I love seeing new places but I don't like to meet new people.

I like dark-haired Argentine women.

I don't know what you mean by "mimosa". Tell me.

The cold doesn't bother me too much.

I do not have possessive tendencies.

I am very sharp-tongued.

I like to go to bed before 11pm and get up before 8am.

I am fundamentally mean but cloak this with occasional bursts of generosity.

I love to get drunk from time to time.

I never miss my family, but my friends dreadfully.
I write even better than I talk.
I am very modest, sincere and never lie.
I read a great deal and imbibe 1-2%.
I am not affectionate.
I like very much a girl whose initials are ANK.
I have a very passionate nature.

At this particular moment in time I have a very, very strong desire to make love with a girl called Alicia, who has dark-hair, beautiful lips and, so she says, a passionate nature. I miss the same girl very much.

All my love,
Steve

—⁓—

Buenos Aires
9 December 1966

My very dear Steve,
    This is going to be a very sad letter, my love. Perla has died. It sounds absurd, incredible, but that's the reality. She had an operation on the afternoon of Wednesday 7th, it wasn't a complicated operation and apparently everything went all right. By Thursday morning, it was all over. During the night she had what doctors called 'an irreversible haemorrhagic shock', and nothing could be done. It was internal bleeding, and the doctors had decided to operate again to see if they could stem it, but her blood pressure dropped to almost zero and the shock happened before they could start

the procedure. It seems unbelievable: the surgeon, the clinical doctor, the doctors on duty in the hospital, several nurses, her son the doctor, doctor uncles, doctor friends, were all present, and she slipped away from their grasp to everybody's terrible feeling of powerlessness. She already had a low blood pressure problem, so they had taken all sorts of precautions, but it was all in vain.

So here we remain, Perla has gone, and there is a vast emptiness. I have lost a mother for the second time. Both of them so different from each other, both much loved.

Perla, who was so dynamic, so energetic, so chatty, so affectionate, so full of life. It doesn't seem true that from one day to the other she simply vanished. She was reading "The Tin Drum", it was left halfway through, she could not finish it. A few days ago we were talking together, she asked me about you and your plans for the future. She asked me that when I write to you, I should tell you on her behalf that you should come and work in Argentina – she did not like having her children far away!

This lunchtime Carlos phoned, her other son, from Israel, we had sent a telegram to some friends of his and asked them to break the news to him. Poor Carlos, so far away, so powerless, in such pain! The line was very poor at first, then it improved, but the whole thing was desperately distressing.

Just now I am alone. They sent me to sleep, after having had a proper meal for the first time in nearly two days; last night I hardly slept. The house was full of people, hundreds of visitors came, I didn't know, or didn't recognize, many of them. I must have walked kilometres, from the pain in my legs – I walked from one room of the house to the other like a sleepwalker (so I've been told), trying to miss out people, but occasionally bumping into somebody, which made me shudder, then I leaned on them and started to cry. The most difficult thing is to comfort my father. He's 63 and he's now alone for the second time, he's a man who is not used to being on his own, with health problems in spite of his external dynamism, and in great need of company. My younger sister, Ester, has luckily now dropped off fast asleep, she's also so distraught, poor girl. And Horacio and Haydée… it's terrible for them, they got married only a fortnight ago! The same people that attended their wedding two weeks ago have come back yesterday and today for such a different, sad occasion.

Perla seemed to have premonitions of her death: they should have operated a month and a half ago, but she adamantly refused to have her operation before her son's wedding. And yesterday a friend told us that three days ago Perla turned up at her house to meet her newborn daughter, although the doctor had ordered her to stay home. And when her surprised friend asked her why she had come against doctor's orders, Perla answered: "I didn't want to die without having seen your daughter". She had been saying things like that for several days…

Perla always thought of others first. When she woke up from the anaesthetic, after the operation, she said she felt OK, and started asking anybody that came round some personal question. In my case she asked me how I had fared in my exam, which was on that same Wednesday.

The slides of the wedding are wonderful. Seeing Perla on them, so well and looking very healthy, nobody could imagine that under that calm mask were hidden heavy bleeding and strong pain.

Now I feel a great burden of responsibility resting on

my shoulders. As my uncles and aunts say, now I am head of the family for the second time (and each time somebody tells me that, I start to cry). I am in charge of a lot of things now, like looking after my sister, and especially taking care of my father.

And you are so far away! Steve, my love, I need you so much with me here today, so I can cry on your shoulder! I can't stand the crowds, but I don't want to be alone either, because the grief is too unbearable. Some really good friends have been keeping me company.

And we haven't gone through the worst yet. We are still so stunned by the suddenness of the event that its real magnitude has not caught up with us yet. We'll start to realise it when we start noticing Perla's absence in small everyday things. We are going to miss the person who looked after us, that could take care of twenty different things at the same time so we could feel more comfortable, from personal problems to politics; the person who was everywhere, who chose delicious meals for us every day and who told us off when we left things all over the house, and when we put our feet up on the new sofa; or who complained that we were on the phone for hours on end. The everyday things, it is there where it most hurts, a continuous ache.

Perla will not be able to find out now in which language you chatted with the Lama. She won't ask me again what nice things you tell me in your letters, nor will she be asking me any more to tell you to come to this country. She was very keen to meet you!

My love, I'll stop now, I can't see what I am writing for the tears. I anxiously wait for your letters, I very much need them just now.

A hug and a kiss, Alicia.

PS. I am sorry to have unburdened my grief on you, but writing to you has done me a lot of good, I've been able to put on paper thoughts that I find very difficult to talk about. Till soon, my love.

———

New Delhi
11 December 1966

Darling Alicia,

I'm feeling very depressed so thought I should write to my beloved to cheer myself up. One of my defects I did not tell you about is that I occasionally become sad and gloomy, convinced of my own mediocrity and the use-lessness of the work in which I am engaged.

So, some good news. There is an $8^{1}/_{2}$ hour time difference between India and Argentina. I am going to telephone you at 8.30 pm Indian Standard Time on January 1st 1967, that is, at noon in Buenos Aires. Does that suit you? I am worried that the reception may be unclear and that we will not understand each other, being as we are 15,750 miles apart. So we must both speak very clearly.

It is a rather strange fact but I never enjoy telephone conversations, and the history of my dislike is interesting. When I was a boy my parents were not wealthy, not even well off, and since we had no telephone, I had never used one. At about the age of 14 I took a job at my uncle's butcher shop as a delivery boy, tea-maker and so on. Whenever my uncle was too busy to answer the telephone, because, say, he was cutting up a lamb, he would have me do it. However, the telephone was located right next to the main room of the shop, always full of house-wives jostling each other, shouts for sausages, ringing of the cash register, sound of the meat chopper crashing through pork chops. As a result I could never understand what the caller was saying and inevitably had to call my uncle over to take the phone. You will see next year how abrupt I am in telephone conversations. Perhaps your dulcet tones will cure me of my anxiety. What are your own characteristic phobias? The dark? men? loneliness?

I play no musical instrument, but sing like Caruso or Sinatra, as I please, in the shower.

I have several attractive pullovers which will look even more attractive on you, my sweet. I have absolutely no desire to wear any article of feminine apparel. (Do you remember the thug in "Tirez sur le pianiste" who enjoyed so much wearing his sister's silk panties?) I hope this reveals no trait of abnormality. Perhaps you would rather be a man? We'll convince each other of the delights of retaining our own gender – vive la différence!

Sorting through some old letters I came across several photos of Joan, Teresa, Mariella, Alba etc. I showed them to Paul and when I explained that Joan had been my sec-retary his eyes glowed green with envy, and he refused to believe our relation was entirely boss/secretary! Oh! how unfavourably Indian secretaries compare. They type badly, can't spell, never work, and worst of all are entirely – male. I wonder whether my relation with my secretary would have been so innocent if you had been delegated to that noble position? Incidentally, I have often wondered why you didn't bother to come to the airport when I left

Argentina (what a mean question! You don't have to answer it, I know why you didn't).

I have just written to the LSE to ask for an increase in my income when I return to England from £1445 p.a to £2000! If my professor reads the letter over coffee, he'll choke himself to death. I'll let you know what they say, if it bears repetition.

When did you first get engaged to your ex-fiancé? Let me now tell you very briefly why I am depressed. I'll tell you at much greater length next year over several pints of "Guinness" (the liquor of the gods). When I first decided to interest myself in 'the economics of development', I did so because I believed that the low-income countries were full of so much misery because of a shortage of physical and human capital, because of a constraint on their value of exports, because of a continuing increase in population, because of the vicious circle of poverty, but that essentially they were fairly unified, and struggling to improve the well-being of their nations.

This is false, and I now realise how naïve I was – in so many ways – at Oxford. They are nations of conflict, where the grouping of combatants turns on clans, or religion, or location, or race, or caste or all these things. Nor do the majority, almost the entirety that I have met, strive to achieve the welfare and wellbeing of the nation. They are indolent, inefficient, unenthusiastic and selfish.

This has been brought home to me very strongly by the approaching famine in Bihar, which if it comes will be entirely the fault of the Indians, for not digging wells and canals in the past, for not maintaining tube-wells which were provided, for not striving now to overcome these defects but instead the politicians devoting themselves to internecine caste struggles in the attempt to get nominations for a Congress seat next February in the elections, for not giving surplus food grains to Bihar, and to the people, the vast, illiterate, caste-bound peasantry, for not attempting to destroy Congress, and the State bureaucracy, and the capitalists who crush them.

Why should I attempt to forecast the required number of agricultural engineering graduates in 1975-76, what earthly good would it do?

Write to me soon, honey, I'm in a black humour.

I kiss your lips,
    Steve

—◦◦◦—

Buenos Aires
11 December 1966

My dear Steve,

It has been such a relief, in the midst of the general depression, to receive three of your letters, together. Today my mood is better than it was when I wrote to you on the 9th, so I'll try to be a little more coherent in replying to your questions and responding to your stories.

I hope that one of these days you'll explain to me at last what your work project is about. I don't really understand what kind of work it is, whether it is a scholarship, a work contract, a research subsidy, or what.

Another thing that I need you to explain is your student career. I have already noted three universities in which you seem to have studied: Nuffield College, LSE,

Bristol University. I know of course the European system of studies is different from the Argentine; here a student does not change universities often, in Europe it seems they do. Would you please clarify this?

Food in London: yes, truly, the Argentines who have been in London tell me that it is not exactly delicious to the Argentine palate. But there are other possible solutions in addition to Chinese food: to go from time to time to the hotel in Marble Arch where my parents stayed, and where they served wonderful barbecued meat – or alternatively for me to cook the dishes that I am used to.

I'm not in the habit of having breakfast in bed, but I quite fancy the idea of doing it occasionally.

If you are intent on nibbling my earlobe, I'll nibble your chin. Agreed?

Who is the author of that poem that you wrote for me, and from which was plagiarized my "Catch a falling star"…?

Music… I love Mozart's Clarinet Quintet, the one played in the film "Le Bonheur" – do you like it? My other current favourites are four lovely Telemann concerts, and "Shenandoah" sung by Paul Robeson.

Mr. Merrett, how dare you tell a lady dirty jokes? It is unpardonable! … (I felt very frustrated because you stopped in the middle of it!).

Today is 11th December. One year ago today you left Argentina. Today my mother (my real one) would have been 56. She died when she was 49. Today four days have passed since the death of Perla, at 52. I tell you these things, but they do not seem very clear in my head. I am a little bewildered, it seems these things did not really happened, that they could be reversed. But death is a barrier against which humanity's weakness shatters. But distance is not such a barrier: that we can overcome.

Now things are different. My responsibilities are greater, decisions are more difficult, because they involve others. Everyone tells me: 'Now it's up to you to look after your father'; 'Now you have to look after your sister, poor thing, she is pale and thin', 'Now it is your turn to run the house and see that everything runs properly', 'Now you are the head of the family'. I feel that that's how it is, that I'll do it, but it is painful; and sometimes I want to scream out in desperation: 'And me, who's going to look after me?'

I cannot understand what happened to my letters, whether you received a very long one dated November 16th; maybe you did, because you have replied to some of my questions in it, but you haven't said anything about the possibility of your coming to Argentina. It is probably too early to tell, but this latest, painful event affects my life considerably, I have to rethink many things. I do not know how long it will take me to start thinking straight in the midst of this general confusion, and see how I will organize my life, and which will be my role in this new situation. I ask myself how, where and when will we meet again. (And it must happen). I ask you as well – I ask you to think about it and help me think too.

Would you phone me for Christmas, my love? If you can't – have a Merry Christmas and a Happy New Year.

Until soon. With all my love.
Alicia

PS. I love to spend evenings sitting in bed reading books, especially if it is very cold outside.

New Delhi
12 December 1966

Darling, darling, darling, Alicia,

You see how quickly my mood changes when I receive one of your letters: I become gay and effusive. I am afraid you have placed me under some kind of bittersweet spell with these long affectionate letters of yours. If I were Nigerian, I would suspect you of being a witch (a very beautiful one).

Recently I went in to the British High Commission to collect some information on your entry into Britain, and work visa. Whenever we get you a job we shall ask your employer to apply to the Ministry of Labour for them to issue to you a work permit. The bureaucracy may last about 12 weeks but apparently the fact that you are Argentine helps a great deal as there are not a lot of people from Argentina trying to get into the UK.

My religion? I am an atheist, but to put it in a way more satisfactory to the psychologist, I am a socialist.

A cocktail party is a quite distinct social event from a party. The former lasts generally from say 7pm to 9pm; the latter start about 8pm-9pm and last well after midnight. But your description of London after 11pm (or more accurately after the theatres, cinemas and pubs close) is pretty accurate. The streets echo to one's pace, and the pavement glistens silently in the light of the lamps as the drizzle falls. But before 11pm the public house – "the Magnet and Dewdrop", "the Blind Beggar" or "the Mayflower" bustle with life.

I have consulted some experts on your hair. Apparently you should apply some di-ammonium phosphate, about 20kg per hectare, in the second week of January, and then drill in some liquid ammonia in the middle of June, and your hair, according to the latest agronomic data available to us, will grow to a length of some 9-11 feet, and will flower in late July! Why, you'll make a kind of mad Argentine Ophelia my love.

Now let me tell you briefly about my parents. My father was born during the first World War, like my mother, and at the age of 17 emigrated to Canada, but stayed only a few years and then returned to Hackney, in the East End of London, where all the family live. They are, or at least were – for times change – working class "cockneys." A decade or two ago they were very closely knit, living near each other, drinking together in the local pubs and sometimes fighting together. My father is the eldest of them, and very distinct. He is a gentle man, rarely shows any emotion, never drinks and in fact rather disapproves of it, hates disturbing his own status quo, is rather mean. My mother also comes from a working class family, one of six or seven brothers and sisters who were deserted by their father who went to Australia. Her mother, whom I can vaguely recall, died of cancer about 20 years ago and this was a profound emotional shock to my mother. She seems to have been a remarkable strong-willed, loving woman. My mother is very hard working, vivacious, generous, possessive (a quality I loathe in women), and yet makes enemies too easily. Her sister – Aunt Lal – is a wonderful character with a rather brilliant son called Joe.

They are all interesting people, and will be fascinating for a young Argentine sociologist in that my father's side is an illustration, I believe, of the destruction of the East London extended family.

I learnt this morning that my boss is coming from London to Delhi tomorrow and is bringing all my colour slides of the Himalayas and the Taj Mahal and a small projector. If the photo of me with my late beard comes out well, I'll send you a copy.

All my love,
    Steve

—⁓—

Buenos Aires
12 December 1966

My dear Steve,

This morning I received your delayed letter of 1st December. You say that it is not possible for you to come to Argentina. Your logic is crushing. I haven't any counter-arguments. But I think that this whole relationship of ours is beyond logic. If somebody had said, a while back, that something like this would happen to me, I would have thought they were mad, that such things happen so rarely – and that it could not happen to me. But here we are. Thousands of kilometres apart, and yet thinking that something of each of us is in the other – seeking a way to reunite these pieces.

I am not trying to reply to anything. I just want to tell you that I received that letter, that I read it, and that I consider it coherent and logical. But that it hurts me that it is that way.

By now you will have received my last two letters and will know of the death of Perla, my emotional state, and the new problems that have come up and the responsibilities that rest on my shoulders. You will have noticed that at this moment I cannot think of anything, I cannot say anything, but can only try to get over this immense pain, and try to be close to my father, who is left so alone.

You are as important to me as ever. Perhaps I need your presence now with greater intensity, because I feel sad and alone – despite being surrounded by people. They say that one of the most painful experiences is to lose a mother – this situation of losing two mothers, first one and then another, is worse. I live not just the present but also relive the past.

Today I went to the Faculty, I have to sit some exams that I missed last week. It was good to go out, to see people, to do things. Tomorrow I have to get back to studying. It will be tough, but I believe that I must do it.

I see that a scholarship is impossible. To work....yes, I think that you have to try to let me know what are the possibilities of getting work. It seems complicated – but perhaps what's really happening is that today everything is black.

I believe that you should continue with your enquiries – anything can happen, there are many alternatives. Maybe I'll go in April, or at another time; it may be that making a huge effort I can graduate in July (I'll know in mid-January what the chances are, when the new University Statutes are published); it may be that when I talk to my father new options will arise, he is always perfectly logical; also maybe you will somehow be able to come here after all. We must not give up hope – something quite unexpected may come up.

I think you'll like my father a lot. With all my love,
Alicia

—◦◦◦—

Buenos Aires
14 December 1966

My very dear Steve,

Five letters in four days! You're beating all records! Today I received the fifth, dated December 5th. And I am writing to you for the third successive day. Really these letters have had a fantastic effect on me, they arrived in the midst of a period of depression, and they are the only things that can make me happy at this time.

It has been a pleasure to read the list of the 'infinite virtues of your personality', and especially to know that you are modest, sincere and never lie. In honour of this, I've decided to give you the nickname of 'Modesty Steve'. But this new statement of yours contradicts a previous one, when you told me that you are an 'inveterate liar'. Which one should I believe?

You don't like people to talk to you during breakfast, and until you have finished reading the papers. Very well. I will *never* talk to you at breakfast time. I'll only make faces at you and tickle you. (If not, I'll be so bored!). Agreed?

So you are not affectionate? This must be very much an Anglo-Saxon characteristic. I hope you will overcome this shortcoming, at least with me. (If you treat other people rather frostily, I don't mind).

You tell me you are frank…that I do believe! considering what you say at the end of the letter! With me, shyness stops me from being too frank. (But don't take it too seriously).

I hope that you only get drunk infrequently, only on special occasions. I have never got any more 'drunk' than what I can control. After three glasses of wine, I have enough of drinking. Moreover, as there are few alcoholic drinks that I like, it's difficult for me to get drunk.

Will you leave your scooter in India or take it back to London? If you bring it, will you let me drive it? And if not, why don't you bring a buffalo instead ?

I'd love to see you in a sulk. I think you must look very funny, and then I'd cover you with kisses.

It seems very reasonable that one should go to bed at 11 pm and get up before 8 in the morning, especially if you have to work or study. I often do the same. But what I do not understand is that anybody should *love* getting up so early. It does not make sense! It's so nice to stay in bed late in the morning!

According to Appleton's Cuyás Dictionary, 'mimar' (a verb) means 'to pet, fondle, spoil (a child)'. A 'persona mimosa' is, above all, someone who likes to be petted. But to understand the meaning that I give the word, you have to add to that a tendency of the person in question to act sometimes like a kitten, and also include a dash of tenderness and loving that must be offered by another person. And there are other elements involved that I don't know how to explain. But I hope this will give you some notion of what I mean when I tell you that I am 'mimosa'.

I think that one of your greatest virtues is to enjoy washing up! You are a marvel! Such things are rare.

Do you think that in London it is possible to work and study at the same time? That would be the ideal formula for me – it is what I do in Buenos Aires, but I guess that the English approach to study does not allow for that. Today I took my partial exam in Industrial Sociology, but it went quite badly, because I had studied very little (I haven't touched a book for nearly a week), and moreover I felt quite depressed. But I hope to pass, even if not with a high mark.

I am dying to see this photo with you in a beard that never arrives. You are a very bad boy. I think you ought to make sure to have a humongous marvellous photo taken and send it to me fast.

At home things are always the same, there are few variations, the situation doesn't change. I'll not go into details because I think that I have already poured enough of my anguish on you, and if I start to write about it I shall recall it vividly again and afterwards I won't be able to sleep. And it will not be pleasant for you either.

So you are going to phone me on 1st January! For a few hours it will be already 1967 for you, while I shall still be in 1966...I hope we can hear each other, otherwise it will be so frustrating. The two telephone calls we had recently, from my stepbrother Carlos in Israel, were very disrupted; at the beginning you could hardly hear, or the line went dead (the link was through Paris), but then it became louder and one could maintain a normal conversation. We'll see what happens with yours...How lovely it will be if I hear you clearly!

As it's already 2.30 am, and no further intelligent or

original ideas come to mind to write about (I'm too sleepy), I better stop and go to sleep.

A sweet kiss goodnight.
With love,
　　Alicia

—⁓—

New Delhi
15 December 1966

Darling Alicia,

I am so sad to hear that Perla has died, partly because I had come to regard her as an ally in my plans to steal her stepdaughter, partly because your letters had revealed what an intimate relationship you two enjoyed, partly because of the distress of your family.

When you receive this letter – at about Christmas – some three weeks will have passed since her death, the initial shock will have ebbed away and it will be clear to you what you have lost. I am certain that already you will have begun to consider "what shall I do now?" In fact you may have already arrived at a decision.

You may have said to yourself "My father has for the second time in his life lost his wife, his two stepsons live abroad, all he has is myself and Ester. I must, in some sense, take over Perla's role and stay by his side. My journey to England will have to be postponed indefinitely."

What can I say in reply? That in order to consummate our love in the sense of establishing it as a physical, as well as an intellectual relationship, we must be together. In a recent letter you said how inadequate words are, letters, in fulfilling the union we wish to achieve, and believe we can achieve.

I fear that if we do not see each other at Southampton in 18 weeks time, we may never meet again. And this will be very sad for both of us. If you come to England and we marry then whenever your father retires he can come to stay with us and play with his grandchildren. So he'll not be alone for long.

I understand what a dilemma you are facing, honey, but implore you not to leave me alone in England. Come, come in April! Darling Alice, come to hear the breezes of Spring over Christchurch meadows in Oxford, and the Isis lapping at its banks.

How glamorous you look in your photo, and how well your new hairstyle suits you. I am afraid the photo I have included is disappointing, but it's all I have.

I love you,
    Steve

Buenos Aires
22 December 1966

My dearest Steve,

This week your letters have been held up, and after the batch of five in a row, nine days passed until your letter of December 11th arrived today. It's odd: it seems that you were very low more or less at the same time as I was feeling so bad here, because of Perla's death – that is, more or less from the 8th to the 12th of December. If one believed in telepathy...

The time you have chosen to telephone Buenos Aires seems excellent. I really hope that we can hear something. The history of your phobia for telephones is odd for such a useful machine; I hope it is soon cured! I'll do my best to help. For me, on the contrary, the telephone is something indispensable, a part of me; my record is a two-hour long conversation (but not long distance!). The problem with our forthcoming conversation is precisely the shortage of time available. It would be more reasonable if the call could last 15 or 20 minutes rather than three minutes. I am slow to warm up in verbal communication and three minutes is so little time! Still, I believe it is worth trying.

You ask me what are my phobias. The dark? No, I don't think so. Men? No, not at all! I love men! They have always been my best friends! They are not untrustworthy gossips like many women. Solitude? Yes, probably. Something that causes me particular tension is to be in a deserted place very far from any sign of civilization, even when it is with a group of people. But that's not insurmountable, I am trying to find a cure. And what are your phobias?

You also ask me if I would like to be a man. No, never! I feel very happy being a woman, I think I am quite feminine, and furthermore I believe it is much easier to be a woman than a man – it carries less responsibility (maybe not that literally). You wondered why I said I'd like to wear your jumpers. Well, it has been very fashionable in Buenos Aires for girls to wear men's sweaters, and I do like it. But if we are looking for subconscious motives, you could hazard the hypothesis that wearing your pullovers, that is to say, having a part of you with me, I can feel that you belong to me more…probably related to my possessive tendencies. Anyway I am happy that you agree to lend them occasionally. If we delve deeper, there may be other motives – the unconscious is so complicated!

In contrast with your friend Paul, I really believe that the relation between Joan and you was strictly boss/secretary. Not because I know you – really I don't know what could have been your intentions towards a girl as pretty as Joan – but because I know Joan a little. I believe that rarely have I known two girls so incredibly childish as her and Teresa (that's not a shortcoming, it's simply a way of being). On what could have happened if I had been your secretary, I think that by this time it is not worth speculating about it. I'll just say one thing: what a pity I wasn't your secretary!

You ask me why I didn't go to the airport to say goodbye to you. There are several reasons, objective and subjective. ('No relation is totally causal in this world; every phenomenon is the result of the influence of many variables.' Source: Research Methodology by Pearson). The principal objective reason I explained to you when I said goodbye: I had to study. It was not just a pretext: I had an exam just a few days later, and it was the first exam I was taking after a year's almost complete interruption of my studies. So that made me very anxious. The subjective motives, they don't really need to be laid out here – we can talk about them some day perhaps, face-to-face. But I confess that I had fits of regret, and a great wish to go…I almost went…but then I didn't. Today I think that, in spite of everything, I should have gone.

You ask about my ex-fiancé. Briefly, we started going out together around August 1963. In May 1965, we formally decided to get married when he graduated as an engineer, which was still about another year off. A few months later, from around October, things started to go wrong – for a number of reasons. However, the relationship continued – although in an up-and-down way – until March 1966, when it finally ended.

And you? What about your relationship with Mariella – how did it begin, how and why did it end? Apart from that, did it ever occur to you to count how many girl-friends you have had in your life? Was any of them particularly important?

I have read in the papers about the problem of hunger in Bihar, the hunger strike of Sikh Fateh Singh in Chandigarh, and other similar things. India will explode soon, you told me. I hope it doesn't happen before you leave for London, the situation could turn very ugly for foreigners.

I do have a feel for your depression, it has happened to me too. Especially when I was part of the University's political movements, and I felt very disappointed by the lack of unity amongst people, the unproductiveness and the charlatanism. I understand and share your disillusion. Perhaps it is to feel in a small way the failure of adolescent ideals; reality does not match ideals, it is oneself that has to adjust to reality. And sometimes it hurts, and depression comes.

You say that one of your defects is sometimes to feel sad and low, and convinced of the uselessness of your efforts, etc. I don't think it is a defect. I think that is a very normal reaction, and quite common. I detest people who are always smug and convinced that all they do is right –

I think in part it is a mask to protect themselves.

Anyway: cheer up, my love! Things are not going so very badly (yet). Being depressed gets you nowhere. I am with you, if only in imagination, I kiss you, embrace you, distract you and – there we are! No more sadness or depression!

Life at home, no change; today I am in quite a good mood, so I'll leave that subject for another day.

My sweet, my beloved Steve, I hope that this letter finds you well and happy, and not depressed. Write to me soon, I don't like to have to wait too long between one letter and the next.

All my love.
Alicia

———

New Delhi
22 December 1966

Darling Alicia,

I have just received your letter of December 11th. I see that by now you will have received my two letters on what we should do; in case they have gone astray I'll try briefly to put together my thoughts.

I love you. You love me. We need to be together for some time to decide whether we should marry. Thus I must go to Argentina or you to England.

It will not be possible for me to go to Argentina because I cannot afford the return air fare London-Buenos Aires, and because I feel we shall need 4-6 months together to make up our minds, and could only come for three or four weeks because of my obligations to the London School of Economics.

It is difficult for you to come to England for a number of reasons. You do not have the money for the fare. But I have already said I'll pay your out-bound fare; the return ticket it seems unlikely we'll need.

You have no money to live in England. But you'll be living with my parents, so board and lodging will be free as long as you wish to stay with them. Also I believe the chances of your getting employment as a translator or research assistant are excellent.

You will have to give up family and friends. There you have to make a choice: to give up them – or me.

You will have to leave your father alone. Yes, but if we marry, he can, if he wishes, come to live with us.

My great desire is that you come to England next April; if you do not then I believe we shall never meet again.

Now let me answer two of your questions, I'll write you another letter tomorrow answering the rest.

I left school in 1957, when I was 18, and went into the Royal Air Force, to the pilot training school at Cranwell in Lincolnshire. (Got a map?) I left for a whole series of reasons, which I can reminisce about at length but the major one was – or was it? – the fact that I was a very incompetent pilot. (Similarly I drive a car or scooter badly – but effectively.) I decided, for want of anything better to do, to go to University and one month after leaving the R.A.F. (May 1959) was accepted for the 3-year course in Philosophy and Economics at the University of Bristol. I graduated in June 1962, and at the same time was accepted by Nuffield College, Oxford to a post-graduate degree in

Economics. Both at Bristol and Oxford I had scholarships covering my board, lodgings and fees from the Local or Central Govt. (Which is one reason I'm a socialist.) I graduated from Nuffield in June 1964 with a Bachelor of Philosophy (Economics.). Soon afterwards I accepted a "Research Fellowship" at el Centro de Investigaciones Económicas, initially for one year but on the understanding that it could be extended. I did not like Buenos Aires, nor porteños and therefore decided to leave at the end of my year.

A few months before I left I met a pretty girl called Alicia Kaner to whom I felt very much attracted. However, at that time I was going out with a fine girl called Mariella, whom I knew would be broken-hearted if I left her for another girl, and therefore never asked Alicia to be my girlfriend, the deciding factor being that I was to leave the country within a few months. But I never could forget this girl – even though she did not say good-bye to me.....

A short time before I left Argentina I had decided that the kind of research in which I was really interested is "Manpower Planning." At that same time I was offered the post of "Research Officer" at the London School of Economics on the understanding that I would proceed, with all possible haste, to New Delhi to start work on a project in education and manpower planning. I accepted, returned to England via the wonderful island of Cuba on December 24th 1965, joined the academic staff of the London School on January 1st, and left for India on February 2nd. But I still could not forget this girl Alicia...

This famous project. Myself and David Ovens, my colleague from the LSE, are making a study of the Indian nitrogen fertiliser industry with our interest centred on the variables: net output at capacity, capital stock, the occupation profile of the labour force by establishment, the formal education derived by each occupation group. We wish to predict for the next 10 years the size of the industry's labour force and its occupation structure and the formal education that will be necessary for these occupations to be carried out efficiently. Finally we want to try to generalize from this industrial study, to say how predictions of demand by manufacturing industry for educated manpower can be most efficiently made. At the moment we are working on the monograph and hope to complete it within 4-5 months. In any case I shall be leaving India in February to go home to my own country.

Alicia, listen to me carefully. I want to be with you. I want to go to see "The Lady with the Little Dog" with you and talk about it over coffee. I want to take you around my favourite pubs in London. I want to watch you cooking a 'bife' (steak) and eat it with you. I want to introduce you to my friends and see you win their affection: Stewart & Coral, Keith & Sheila, Peter, Oscar & Sonia, Mark and Cat, Joan, Jorge, Anne and Jean-Michel, Bob, Ted. I want to take you to see "King Lear" and "Hamlet" and "The Homecoming" and tell you why I enjoyed it and hear your views, over a Chinese meal at the "Hong Kong". I want to sit in bed with you on a cold evening and persuade you to put down "The Tin Drum", just for a little while. I want to lie entwined in your arms, make love with you and tell you I love you.

But I want *to do* these things not just to *write* them.

And we can begin on April 26th at Southampton dock, *if* you come.

Come!
All my love,
   Steve

—◦◦◦—

New Delhi
23 December 1966

Darling Alicia,

Lots of questions to answer, so: I deplore drinking tea or breakfast in bed; immediately after washing I have to read the papers whilst stuffing food into my face with a free hand. Can you cook scrambled eggs well? If not, you'd better start learning. (I'll wash the dishes.) I'll come to a compromise on the hours of retiring and rising. We'll go to bed before 11pm and get up after 8am. The ideal existence! Now that I think I understand what you mean by "mimosa", every night I'll put out for you a small plate in the kitchen full of chopped liver and herrings; and in the mornings a saucer of milk. Agreed? Do you have a very sexy purr? When I told you I never lie I was lying, and when I told you that I am an inveterate liar I told the truth, but it is false that I lie always.

I am planning to return straight home to England in February and start looking for a flat. I am going to sell my scooter to Paul for £99. My father has a ten-year old Ford Anglia; I'm sure that with a little gentle persuasion he'll let you drive it. Very handy thing for holidays in Britain, e.g. Cornwall, Scotland, the Lake District, and for trips to Oxford and Bristol. The poet who wrote 'Go, and catch a falling star' is: John Donne. (Pronounced DUNN.)

As far as study goes, I should say the two most obvious possibilities are: evening classes if they are given in Sociology or Social Anthropology, or that you attend a British University full-time, while I work. But that we can discuss when, if, we meet again.

Paul and I are having a competition to see who gets the most Christmas cards. A string runs across one wall of the double-room we share together and we are hanging the cards on that. As the number of cards increases the string gets lower with their weight, however Paul has devised a brilliant technique by which an empty (alas!) whisky bottle is used as a counterbalance; this can be filled with water as its optimal weight rises.

Paul and I are getting along really very well now; my vulgar language, extreme political views and harsh atheism has knocked the edges off his prudery and Christian poses; on the reverse side of the coin I have begun to enjoy his dry humour, natural friendliness and fascination for India. I'm always telling him about you and how you're breaking my heart; he must be quite fed up with it, poor chap.

A few days ago we had an earthquake in the middle of the night; a low rumbling sound, the beds shivering, the double-windows rattling. All over in about ten seconds and no harm done.

Now let me introduce you to one of our little community of technical assistants. Sir Robert Rae. He's about 72, a Scot by birth, fought in the First World War on the North-West Frontier of India – at that time part of the British Empire. Knows a very great number of distinguished men and women, especially scientists, including "Winnie" (Churchill). He's the kindest, most warm-hearted man you could wish to meet, always willing to listen to your point of view, and hear out a young man 45 years younger than he. An "old-fashioned Liberal" as he calls himself, full of amusing stories about country-folk in Britain.

Well honey, it's 10.55pm fast approaching my bed-time so I'll say good-night.

I kiss your lips,
    Steve

Buenos Aires
Undated

My very dear Steve,
    Today the post delivered the following correspondence:

1. A very sweet letter from you in reply to mine in which I told you about Perla's death. I'll reply to that shortly.
2. What a surprise! A Christmas card signed by Mr. and Mrs. Merrett, Leytonstone, London, England, and which my clairvoyant powers linked to a correct use of the hypothetical-deductive method lead me to suspect they are your parents.
3. A note from the New Vision Bookshop informing me that the balance of my account is $.... (Oh! Sorry! That was a slip, something I don't believe will interest you much).

To which I have replied as follows:

1. That's where I am now.
2. I have sent them a New Year's card in reply to thank them for their warm gesture. Do you think that I should write them a letter? Or maybe a bit later, when I know for sure whether I shall go to London – and when. I await your instructions because I don't know what the English custom is.
3. I'll go by one of these days to pay my December bill. Unfortunately each time I go and pay, I come home with another load of books! So the balance of my account gets higher!

At last the Himalayan photo arrived! Sure it is a bit dark, your face especially, but it looks very attractive (and not exactly for the view behind you!). I think I prefer you without a beard after all (and without a hat). In fact, I prefer you in person and not in a photo. But, for the time being, we'll make do with the photos.

In your letter of the 15th you reflect on the influence of Perla's sad death on my decision to go to England. It really does have quite an effect, as I told you before. I'm always thinking about it all and it makes it very difficult to arrive at a definite conclusion. Everything is mixed up: most importantly it is not easy for me to up sticks and leave my father and my younger sister alone – not to mention my own concerns and uncertainties. My mind is full of contradictions: on the one side, yes, I should stay with my father, it upsets me terribly to see him so alone; sometimes, at night, when I am up studying, I hear him walking up and down through the house, and I can't stop the tears. I now fulfil a series of roles formerly carried out by Perla – formal roles; but of course I cannot fulfil them all, nor am I the ideal companion for him, and although he feels very happy having me and my sister around, I don't think for a moment that he intends holding us with him indefinitely – however much it may hurt – he is a very intelligent and sensitive man. And at the other end of the spectrum: why shouldn't I go to London? My father is 63, and I am only 24, my life is just starting, I cannot stay still and vegetate, I have to live life, intensely, try to be happy, not tie myself to memories. As Perla said, we have to move forward, come what may.

As you see, my moods and my thoughts seem to vary, rushing from one extreme to another very quickly, like the pendulum. So I feel I am not in a state to take a decision just now. My love, you tell me that you are afraid that if I do not go in April may be we shall never see each other again. That's not true – the actual date of our meeting is not important – we'll resolve this situation one way or another, and we will eventually meet – whether it is in April, May or even July. Because I feel as strongly as ever the desire to see you, to embrace you, to be with you and to establish between us a relationship that is real, physical, concrete, complete, not only intellectual. And I believe that is what we must most care for – to maintain this inner force that drives us together. Then, external difficulties become easier to resolve.

With respect to my father, I really believe that the only thing that could fulfil his life now are grandchildren; unfortunately, Carlos's two sweet girls – Nurit, four years old, and Yael, three – are in Israel, far away. And we other three children have been quite slow so far in delivering grandchildren…

Dear Steve, I would really like you to write a short letter to my father, if you don't mind. He is a very private man, seemingly distant on the surface, nevertheless small attentions and affectionate gestures really touch him. I don't know what you could write to him about – you could say that you have invited me to spend a couple of months in London, living in your parents' home, and that you would be pleased if he agrees and can help me to do it. Or something like that. I leave it to you. My father has similar features to you in some senses: he is quite 'sharp-tongued', does not easily establish deep relationships with new people, is brief, concise, mathematical, ordered, precise in his sentences and in his ways of acting.

My brother Horacio and his wife are still in Buenos Aires, they are off to Europe soon, in April 1967.

I'll write soon. I love you dearly.
Alicia

—∿∿—

Buenos Aires
Undated

My dearest Steve,

Hip, hip, hooray! Today is a day of great and magnificent news! First and fundamental: I have just had a long talk of about two hours with my father, and he is *totally in agreement with my voyage to England*. Isn't that extraordinary! I am so pleased that I don't know what to do to fully express my excitement, I want to jump, dance, scream, and above all I want to tell you about it. Luckily the day after tomorrow is January 1st 1967: and I'll tell you by telephone! (If we can hear each other!).

I'll try to sum up as best as possible my father's reasoning and the conclusions to which we arrived. As I told you in a recent letter, you can expect anything from him, and he is always perfectly logical. His fundamental premise is that children cannot always live tied to their parents, they have to leave home, work out their own way and live their own lives. Therefore, he considers that my idea of travelling to England, independently of any other motive, is a chance to enjoy positive experiences: to live by myself, make my own way, get to know a different environment and new people, improve my English, and learn many new things that you do not learn from books but from human contact. And that it is not madness (as my stepbrother said, so incorrectly). As to other reasons: he accepts gratefully that I should live for a time with your parents, and has no opinions of his own in that respect, first because he does not know you and second because he considers that is a path that I have to choose and you cannot foresee now, with absolute certainty, what may happen between us. Sure, he asked me what you are like, what you do, how old are you etc., to get to know you. There is only one thing in which we differ, and that is he believes I should graduate before leaving. After discussing this issue, we arrived at the following conclusions: once the new University Statute is out, which I hope will be next month, in January, and we see what will happen to the degree in Sociology in Buenos Aires, I will see what are my chances of graduating in July 1967. If that is feasible, I will delay my journey by three months (if you agree), and I will graduate in July. If that isn't possible, then I will leave in April or May – really there would be no justification in waiting for a year if that is what it may take to graduate.

Re – financing my trip, etc.: there will be no problems. It is a pity that this year we are expecting an economic crisis, because my father says that if things go well in his business, he perhaps could pay for a complete year of studies in England. That surprised me enormously, it is very unusual for him to be so free with money. But this is how it goes – he even made a budget, which came to somewhere between 80 to 90 pounds sterling per month to cover lodging, food, books, University fees etc. I think I may be able to live on less, maybe £60–70. In any case it is a huge amount of money! And of course it is not absolutely sure that my father will be able to send me money every month, the economic situation can change a lot, for better or for worse. Today there was a raving speech from Onganía, who instead of talking about the mounting economic problems and the recent ministerial resignations, spoke of the greatness of the country and other similar stupidities.

Re – the chances of my graduating in July: I sat an examination yesterday, I will sit another one on 3rd January, and another on the 12th. I have also followed a course on Industrial Sociology, which is to be examined in March, and after that I will have 7 more courses to complete, two compulsory and five elective ones. Normally I would need another year to attend the courses and sit the exams. But if the University situation permits it (why and how takes a long time to explain, and I'll tell you another time), I could be examined on two more subjects in March, 'free' (that is, without having previously followed a course), and the five remaining, attend the courses in the first term of the University year, and sit the exams in May and July dates. And graduate! I would then go flying off to England! – perhaps really flying, if everything goes well I may be able to go by plane (it costs $463 one-way). Do you mind waiting for me three months longer? I'm pretty sure you do mind – and I do too, because I'd like to see you as soon as possible. But it would be sensible to graduate first, my chances of further study and self-fulfilment would really expand. What do you think, my love?

I eagerly await your response to this letter with all your views. My sister Ester sends you her greetings. Until soon my sweet. I love you.

Alicia

———⌇⌇———

Buenos Aires
1 January 1967

My dear Steve,
I received your letter of 22nd December 1966. You first summarize your thoughts on what we must do to see each other, and the reasons why it is difficult for me to go to England. I suppose that by now you'd have received my letter of the 30th of December, about my long conversation with my father, which I can sum up by saying that he supports my going to England, considering that it is sure to be a positive experience, whatever happens, and that therefore he'll help me do it – from the economic point of

view – but that he wants me to graduate first, the chances of which I'll know quite soon – in one or two months – it relates directly to the University situation in Argentina, on the responses I obtain from the universities of London, on the chances to be accepted as an undergraduate, etc. etc.

With this, points 1 and 2 of the practical difficulties are solved: 'money for the fare', and 'living in England (board and lodging)' – partly because of my father's money, and partly because of your parents' invitation to live with them, at least for a while.

Point 3: it requires a decision: 'to give up family and friends – or Steve.' On that the agreement of my father is also important: because the moral support his approval gives me, so that I can choose to be with you, but that does not mean I lose my family: they (my father and my sister, fundamentally), support me, in a certain way share my new experiences, I can count on them, and if it ever comes to my staying on in England with you, perhaps they can come to visit me – and to get to know you.

Point 4: to leave my father alone. That is what I still agonize about. But Perla's death is very recent, and I'm sure that time will wash away a little the pain and the loneliness. If we get married…well, we're sure to find solutions to the problem. In any case, I cannot stay at my father's side all my life.

The last phrase of this first part is: 'My great desire is that you come to England next April; if you do not then I believe we shall never meet again'. In reply I quote from Hamlet: 'If it be now, it is not to come; if it be not to come, it will be now; if it be not now, yet it will come; the readiness is all'. The actual date is not yet known, it depends as much on external factors as on you and me; but the reply is: I'm coming.

I was thinking of telling you all this today by telephone; but you did not call. What happened? I was waiting for your call, as you told me, today at noon – 8.30 pm in India. I have thought of a million things that could have changed your plans, a breakdown in the service, etc. But I didn't get to explain anything, I have to wait for your explanation. But I felt – and still feel – quite depressed and disappointed, I had built up so many dreams about the call. Is it something serious? Is it something simple that can be solved? Can you call me some other day?

In the second part of your letter, at last I've learnt what your famous project is all about! My father finds it very interesting, and thinks that in spite of the problems that exist in the under-developed countries – which at times make you think how the devil can such a project be any use if afterwards the bureaucrats and politicians don't put it into practice – it is essential to carry out such studies. I also note your University career. You already know about mine.

The third part of your letter: what a wonderful panorama you offer me for when I am in London! I agree with all your points. I will add that I want to get to know with you all the odd corners of London, the great buildings, the museums, the narrow streets, the University; the English countryside, the castles, the nearby villages; I want us to go dancing, to read Shakespeare together and the great English poets, and listen to you explaining to me all the subtleties of their thoughts; and that at nightfall we listen, in each other's arms, to the songs of Joan Baez, Gilbert Becaud and Billie Holiday.

Yesterday the family got together for the New Year in the house of my uncle Germán. How we missed Perla, the bright spark of every celebration! In her place, Haydée and I cooked. The dinner turned out very well, but the pain of her absence was very great. 1966 was a very difficult year – among other things, a fire in my father's factory, and serious surgery, from which he took a while to recover. We'll see what 1967 brings. Dear Steve, I hope that it will be very good for you and for me, together.

I'll write soon. With all my love,
    Alicia.

———

Buenos Aires
3 January 1967

My dear Steve,

Today I received your letter of the 23 December 66 with responses to a mountain of questions of mine, and more questions from you. I hope that when you received (a little delayed) my Christmas card, you didn't hang it on the wall with a piece of string (in competition with those of Paul), but that you placed it in some special place of honour.

Talking of Paul, just as you tell me that he must be 'fed up' with hearing you talk about me, so too must my friend Graciela be tired of hearing me talk about you and my planned journey to London. With respect to your friend Sir Robert Rae, from your description he seems to me to be a delightful person and I would very much like to meet him.

You sharp-tongued devil! It seems to me that your interpretation of 'mimosa' does not exactly correspond to mine...

I do know how to cook 'scrambled eggs'; if my way of cooking them is not to your taste, I'm sure I can learn and adapt a little. As long as you wash the dishes afterwards, I'll learn to make all the dishes that you may fancy!

I'll make every effort, with great pleasure, to persuade your father to let me drive his car. For that purpose I'll obtain an 'International Driving Licence', since I guess my Argentine one will be of no use.

Last week, the day on which we celebrated the birthday of my cousin Ana María, we had an interesting discussion with a group of friends. The theme can be summed up by the following title: Man: is he or is he not a monogamous animal? Of course, we discussed this for two whole hours and arrived at no conclusion, but we had a lot of fun. Above all because there was a married couple present, and it was interesting to hear their points of view, and see the glances they exchanged...

I don't think we shall meet in Southampton, but at London Airport. My father informed me today that it is cheaper to travel with Aerolíneas Argentinas than with BUA – only $395.

I see that you are an atheist; I am too; but I insist that I would like to know what is the religion of your parents; or at least your remote ancestors.

I am delighted to accept your proposal of going to bed before 11 pm and to get up at 10 am. That would be perfect. From the bad handwriting of your last two letters, I suppose that you must spend the great part of the day writing. Are you drafting your monograph on the project?

I never did work out the story of whether or not you

are a liar or not, and when. Moreover, since I don't like liars, I propose a treaty: for every lie you tell, I will smoke a cigarette. So that if I become a chain-smoker, it will be your fault. I hope you will be racked with remorse!

I am still concerned about your failing to phone me on Sunday January 1st 1967, as you had promised. It feels a bit like the first practical commitment in our relationship failed...because of that I am quite disappointed. Just as you did not call me, I can feel that you will not be at London Airport waiting for me... (If your first reaction is to throw a book to my head, please don't; take into account that today I am in a dark mood.) And I suppose that I will have to wait a few days before getting an explanation. I hope it was nothing serious; my fantasies run from a problem with the telephone link through to you being sick or something like that.

My love, I am going to stop here because it is 1 am. I hope to get news from you soon.

I love you and miss you a lot.
Alicia

———

New Delhi
3 January 1967

Darling Alicia,

At times, suitably settled into the grubby, smoke-filled corner of some English pub with a half-emptied pint of Guinness in front of me and a sympathetic ear I will discourse sagely on THE TWENTIETH CENTURY, that it is the Age of Communications, that measured in temporal units the world has shrunk in a fantastic way, that the telephonic world has destroyed for ever and a day the glory of letters…

The day before yesterday I was proved wrong. I am a million light-years from you, wandering in another galaxy, alienated from my love. An Island. I spent from 20.30 hours (local time) until past midnight at intermittent intervals, trying to phone you. The line, they told me, just gave out a buzz. The same thing happened last night so I have given up the attempt. Today your wonderful, warm letter of the 22nd arrived and your pretty Christmas card.

Let me tell you briefly what happened during Christmas and the New Year. On Christmas Eve I went to the Laguna with Sir Robert Rac, Sir William Slater, David Ovens and Professor Arthur Steiner (University of Los Angeles) where we had a meal. It was amusing to see these distinguished old men sitting there wearing fancy paper hats, blowing trumpets and passing rather lecherous remarks on the well-shaped rumps jigging about the dance-floor. The sari can be a very erotic form of dress, you'll see – and demonstrate of course.

On Christmas Day I went to have lunch with a British couple from the UK. High Commission. We ate turkey, ham, baked potatoes, cauliflower in sauce, and drank whisky, beer, sherry, champagne. Excellent meal and the first time I had eaten well for some days since the food here at the Centre is so nauseating. On Boxing Day I went to an "old-time musicke hall" at the High Commission, enjoyed the sketches and sang all the "old songs" afterwards.

The first Thursday after Christmas was the best evening I've had in India. I organised a dinner party at the flat of a Welsh girl here working with the U.N. My Bulgarian friend, as vivacious as ever, came (poor girl has been separated from her husband for over a year now), a Hungarian journalist, Paul, Rani, and Sunnil – an Indian boy. It was a very gay evening, with some good French wine (Beaune) and I danced with all the girls in sight for hours on end. For the first time since I left Argentina, I danced "spontaneously" letting my body sway and drift like seaweed in a strong undertow, till the sweat ran into my eyes.

New Year by contrast was very dull and I went to bed by 10.30!! Awful.

You ask me what the reply of LSE was to my request for a rise. Ah! But if I tell you then you'll know my most intimate financial secrets and will extort from me on Friday night when I come home with the weekly wage packet every last penny so that I can't spend it on booze. However, since we are in the age of the salary paid by cheque I can outwit you with these institutional devices, and therefore, Miss Kaner, will furnish you with the information you have requested.

They have agreed to promote me to Senior Research Officer (Oh! Delight) although apparently I shall be the youngest staff member at the LSE with this distinguished title. However, they say they cannot get me my £2000 p.a. so I have more or less decided to leave LSE next May/June when the fertiliser monograph is complete. My reasons are:

1. I want to leave India, so that you and I can decide our lives together, and because I'm almost completely disillusioned with the Indian polity.

2. I've had my fill of research into manpower and education, which is too much on the borderline of economics for my own taste.

3. LSE won't pay me enough. This is relatively unimportant. (If, as the Chicagoans would have us believe, I wished to maximise my income I should be in Washington working for the Pan-American Union and earning $12,000 per annum.) (Doesn't it make your mouth water?)

Te doy un beso, dulce y caliente,
Con todo mi amor
    Steve

———∿∿———

Buenos Aires
Undated

Hi, my love! How are you? If you could be here with me now, you would be listening to Joan Baez singing "I still miss someone"; you could read the recently published book of cartoons of "Mafalda" while I am studying Social History, and I would give you a kiss behind the ear.

And – who won the Christmas card competition, Paul or you?

To celebrate the fifth anniversary of his Ford Taunus, my father crashed it, so it will be in the garage about two weeks (oh, how slow the bureaucracy of the under-developed countries), and he feels like a fish out of water. He is not feeling too bad, but when he is not at work, or out with friends, he doesn't know what to do with himself;

television bores him, he's tired of reading, he walks round and round the house. I do feel for him, I understand what he's going through. We've been talking about many things, about Perla, about my mother, etc. etc.

The other day I was reading once again your article on Argentine engineering students, and on reaching the paragraph: "The first set of hypotheses we shall wish to test is that annual real consumption rises with age and social class, and that family support falls with age and varies directly with social class", I thought of a phenomenon related to that hypothesis: whereas many families of the Argentine upper middle class could perfectly well pay the cost of their children's studies, in practice they insist on them working to support themselves, or at least financing part of their University costs, while on the other hand, many lower middle class families act in the opposite way; parents make many sacrifices for their children to have a chance to study, and do not want them to 'waste time' working. So a wealthy father wants his son not to be 'Daddy's boy', by learning from an early age to take care of himself, while a father from a lower economic level (and a lower cultural level too), wants his son to study, so their children can achieve the frustrated aspirations of the parents.

To switch from this intellectual conversation to something more personal...let's talk, for example, of how I would have liked to have you with me yesterday. I was so beautiful! (As you see, I'm not too modest). I'll describe myself: I put on my new corn-yellow suit: very short the skirt, and a jacket and blouse of the same design: shoes and handbag both white; my hair, which gets longer all the time, loose and collected behind with a bow; my skin lightly bronzed by the sun, since Ester, her friend Blanca and I study together every morning in our garden, wearing bikinis. Today, on the other hand, I am dressed very informally: my hair is all messed up, as I always play with my hair whilst I study, and wear a loose dress so I can feel comfortable while studying: with my feet up on the chair, curled up on the cushions, stretched out on the bed, etc. When I study, I cannot stay still for long; as well as continuously changing my position, I get up to make a coffee, I drink coca-cola, I eat biscuits, I put on a record, etc. In spite of everything, I learn a lot. Of course if I could concentrate better, perhaps my time would be more productive...

Two questions. 1. Do you like "Carmina Burana", by Carl Orff? 2. What do you think of psychoanalysis? – and a request: tell me about your likes and dislikes in English poetry.

I am growing ever more impatient to see you. I am still waiting for your letter explaining the mystery of why you did not telephone me. I kiss you,

Alicia.

PS. I love you, Stevie darling.
PS2. Greetings to Sir Robert Rae and to Paul.

—―∿∿―

New Delhi
11 January 1967

Darling Alicia,

I have received (yesterday) your letter of January 1st, which could hardly be from my point of view a more beautiful way to starting the year. However, your letter of the 30th has not yet arrived, but should turn up tomorrow so I'll reply to the two letters together, and here will confine myself to frivolities.

First: you are a brute. I was preparing for the first time to write you a letter full of anger and scorn, because it had become quite clear that (until 30th December) you had informed neither Perla nor your father of our plans for you to come to England. Unfortunately before I put pen to paper you deprive me of the grounds for my indignation. I believe that a first-class "stand-up row" between two people in love is very therapeutic from time to time so that they can release all the grumbles they have about the other which their very attraction leads them to hide. So now we'll (at least I'll) have to wait until you have been in England for a while; the great advantage of this course of action is that we'll be able to enjoy all the emotional and sensual pleasures of reconciliation.

What an extraordinary photo this is of us together. It must be a very curious camera since it is capable of making you appear much less attractive than you are and me much more handsome than I really am. I'll send you next week a photo of me dancing the Conga at a British High Commission party on Boxing Day, when I was wearing my fabulous Jodhpuri suit.

Now let me tell you about me and Mariella. We started going out together (I think) on May 15th 1965 and stopped courting on December 11th 1965. The rest I'll tell you when I know you better, similarly for the one or two girls I knew before Mariella became my girlfriend.

By the way apart from the fact that *ethnically* you are Jewish, is that also your *religion*?

You remember I sent lots of papier mâché work made

by Jaffa Ali back to England, including a heart-shaped trinket box for you to put my heart in since you own it (Ah! Donne!), well it has all arrived very safely, nothing broken and my mother is delighted with the lamp standard I sent. They wrote to me saying that you are very welcome to go and take over our "front-room" for a few weeks till you get a flat of your own. If you wish to stay with them permanently I think they would like you to take over my bedroom (don't take fright, unfortunately I'll have got myself a flat by that time). The house has only got six rooms.

I know my parents would very much like to have a letter from you (English please! But not too shocking!), and I suggest you write when you definitely know what month you'll be coming. "Make it April," he said, "please," running his fingers down the nape of her neck and kissing her bared shoulder.... film fades out." Of course, if you can graduate in July, you should definitely stay on, and emerge with a degree triumphant. But I'll hate it all the same.

Within the next few days I'll write a letter to your Dad,

All my loving,
    Steve

PS. ¡I miss you!

————

New Delhi,
14th January 1967

Darling Alicia,
    At last your letter of the 30th has arrived so I can give you my response. Your father really does seem to be an extraor-

dinary man, not merely because he is so generous in granting you such a princely allowance, but much more because he appears so willing for his daughter to leave house and home, cross the Atlantic and stay with the parents of a man he has only met on one occasion. He must have great confidence in your own adaptability and to use a Hindi word "dharma" (sort of moral fibre, knowledge and acceptance of a correct way of living. Swamis, gurus and sadhus say everyday in India just now that what the country lacks is "dharma").

If the real possibility of your staying in Buenos Aires until July and graduating exists then you must certainly do so. This for several reasons: that you have studied long and hard and it would be a great shame not to carry the thing through to its final conclusion, that it may facilitate your entering a British University, that in the longer run if you stay with me, the possibility exists of your teaching in a British University.

Recently I said that I intended leaving LSE in about 5 months time. I still intend to do so since I don't believe in studying Indian development problems from a London office. The possibilities I mentioned as alternatives were: (i) to work in Cuba. (ii) to work in one of the British nationalised industries. (iii) to get a research fellowship at one of the British Universities. Cuba must now be counted out, at least for the next year or so, since it would be inconsistent with your getting a British diploma/degree. I think (ii) is now a very strong runner, and when I get back I'll start making enquiries. The only difficulty is that I should *have* to be based in London or Oxford to suit your studying (iii) is attractive, save that if I carry on as an academic I would want to write about low-income countries and again this would entail extended field trips to the country in question. So (ii) looks the best bet just now.

Last night I had a delightful time. At 10 pm after spending the evening with Sir John and Lady Hicks (he is probably the most eminent living British academic economist) I got into bed, put the three photos I have of you right by me and started re-reading all your letters to me right from the first little note that Mariella sent to me – in which you asked me whether I had taught Indian women how to swallow the pill. I know – in my next letter I'll try to give you an account of the progress of the family planning programme. Anyway after 75 minutes I had only got up to letter no. 9 (3 Nov. '66) and I'll carry on with this delightful task tonight.

Well honey, I shall stop now and carry on my history of the Indian nitrogen fertiliser industry.

I am very happy that we shall see each other soon in April or in July and settle this romance once and for all. Tell me as soon as the Statutes of the University have been finalised, won't you?

All my love, honey,
Steve

PS. Do I present the cattle to your father or your maternal uncle?

———

Buenos Aires
15 January 1967

My dear Steve,

I am really concerned because I have not received any letters from you since 3ʳᵈ January. That, combined with the lack of a phone call, is doubly worrying: no telephone call – no letters. I am very apprehensive and fearful when there is no news – in this case, I worry in case something bad has happened to you. I hope to get a reply soon at least to *one* of the seven letters that I have sent you in the last three weeks.

Latest news: First, the good one: I have passed my Social History exam with an 'Outstanding' grade (the highest possible mark), which made me very happy. The second news item is quite bad. A few days ago my father's partner in his firm died; they had worked together for 34 years and got along very well. This, on top of the death of Perla, has really left him depressed.

My darling, at the risk of you accusing me of plagiarism, I'll finish with a phrase of yours: You must have a heart of ice to leave me languishing for so long without a reply.

All my love,
Alicia

—⁓—

New Delhi,
17 January 1967

My dearest and darling Alicia,

Quote Hamlet at me, will you? It is a play that fascinates me; I once knew great chunks of it by heart since I was "prompt" in a production given by my school at the Edinburgh Festival in 1957. The boy who played Hamlet – Derek Jacobi – now plays Cassio to Olivier's Othello.

Unfortunately I cannot give Sir Robert your best

wishes as he returned to England about a week ago. Just before he left I said that I would like to come and visit him on the Isle of Man – a small island off the West coast of Britain – sometime next summer and bring my beautiful (intellectual) Argentine girlfriend. He says we'll be very welcome. I'd like you to meet him as he's such a magnificent old man, the archetypal "English gentleman" (tho' he's a Scot).

After reading you describing your appearance with such lavish praise I began to conjure up in my mind's eye what you'd look like in your first mini-skirt in London. Ah! what a delightful pastime! I decided that my view of the excellent leg show in the picture of you seated in an arm-chair that the mini-skirt will suit you perfectly and am longing to see you try your first one on. Incidentally you *must* bring to the UK the dress you are wearing in the photo I just mentioned – it's very, very pretty.

I've not only not *read*, I've not even heard of Carmina Burana. Sounds like the name of the horse that won the Derby a few years ago, or am I mistaken?

Will continue, tomorrow,

All my loving,
Steve.

———

Buenos Aires
18 January 1967

My dearest Steve,
Aaaahhhh! (great sigh of relief). Finally, a letter, after

two weeks without news! I return to normality. Your letter of January 3rd arrived yesterday. I am now on holidays – no more exams until March. Now I can relax a little (not too much) and get on with other activities, such as shopping, tidying up books and documents, helping in the house, going to the cinema, writing letters, etc. etc. Re-work, I am collaborating in the final editing of the report on Internal Migration, with Mario Margulis, and that will probably go on until March.

Graciela and I have decided to meet up a couple of times a week to read some 'case-studies' in Social Anthropology.

I'm glad that you went to some good parties in December! When in London, you must teach me to dance your way. My way of dancing is different, gentle movements and with a stronger rhythm (but much more 'sexy'). I love Latin American dances, such as the Cumbia, the Brazilian Sambas, etc. (do you?). I also love The Beatles.

Would you tell me what you remember about the Farewell Party for you in 1965, at my house (whether good or bad), and how you felt that day? For me it was very important that the party was held in my house. I remember that I introduced you to Perla and to my father, but I doubt you'll remember them, as it was just a brief encounter before they went out for the evening.

Re- your salary: don't expect that you can dodge out of the situation just like that; I am an excellent faker of signatures, and will be able to manage to get hold of your money up to the last penny, and spend it all on furs and jewels. What do you think of that!? At least they last longer than beer…

Congratulations on your promotion to Senior

Research Officer. I am very proud to have such an important boyfriend! The youngest on the staff!

Yesterday I received a reply from the LSE Graduate School. They sent me a pamphlet and an application form, which I will fill in and send back in a day or two. At the end of the leaflet, in the list of Research Staff, I found the following note: «S.R. Merrett, B.A. (Bristol), B.Phil. (Oxon.); Research Officer, Unit for Economic and Statistical Studies on Higher Education». Isn't that name familiar to you? ... I can't remember where I met the guy...

The most interesting course they offer is the one-year M.Sc. in Social Anthropology (while the Diploma takes two years to complete) – it starts in October 1967.

The situation in Buenos Aires: I haven't yet heard anything about the new University Statute. I speculate on the possibility of graduating in April or at the beginning of May – but then I would have to sit exams in not less than five subjects in March (a mad total) so that when only three remain, I am entitled to request to sit exams under a «special examination procedure» (meaning they would be set up especially for me) – they could take place between the end of April and the beginning of May. Perhaps you are wondering why I am now so keen to graduate. It's because I realise that having a University degree will enormously facilitate my chances of getting scholarships or jobs or research work in any country in the world.

Write to me soon. I send you a kiss, sweet and *hot*.

With all my love,
    Alicia

New Delhi
19 January 1967

Darling Alicia,

In re-reading your letters I think that although you have mentioned the research projects on which you are working several times, yet you haven't given me any details of the objectives of the studies or preliminary results. I'd like very much for you to tell me a little about the one on urban-rural migration. One phrase which you have introduced to my vocabulary is "participant observation." Tell me now, on what occasions have you engaged in this kind of research, and among what groups of people? Somehow I cannot imagine you easily integrating with gauchos and their families or a group of Indians, too much of a well-fed, pampered city girl. But then I could easily be under-estimating your adaptability and resilience. Which reminds me, I thought that quite apart from our visit to E. Europe this summer we might spend a week walking, say in August or September, in the West of Scotland sleeping in a tent or any small hotels which might exist, either on the coast itself or around some of the great "lochs." We might even catch the Loch Ness Monster and you could grill it for supper. (How do you like your monsters, grilled or fried?)

I'm very ambivalent about your date of arrival, as you are too, I know, honey. I want to lay my hands on you just as soon as possible and kiss those voluptuous lips of yours, but the chance of a degree in July is much too good to miss, since it will mean that in the future you'll be able to fulfil your own handsome talents as a fully-qualified teacher or researcher.

Paul and I tied with 29 each, but between you and me I cheated because I didn't tell him your Principito *(The Little Prince)* card was not a Christmas card. Still in his mail today (he's still at the Planning Commission) there's an envelope which looks suspiciously like some kind of card arrived late. So it may be that justice will be done.

By the way I think our musical tastes differ to some extent – I think Joan Baez is a very pleasant entertainer, sings some wonderful ballads, but is not a great singer – her voice is too piping, and limited in range. Never would I put her in the same class as Lady Day (Miss Billie Holiday).

My parents are both "Church of England", one of the least virulent forms of the protestant ethic.

I'm glad you're going to bring your international licence to drive a car; I was going to suggest you do just that. Don't forget that in England we are much more sensible about traffic direction and drive on the *left*. (It's much easier that way to overtake in a car with the driver's seat on the right-hand side, and it is also much easier to turn left than the Continental fashion. But doubtless these hot-heads in power in England will want to decimalize even our traffic system before long.)

Which reminds me, in little England we have an admirable currency system (2 ha'pennies = 1 penny. 3 pennies = a three-penny piece. 6 pennies = sixpence. 12 pennies =one shilling. 10 shillings = 1 ten shilling note. 20 shillings = one pound.) Got it? Now answer the following question.

¿How many *ha'pennies* are there in *three pounds, seventeen shillings and threepence ha'penny* on a Sunday morning? (Answer at foot of page *.) Foreigners can never make head or tail of it, so if you like you can give me your £60/90 per month and I'll spend it for you.

I am sending you, under separate cover, a letter from Sir Sydney Caine on the philosophy of LSE (please keep) and the review of a concert I attended last night by Ustad Vilayat Khan on sitar, which was the most moving I have ever heard. How I wished you were there, to hold your hand and have you share my emotion and me yours.

Ah! my dear, how cold and emotionless you Latinos are. I compromise on 11 hours in bed out of every 24 and you agree enthusiastically on the grounds that "Alicia wants to sleep." Creature of ice, cool, cooler, coolest iceberg, snowwoman.

Bye for now, darling,
I love you,
    Steve

—◊◊◊—

Buenos Aires
19 January 1967

My darling Steve,
    I've made up my mind: I'll attempt to sit five subjects in March so I can graduate in April-May. I have begun to cast my net wide to get the notes, books, reports, etc. for various subjects that I can take in the 'free' sittings.

Answer: None, because you spent them all at the pub on Saturday night!

When do you return to London? When you do, should I write to you at 32, Mayville Road, or to any other address?

The weather is crazy in Buenos Aires (and seemingly in the rest of the world too). After a week of unbearable heat (35°C) came a wave of polar cold air that pushed the temperature down to 17°C, exceptional for the month of January. But today it was even worse: I left the house at 11 in the morning with the temperature at 28° (and therefore wearing a light dress) and came back at 8 pm with 17° (frozen).

My typewriter appears to be weary of so much work, and yesterday it began to fall slowly apart. My father tightened all the screws. I hope that it will last through to April. Do you have one in London? Because I'll need one to write to my family and all my friends…(but not to you! How lovely!).

You ask about my religion. I already told you that I am an atheist, in the sense that I do not believe in God and I do not practise nor believe in any religion. But I suppose that the circles within which I move cause me, rather unconsciously, to participate in certain Jewish cultural traditions. And you? How are your traditions influential?

I agree that to fight from time to time is very therapeutic, but I hate being insulted without explanation. So I reply to you with an old French proverb from my childhood games: 'El que lo dice, lo es" (if you say it, you are it).

I forgot to tell you that my father doesn't understand a word of English. If you don't feel up to writing to him in Spanish, you can do it in Russian, Bulgarian, Serbian, Ukrainian, German or French. And if not…well, I'll translate your letter for him.

0.45 am. Bed-time. Now I am in semi-holidays I try to go to bed earlier and sleep longer and better. So I say good-night.

Lots of kisses.
        Alicia

PS. I love you so much.

———~~~———

Buenos Aires
24 January 1967

My darling Steve,

Yesterday I sent to the LSE the completed application form and the other documents that they require to be able to review my case and decide whether I will be accepted for the M.Sc. in Social Anthropology. I felt very emotional because I felt that I was taking an important step towards making my journey to England a reality.

I've spent a couple of days in bed with a fever; I don't yet know whether it was because of the cold spell I experienced last Saturday (it was 13°C, in the middle of summer! that's incredible) or due to eating a chocolate cake covered with strawberries that I ate the same day. I had both a cold and an upset stomach. But I am much better. Just as you like to spend a day by yourself from time to time, I like to spend one or two days at home without going out, reading, listening to music, resting or sleeping, and having people to spoil me, and to be a bit ill is a good pretext!

On Sunday it got warmer, and the evening was lovely; I turned the lights off when it got dark, and from my sick bed, through the garden window, I could see the enormous, brilliant moon in the sky; my room was totally lit up. Later, when the moon couldn't be seen any more, I could see the white laurel flowers in the garden shining against the dark sky.

Last Friday was Haydée's birthday. Horacio took her out under false pretences, and while they were out, me and a group of friends went into the house, placed a birthday cake and other eatables and drinkables on the table, and hid in another room. When they came back we all jumped out singing "Happy Birthday". Haydée was quite amazed as she wasn't really expecting any celebrations; she was so pleased! We had a great evening – we listened to some highly political Brazilian songs by Nara, and because her music is so popular, everyone sings them – Brazilians, Argentines, etc.

Today I went out shopping. I love to go shopping! (like all women I suppose). I bought two machines: a portable radio (the one we had was stolen on the day our house was burgled) and a small slide projector.

Your letter of Saturday 14th, which I received today, is one of the most beautiful ones that you have written – I feel so happy after reading it! I really believe we can spend a lovely summer together…

You must present the cattle to my father. In return you will probably receive some very nice and valuable gifts.

Haydée lent me some books of English poetry, and in it I found "Go, and catch a falling star."

A kiss. I love you.
Alicia

New Delhi
25 January 1967

Darling, darling, darling Alicia,

Today I feel desperately lonely without you by my side, and your letters, far from comforting me, reveal as they do your tender and gay nature and increase my sadness that I can't be with you. Just for a few hours.... Still, pathos is not a quality in men that you find attractive, I'm sure, so let me tell you what's been happening in Delhi.

First, as you must know by now I have written to your father, re-introducing myself and telling him what he already knew, that you are coming to England soon to be with me. *Please* be my spy in the House of Kaner and tell me what your father's reaction was to the letter. Also, if he shows you the letter please point out to me the grosser mistakes in my Spanish.

Yes, we are writing the monograph, and I've even given it a provisional title: "Educated manpower for Indian Economic Development: a case study of the Indian nitrogen fertiliser industry." I guess it won't sell as well as "From Russia with Love", tho' we might push up the royalties if we show one of these handsome bare-breasted tribal girls carrying a basketful of gypsum on her head, and put it on the dust cover.

An advertisement appeared in the papers the other day for economists to work in the British government, in ministries such as that of Overseas Development, Transport, Power etc. etc. I've written off and hope to get a reply soon. I have now decided pretty firmly to leave LSE after the book on fertiliser manpower is done, in which case they'll obviously not promote me to Senior Research Officer so your congratulations are premature. I'll let you know as soon as I hear from the UK. government but the prospects seem excellent.

The other day I strolled down to the shops in the centre of town and have bought: one emerald-green sari for my aunt (a really wonderful person) who lives at 34 Mayville Road; one pale pink sari for my mother; one maroon sari for the girl I love and one pink off-the-peg churridar and kameez likewise for the girl I love (you). So we must all go out in our "clobber" one evening soon after you arrive and have an Indian meal in town.

My very warmest congratulations on your "Outstanding" in Social History, you're obviously a very brilliant student. If you really can pass 8 exams in March/May, that would be magnificent. As you will have seen from my last couple of letters we are in complete agreement about your graduating before you come to England. Let's keep our fingers crossed – that's all I *can* do, I wish I could help you honey. Let me know as soon as you can what the chances are of you graduating before July.

A bargain! For every lie I tell you may smoke one cigarette *provided* for every cigarette you smoke (unprovoked by my mendacity) then I may tell one lie. Fair enough?

I have now provisionally booked my flight on the VC-10 leaving New Delhi on March 3rd and arriving in London on the same day (which is my father's birthday). My trunks went out on the long sea-journey today.

I *hated* the farewell party in your house, though of course it wasn't your fault (in fact I remember planning to catch you alone in the house and to give you a kiss, just to see what would happen, but then decided against it as it seemed rather callous). The majority of the people seemed so incredibly lifeless, remember how no-one save Donald and myself would sing any songs. I walked home muttering "Oh! these bloody porteños" whilst Mariella tried to comfort me. My best friends in Buenos Aires were a Belgian couple called Willie and Nicky Van Ryckeghem, both in their late twenties with two handsome children. I would often visit their house at weekends and swim in the pool, sunbathe and eat steak. Very nice! What a pity you and I, my beautiful, have no memories to share of Buenos Aires.

Well, I feel much better now that I've written to you, a little less alone, a little closer to you. I'll write again very soon (not every day because some days I just hate writing letters or communicating at all).

I love you, I love you, I love you
I still feel that same terrible desire,
  Steve

Buenos Aires
26 January 1967

Darling Steve,
  After two weeks without news, it is lovely to receive so many letters one after the other.

Carl Orff is a contemporary German composer of striking originality. Carmina Burana is his best known piece, sung in Latin and German; composed in 1937. It is inspired by poems written by the "goliards", clerics or strolling students, at the end of the 13th century, which were brought together in a collection of manuscripts entitled "Carmina Burana", discovered in the Bavarian monastery of Benediktbeuren in 1847 by Johann Andreas Schmeller. It is part of a triptych, along with "Catulli Carmina", and "The Triumph of Aphrodite". I like it enormously; I hope you can listen to it soon and tell me what you think.

Next week Julio's photos of me will be ready, and also the ones taken at Horacio and Haydée's wedding, so I will choose a nice one to send you. I eagerly await your Conga photo.

How are things in England? I read in the papers that there are 600,000 unemployed and that the situation is critical. What do you think? I understand very little about the English economy.

Re-Shakespeare, I have read only Macbeth and Julius Caesar in English, when I was studying English; I've read only Spanish translations of some of his other plays. The quotes from Hamlet were from Gielgud's speeches in his record "Ages of Man". Haydée is going to lend me some of the English originals, so I have promised myself to read Hamlet and King Lear soon, so I can choose quotations with a better foundation.

You saw my sister Ester at the December 1965 party; she arrived right at the end with her then boyfriend. She's very pretty, dark-skinned with green-blue eyes, very slim and smaller than me. She's studying Psychology, but not with great enthusiasm; she prefers to paint, to draw, make mobiles, and other artistic activities. She is very quiet and introverted, has difficulty in establishing relationships with people, but once you get to know her you find she's sweet and 'simpática'. She'll be twenty in a few days' time. We get along fine; Ester was one of the first people who supported with enthusiasm my plans to go to England.

Re-mini-skirts: After making a study of my figure, I think the ideal skirt length for me is one that ends around 5 to 8 cm. above the knee. What do you think? The dress in the photo that you like so much, is one of my favourites and of course I'll take it to England. The original colour of the flowers is blue-turquoise, white and yellow.

Some days I feel desperate to go to England as soon as possible, while on other days I think that I should not let my enthusiasm carry me away, that I should study and graduate first. And on other days (rarely!) I'm grabbed by fear and panic, and I feel how much more comfortable and risk-free it would be to stay at home and look after my father. But don't worry, I've taken my decision and I will be travelling to England as soon as possible; my desire to see you overwhelms all my ambivalence and fears. However I know that about a week before leaving I will very likely become hysterical, get ill with nerves and feel a strong fear of the unknown. But that's nothing to worry about – I feel the same way before any trip! Of course, this one is much more important than any other I have under-taken so far, and it could be a decisive one in my life, so it could be worse…. But once I arrive at my destination I calm down immediately – it is the transition that vexes me.

I think there are three distinct Steves, which however are also the same: the Steve I knew in Buenos Aires in 1965, the Steve who writes such wonderful letters, and the Steve that I am going to meet in England within a few months. They are distinct because clearly any person changes and evolves with the passage of time; they are the same because their background is always the same. But fundamentally they are distinct for me because of the different type of relationship and degree of understanding that I have of them; in Buenos Aires it was to see each other but not to know each other; by letter it is to know each other but not to see each other; in England everything will come together, to know and see and love each other – or not? I think that we shall have to adapt to each other, a readjustment that will take time; to establish a good personal relationship takes time, in spite of all that's gone before…But I think that everything will turn out fine.

Today I say farewell with the words of Catulli Carmina: Eis aiona – tui sum! (Always, eternally yours).

All my love,
Alicia

———

New Delhi
29 January 1967

Darling Alicia,
The last few days have been very pleasant because Jan 26th is India's Republic Day. Crowds lined the Raj Path, the great avenue in New Delhi that leads to the vast Central Secretariat buildings made of red sandstone with towers, domes, flights of steps, parapets. The Vice-President took

the salute, and we had a long procession of marching soldiers, pipe bands, tanks, folk dancers, elephants and best of all a corps of camels, unusually graceful with their long necks and beautifully groomed light-chocolate fur. A fly-past brought it to an end, including British "Hunters", Soviet "Migs" and Indian "Toofanis." The crowd seemed unresponsive to all the pageantry. Perhaps times are too hard and the future too uncertain for gaiety or the surge of patriotism that such an occasion should call forth.

Yesterday I watched the festival of Folk Dances from all over India, the majority of groups coming from the hill peoples of Himachal Pradesh, the North East frontier agency, and the aboriginal peoples of the plains. Whilst this was full of colour and rhythm it seemed ineffectual in the centre of the National Stadium, surrounded by a crowd of perhaps 30,000 with the arc-lights glaring. It gave me a strong desire to see such dances performed of the people by the people for the people in some clearing in the jungle, far from the hypocrisy and materialism of New Delhi.

Please give my warmest regards to your father, your sister and that incorrigible brother of yours, Horacio. And also Gracielas No. 1, 2…∞, Haydée and the photographer *whose photos 'for the Englishman' I have not yet received.*

And for you one kiss, or two, or three… I miss you very much and you are constantly in my thoughts,

Hasta pronto,
　　Steve

———

Alicia studying at a friend's house.
Buenos Aires, 1966.

Steve in the garden of the DiTella Institute.
Buenos Aires, 1965.

Alicia on the balcony of an apartment where she
studied with friends. Buenos Aires, 1966.

Steve during his travels around India. Himalayas, 1967.

Alicia at a party – a photo that Steve liked very much.
Buenos Aires, 1967.

Steve and Alicia outside a pub on the Thames, shortly
before their wedding. London, 1968.

Trafalgar Square. London, 1967.

Ester, Steve and Alicia wearing their Indian clothes for a party. London, 1968.

New Delhi
29 January 1967

Darling Alicia,

Today I received your letter of the 19th to which I have lots of answers to make.

Even if your father does not support you during your year of study 1967/68, it doesn't matter because we can both live on my salary. O.K?

From March 3rd my address will be:

Unit for Economic and Statistical Studies on Higher
Education
London School of Economics
Houghton Street,
Aldwych
London W.C.2

Yes, I do have a little portable typewriter which you can use all the time since I never touch it.

I think that you should send all the things you can't take on the plane by sea, as unaccompanied personal effects, and put it on a ship going to London. The docks are not too far from Leytonstone. My feeling is that we should assume implicitly that everything is going to work between us, not delay taking decisions whilst we examine each other with infinite care as a suitable spouse. That would be a gross psychological error, for each will have marked faults in his or her character if one waits and watches carefully enough. We must be effortless; relax with each other, enjoy our long-sought-after encounter, and leave the future to take care of itself in this respect, not prepare ourselves for failure. What do you think?

Now, clothing and the English climate. I feel that too many foreigners do the English weather a severe injustice. I think we have two major seasons: November–March when it is freezing with buffeting winds and continual rain; April–October when it is just bloody cold, stiff breeze and only rains part of the time. They say we had a very good summer in 1947. Old men huddle by a blazing electric heater and whisper of those bygone days when the temperature soared to 72° Fahrenheit, and Edrich and Compton dominated the English cricket season. So I should just make do with plenty of blankets, some Wellington boots, two or three mackintoshes (they wear out very fast), ski-ing trousers and heavy jacket for the full glory of summer, gloves galore, an umbrella with carbon steel frame and a portable log fire. Got the idea?

The religion of my parents, I believe, has had no effect on my personality. The fact that they are working class has, but not in the sense that I have specifically working class characteristics such as accent, range of interests, but in the sense that I have an empathy for them.

How long must we wait honey? Writing is so inadequate.

A sweet, hot kiss on your red mouth,
    Steve

Buenos Aires
29 January 1967

My very dearest and darling Steve,
  I keep being surprised by how often we get the same idea. I was about to suggest that we could try and see something of Scotland this summer – and then you suggest the same! I thought we could load the car with the minimum necessary luggage, as I don't like walking with a rucksack on my back – I get tired quickly – take a tent and a couple of sleeping bags, and go off to Scotland for a week. You should decide the itinerary as I don't know much about Scotland. I'd prefer to stay in small inns, when possible (I still am, as you say, "a well-fed, pampered city girl", in spite of some of my Bohemian tendencies), and occasionally in the tent. Cars are very practical for longer journeys, and you can park it somewhere and go walking and fishing for monsters all day long. We'll settle details when we are together.
  Deceiver! (but I forgive you!!). How did the Christmas Card competition with Paul turn out?
  I've spotted we have one difference of opinion: you say that the English are sensible in driving on the left, and I say that they are mad. Why go against the rest of the world? I will have to learn to operate the gear lever with my left hand! Not to speak of your money: imagine! – it has coins that do not exist, like the guinea! At present I'm trying to understand what is the half-crown, but I assure you that when I arrive in England I'll be so clever as to spend my own money, and yours too, and furthermore to ensure that three pounds, seventeen shillings and three-and-a-half pennies on Friday evening are still the same

three pounds, seventeen shillings and three-and-a-half pennies on Sunday morning.

On participant observation and my experience in that area: it is a long story and I'll leave it for the next letter. But I can tell you that the rural population of La Rioja does not consist of gauchos or Indians – these terms are too stereotyped.

As I didn't know what 'pampered' means, I looked it up in the dictionary. To pamper: mimar, consentir. Got it?

My darling, I miss you so much! Today I spent the whole day in the country house of some friends in the outskirts of Buenos Aires, sunbathing, swimming in the pool, eating a barbecue, and in the evening watching the sunset (marvellous!) and listening to the singing of the cicadas and the crickets. Sweet, darling love of mine, how much I want you to be with me, I feel that I enjoy so much of what I see, listen to, feel and live because I feel receptive to every sensation, and that is because I think of you and feel happy, but I lack the half that completes the whole: you.

Do you know something? At times I feel that I am seeing the streets, the houses, the trees, the neighbourhoods of Buenos Aires as if saying good-bye to them, they are beautiful, I get emotional, feeling that I am going to leave them for a long time, and that I'm going to miss them. It is such a strange sensation, of pain and of joy at the same time, pain for what I leave, joy for what I shall encounter on the other side of the ocean.

I wish it were hours, and not months, the time remaining before we meet…

I love you so much. Eis aiona – tui sum.
    Alicia

PS. The next time you call me an iceberg or such similar things, I'll give you a clump of historic proportions.

—◦◦◦—

Buenos Aires
1 February 1967

My dearest Steve,

This letter, super-urgent and out of the normal run, is to tell you that my stepbrother Horacio Breyter and his wife Haydée will be in London shortly and I would like you to meet them, so we need to make suitable arrangements.

Perla had given them as a wedding present two plane tickets for Europe, and they have decided to go now. As they haven't got a lot of time (from six weeks to two months) they'll just visit a few places: London, Paris, Rome, Athens, and Israel to visit his brother Carlos and his family. They are very eager to meet you and of course I am delighted with the idea, so they can send me a report back immediately, and take photos of you. I really feel that it is as if a part of me goes to meet you in advance.

Haydée is delighted with the idea. She speaks excellent English and is a charming woman – I'm sure you'll like her a lot and will get along very well. Horacio is a bit more reserved and speaks little English, but after getting to know him you'll find he's a great guy.

Other good news: my father received your letter and was absolutely charmed by it. He says your Spanish is much better than he had thought. He'll reply to you quite soon. I read the letter as well, and thought it magnificent and very well written (in spite of some errors, which I'll correct personally) and very appropriate. I'll only indicate two "gaffes", although they are not really that serious. First, when my father read that you think that if I graduate in July I have better chances of going to an English University, he said to me: "See? Steve also thinks that you have to graduate before leaving." Which reinforces his idea that I am not going to buy my ticket before graduating. And at times, as I already told you, the urge comes to take the first plane that leaves for India…

The second gaffe: I don't think my father was too happy with the idea that "we are going *together*" this summer to Eastern Europe. He did not make any comments straightaway, but although he is a fairly broadminded person, he has not lost all his prejudices…you should have added "with some friends" or something like that.

News from Buenos Aires: postage prices are set to almost double, so I hope that I'll not have to write to you much longer.

I miss you a lot my love. I kiss you,
Alicia

—⁓—

Buenos Aires
2 February 1967

Dear, beloved, darling Steve,

Sweet, sweet love of mine, your letter of the 25th of January makes me ever more desperate to see you, to be together. You tell me "pathos is not a quality in men that you find attractive". But when you show your feelings that way, when you are sad, or depressed, or lonely, those emotions of yours reach me deeply, I share them, I understand them, I feel closer to you, I learn to understand you in all your moods. I don't want you to speak to me only when you are well and happy. I want to share everything with you, joy, sorrow, euphoria, depression, loneliness, what is beautiful and also what is not.

When you wrote "In fact I remember planning to catch you alone in the house and to give you a kiss, just to see what would happen, but then decided against it as it seemed rather callous", a shiver ran through my body. Steve, you should have done! You cannot imagine how much I wanted at that time that you make some gesture that gave me an idea of your feelings for me – in whatever form. I felt you were distant, I felt very tense every time I spoke with you, I was afraid – not of you but of myself – and I wanted to get closer to you but I didn't know how to. Not because I thought that it was good or bad; as Hamlet says, "There is nothing either good or bad, but thinking makes it so"; rather because I had no idea what your reactions might be. The truth is that at that moment I didn't care about Mariella, my fiancé, or the fact that in a week you were leaving for India, and I would have given you all the kisses that you wanted, I would have made love with you. But you didn't ask me. Pity!

I agree with you that the farewell in my house was not a great party, but it wasn't my fault: the guests were a mixed bunch, some not very agreeable – certain porteños can be incredibly lifeless. But not all of them – and not all the time. That day was important for me, not because of the party, but because you were in my house – as part of me is reflected in the place where I live, I love it a lot, and it pains me to think that I am not going to see the house for a long time.

I already told you that my father was delighted with the letter that you sent him; he immediately told Horacio that he should visit you in London, as well as your parents. My father's name is Abraham, but as he does not like his name (nor do I) he doesn't use it. Almost everyone calls him by his surname, save for a few intimate friends who call him by the diminutive of Abraham in Russian: Abrasha. Héctor, my sister's boyfriend, who has a very sharp-tongue, calls him "the Great Kaner", or "the Great Ka" for short.

I am touched by your decision to stay in London for the time being, so that I can study there. It makes me feel very close to you and feel the strength of your affection. If it wasn't for me, maybe you would now be making preparations to go and work in Cuba – enormous changes in both our lives… I am really emigrating; and after studying the subject of migration for a year (from the social, anthropological and psychological point of view) I know what it means: the need for "elaboration of the grief of separation from known things", as we refer to the process; the problems of assimilation and integration in the new society, etc. But I don't mind, I know that you will help me to overcome all that. Keep me in touch about your negotiations about getting a job with the British government.

Bargain: as I believe that it is wrong to forbid you from

telling from time to time one of those little amusing lies of yours, and on the other side I believe it would not be correct of you to prohibit me from smoking, I propose a new conciliatory contract: I have the right to smoke two cigarettes a day – or up to three in extraordinary cases that are properly justified. And you have the right to tell two or up to three white lies each day. If you tell more lies than those stipulated, or I smoke more cigarettes, then we revert to the previous pact. O.K?

Statistics: I read each one of your letters, on the day it arrives and before answering it, about five times. I think it would be impossible for me to estimate how many times I read them afterwards...

Today I'll say goodbye with Hamlet once again:

Doubt thou the stars are fire
Doubt that the sun doth move
Doubt truth to be a liar
But never doubt I love.

I love you so very, very, very much. I share your terrible desires.

Alicia

———

Buenos Aires
3 February 1967

My dear Steve,

These days I feel a great need to communicate with you – that's why I am sending so many letters in succession. How much I want us to be together!

Today Ester was 20 and we went out to dinner to celebrate, with my uncles and siblings. All these celebrations – the New Year, birthdays, etc. – hold a tang that's so different this year; in them we feel so much the absence of Perla!...Ah, what a terrible thing! How unfair her death! How absurd! Let's leave this, as you say, "pathos is not a quality…"

I'm sending you a crazy card and two photos. In one of them, I am with Horacio and Haydée, so that you can get to know what they look like, as you will see them soon. Haydée complained about it because she says that in this photo she has 'the face of a morphine addict', and that she is much more beautiful (that's true), but I could not find another suitable one. It was taken in our garden in November 1966. The other photo is one of me in casual clothes, taken with my new camera, also last November. Although it is a bit dark, I think it is a good one to send to you. It was taken in my bedroom, and behind me are three of my posters. I already told Haydée to keep space in her suitcase on my behalf so that I can send you some presents (surprise!).

Bye, sweetie. 2 am bed-time. All my love.
Alicia

—◉◉◉—

New Delhi
4 February 1967.

Darling Alicia,
Oh my prophetic soul! Last night I dreamt that I

would receive 3 or 4 letters from you in the mail. Lo and behold! Three letters turned up today.

On the subject of a holiday in Europe. Poland versus Czechoslovakia versus Hungary versus Yugoslavia? Sounds like the semi-finals of the World Cup. (Did you notice, my sweet, how the Europeans thrashed, not to say massacred the Latin Americans in the World Cup?) Let's compromise and make it Czechoslovakia and Hungary. Tho' in fact it may be difficult to spend two weeks in each since the Labour government, because of the severity of our foreign exchange crisis, imposed a limit on the currency available for tourism of £50 per annum. This might limit us to 2/3 weeks in which case we could spend all the time in Czechoslovakia. Let's discuss it in London.

Thanks for describing to me so succinctly the difference between modern Social Anthropology and Sociology. For me, the former has the stronger appeal simply because it deals with social sub-groups in their entirety, and partly because I feel that participant observation, whether by economists or social anthropologists, can be capable of greater originality and have greater implications for social policy by governments.

I miss you, as they say in India "too much".

Te adoro,
    Steve

—⁓—

New Delhi
Undated

Darling Alicia,
   Happy Birthday.
   Have bought you a pretty necklace made of coconut shell
(must be worn with a grass skirt and coconut brassiere).

   All my love,
      Steve

———∿∿∿———

New Delhi
8 February 1967

Darling Alicia,
   Lots of news and views to tell you about, but in order
to get this letter to the post this afternoon, I'll limit myself
to the G.E.S.

   G.E.S. = Government Economic Service

I have sent an application to the Civil Service Commission
in Savile Row for the post of "Economic Adviser." If I am
selected for interview, this will probably be sometime in
March. If, after the interview, I am selected for the post I
would start work, I have said, on September 15th in
London. Salary would start at £2,335 (!) p.a. 41 hour week.
5 weeks holiday p.a. I have said I would like to work, in
order of preference, in

   (i) Ministry of Technology

(ii) Board of Trade

(iii) Ministry of Power.

I would take out a 5-year contract initially. Major diffi-culties: (i) I am 4 months below the minimum age for entering the grade of "Economic Advisor." (ii) The com-petition is likely to be very severe for the limited number of posts available. (iii) No work "vital to the security of the State" can be entrusted to, amongst others, Communist sympathizers, and clearly I *am* a C. Symp. So we'll have to see how rigidly they interpret this clause. I would have thought (i), (ii) and (iii) could all, in certain circumstances, be considered "vital".

Vamos a ver.

I love you very much and feel lonely without you.

S.

New Delhi
10 February 1967

Darling Alicia

Well, honey, on Sunday I am taking the train to Sindri in Bihar, then on to Calcutta in West Bengal, then Konarak in Orissa, then Benares in Uttar Pradesh then back to Delhi. I'll be gone for about 2 weeks. I'll write to you whenever something exciting or moving happens, but posting the letters may prove difficult, so if you don't get any mail for a week, don't fret.

Please come to England as soon as you can, do your

best to graduate in April, if not (alas!) July. I don't want to be separated from you for so long,

All my love,
  Steve

———

Buenos Aires
12 February 1967

My dearest Steve,
   So that you don't keep on complaining, I am sending you one of the photos "for the Englishman", which was ready yesterday. I don't like the others, so I won't send them. I haven't received your Conga photo yet, which you promised me a long time ago, and while I have already sent you *six photos of me* (including two last week and one today) you've sent me *only two*. I present a formal complaint!
   Your review of London's climate makes me shiver with cold. Are the houses well heated? Does it snow much in London? I have only seen snow once in my life, in Paris, and it was a very gentle snowfall. I am not equipped to face the cold, I do not have Wellington boots, nor a portable log fire (?) etc. On the other hand I do have a lovely collection of summer dresses, so I imagine you'll take me to the Cote d'Azur or to the beaches of Yugoslavia so I can show off. My only raincoat, bought in Paris, is as good as new as I have hardly had an opportunity to wear it in Buenos Aires. A final consultation: is it worth taking my otter fur coat, or will it get ruined in London's rain?

About us: of course I am totally in agreement that we should relax and just let things work out. But what happens is that sometimes I am scared and it shows....

My love, your offer to support me whilst I study, if my father cannot do it, has moved me deeply. All the external difficulties are practically solved, all that remains is that I study hard and graduate and am accepted as a student at the LSE.

Today the CGT* which is already in open disagreement with the government, has announced a 'plan for strife', which includes large meetings, general strikes, demonstrations, etc. It is due to start within a few days, and it will last until the end of March. If the students and some of the lecturers decide to join the strikes, the Faculty will be in total disarray (not to mention any awkward clauses in the University statute, which has not yet been published) so exams may not even happen. In September 1966, for example, you could not sit exams when the Students' Union was on strike.

I guess Horacio and Haydée will be in London in the second half of April. I'll confirm the dates in due course. Please send me your telephone number.

My father, Ester, Graciela and Haydée, all thank you and return your greetings. Horacio, as always, complains. This time, because you called him "incorrigible". (I should not have told him, but it was too late...) Don't take this too seriously, his complaints are a bit of a show off, he doesn't want to admit that he likes you a lot.

2 am – bedtime. I wish you were here with me! I want us to meet soon, very soon, I miss you, it seems I've got

*Confederación Nacional del Trabajo, the Trades Union Congress

"ants in my pants" and want to leave for London straight-away. I long to throw my arms about your neck and kiss you.

I love you,
    Alicia

———

New Delhi
12 February 1967

Darling Alicia,

David Rubin has promised to post this letter for me tomorrow, so that I can give you some idea of my itin-erary. In my next few letters I'll answer whatever ques-tions seem to remain unanswered, but here are some 'quickies.'

The day *after* I received your letter of the 3rd I got the letter of the 2nd: I note your frankness is beginning to equal my own!

I have now postponed my departure to England until Friday, March 10th, and suggest you mail your last letter to me in India on February 28th.

The other evening, just after I finished my last letter to you I had dinner with David Ovens and his wife Margaret and with Professor David Glass and his wife Ruth. I was feeling very miserable, as you might have guessed, because I want to touch you, kiss you, talk to you, and the thought of meeting Horacio and Haydée in April and not *you* depressed me, sharpened the sense of loss.

My train leaves in 1 hour and 20 minutes. My itinerary is (Got a map?):

12/2 New Delhi – train – Sindri (Bihar)
15/2 Sindri – train – Calcutta (West Bengal)
18/2 Calcutta – plane – Bhubaneshwar (Orissa) – Bus –
Puri (Orissa)
19/2 Puri – Bus – Konarak (Orissa)
20/2 Konarak – Bus – Bhubaneshwar – Plane – Calcutta
21/2 Calcutta – Plane – Benares (Uttar Pradesh)
23/2 Benares – bus – Allahabad (Uttar Pradesh)
25/2 Allahabad – Taxi + Bus – Khajuraho (Uttar Pradesh?)
27/2 Khajuraho – Bus + Train – Delhi

Must pack,
Study hard!
I love you so much
  Steve

Buenos Aires
14 February 1967

My dearest Steve,

This crazy mail service! Today I received, all at once, your letters of the 3rd and the 8th. So – you may have to postpone your return to England by one or two weeks. Are you very keen to go home? You don't say, but I feel you must be keen to get back to London.

I've got plans to sit five exams in March-April, and at the beginning of April I'll request permission to sit special exams for the remaining three subjects. I'll also need to sort out the "research hours" which are a degree course require-ment in the Sociology syllabus. If all goes well and there are no hold-ups, I could be in London in the middle of May.

The worst part of the situation here is the complete uncertainty that reigns in University circles. Nobody knows anything, rumours fly around from all directions, giving a thousand different versions of what is likely to happen.

"Economic Adviser"! I hope that despite the drawbacks, you get the job! I think that working in the Ministry of Technology would be the most interesting option.

Today I have settled myself in the dining room, with my typewriter and all my papers, because the carpenters have removed my writing desk to fix the damage caused by the thieves in forcing the locked drawers. It will take a week to be ready! I feel uncomfortable and frustrated (well, not too much) without my desk, from which you can see the garden, the flowers and the sky.

After my poetry period, and reading Hamlet in English, I've taken up again "The Tin Drum". I hadn't picked it up for two months, Perla left it in the middle and I could not begin reading it…Well, so far I feel extremely enthusiastic about it. I alternate it with reading "The Lord of the Flies", Homans and others.

My sweetie, I'm going out right now to the post box, I'll continue tomorrow. These days I miss you a lot, I would like to be with you, I feel incomplete without you. Your letters do not calm this need which becomes ever more powerful.

I send you lots of kisses,
Alicia

PS. Shall I send your father a birthday card for March 3rd?

Buenos Aires
17 February 1967

My adored Steve,

My love, the post is completely upside-down! Yesterday I received your letter of the 4th, and the day before yesterday the one of the 5th. Today I received none and that made me sad. And for two days I have been trying to sit down and write to you, but I couldn't find the time, which drove me to desperation!

The other day I saw in Cine Arte a film I had missed last year: "This Sporting Life", by Lindsay Anderson, with Richard Harris. Terrific and very striking. Have you seen it? The guys talk an outlandish English, badly pronounced; I suppose it's cockney?

It also occurs to me that your relationship with your parents is very different from mine with my parents, especially as my character is Latin and yours (at least in this respect) is Saxon; you have been living quite a long way from them for many years, while I still live with my family.

All the people who hear I am going to England soon congratulate me and envy me a little. I wish I were with you now, my sweet love. I love you.

Alicia

Buenos Aires
20 February 1967

My adored Steve,

David Rubin (who is he?) kept his promise and today I have received your letter with the itinerary and the 'quickies'. What a lovely journey you are having through India! I'd love to be with you! Is the journey for pleasure only, or also for work?

Time to go to Mario B.'s to study! My darling, I'll try to write to you as often as I can, although it is not very compatible with your recommendation of "Study hard!" (which is what I am doing anyway). But yes, probably my letters will be shorter because a long letter takes me three to four hours to write, and now I do not have so much free time.

I miss you, I want to see you soon, I kiss you, I hug you, I love you.

    Alicia

———

Buenos Aires
21 February 1967

Today my father was in a very bad mood and scolded everyone and complained about everything; he confessed that he has not yet replied to your letter, he finds it a very difficult task. My interpretation is that it due to his subconscious resistance to my leaving (but I said nothing to him because he hates psychoanalysis).

News from Buenos Aires: the new Plan of Strife of the

CGT began on Monday, with stoppages of two or three hours, and occasional demonstrations. The government issues briefings and says that it will revoke the judicial status of those trade unions that sign up to the Plan. The CGT is theoretically going ahead, but in reality it has little popular support. People don't have the stomach for a fight.

Graciela, who graduated in January, is now doing the paperwork to get her title of Licentiate in Anthropology. Do you know how long this paperwork takes? Three to four months! And there's no way to speed up the process. She is desperate because she needs the degree papers to apply for a scholarship in the USA. This is a matter of concern, because I can see that I'll have to face the same problems, and who knows when I'll get hold of the degree papers to submit to the LSE. I shall have to find someone to help, as you can imagine that I am not planning to wait for all this administrative stuff to be completed before I leave; I'll simply start the process of finding out what documents are required. Argentine bureaucracy is beyond belief.

Bedtime! Bye, sweetie, must go to sleep. I miss you. I love you. I wish you were with me. I kiss you.

All my love,
   Alicia

—⁓—

Buenos Aires
26 February 1967

My dearest Steve,
   Unless I hear any different by tomorrow, this will be

the last letter I'll post to India. The next one will be to London! Are you sad to be leaving New Delhi, and exotic India, your friends there, etc.? Tell me what your feelings are when leaving, and when arriving back home.

I am studying at full speed: from 9 in the morning until 5 in the afternoon I am preparing a seminar in Argentine Sociology, from 6 in the afternoon until 12 midnight I am studying Statistics II and Statistical Sampling. Next week I begin to read some of the material for Political Science, and after my first two exams (on 10th and 11th March) I'll begin to study Social History – Special Subject (Socio-economic Aspects of the Development of Argentina from 1880 to 1914 – which sounds extremely interesting). If I pass all these subjects, only Social Psychology will be left, plus one elective subject. They'll have to organise a special sitting for me, given that the Social Psychology Professor resigned in the middle of last year. When the exams are finished you'll be able to gather my remains in a spoon!

It's not so bad, really. The Faculty staff is favourably disposed towards those students who are very close to graduating, and are not too demanding in the exams; they think it is necessary to make it easy for those students to get their degree, considering the general chaotic situation. In contrast, the chiefs and staff of the Faculty's administration think differently, and they seek to create difficulties for the students by bureaucratic means. For example, they have placed limits on the number of subjects in which one can register to be examined "free"; when in fact there are no administrative regulations to prevent students from studying as many subjects as they wish, at the same time.

On Friday, after a week's intensive study, we got fed up studying statistics, and at 10.30 pm decided to go to the cinema and relax our minds a little. We went to the Cine Arte to see Tony Richardson's excellent film "The Loved One", starring Robert Morse, John Gielgud, Robert Morley, Rod Steiger, and many other good actors, many of them in cameo roles. Have you seen it? A sharp critique of family, the army, country, religion, propaganda. Black humour, extraordinary close-ups taken with a wide-angle lens, and really fine performances.

I suppose you will already have received my father's letter. What did you think of it? He asked me to type it. I do that for him regularly when it is personal correspondence. He's asked me to tell you to thank your parents very much for their invitation for me to stay in their house, and he asks you to give them his respects – he forgot to include that in this letter.

The Plan of Strife of the CGT goes ahead, but with little success; there are few people on strike, as strikers are sacked either by the government or by the private firms that employ them. The working masses seem to have lost most of their oomph, the government's control is really quite strong. Not an encouraging panorama!

An odd question: what languages do you speak, apart from Spanish?

I have to carry on studying, although it is Sunday. I look forward to receiving your letters from the exotic places that you are visiting, Calcutta, Benares, Allahabad (or something like that), Puri, etc.

Until my next letter, my love. Perhaps it will reach you in London… I hope that you do not have to postpone your departure yet again. I love you.

Alicia

India
February 1967

Darling Alicia,

The Vestibule Express takes 22 hours to reach Dhanbad in Bihar from New Delhi, and during the course of a long, sticky journey one crosses Uttar Pradesh and Bihar. The route follows the plains of the holy rivers Jamuna and Ganga, and intertwines itself with the Tropic of Cancer. We stop infrequently and can take a cup of tea, already milked and sugared, from a small, imperfectly cast, clay cup that is smashed after one has finished.

David Ovens is reading our friend David Rubin's first novel, 'The Greater Darkness', Margaret Ovens with her ready, bright smile, picks involuntarily at the heavy necklace she is wearing, Paul sucks symbolically at his pipe and I skip through Dr Chakravorty's "The Theory of the Universal Spherical Wave," stopping occasionally to scratch at my groin. It is hot, the sun glares, the carriage rolls and we begin to shift restlessly.

Three and a half hours later we arrive in Dhanbad, and after giving each of the porters one rupee for carrying our bags to the car I notice that they turn away straight-faced but soon scud along, their eyes bright with pleasure and controlled excitement, for we were paying about four times the market rate. We soon arrive at "The Fertiliser Corporation of India, Sindri Unit," and are shown to our mosquito-net shrouded beds.

Paul and I are shown round the Planning and Development Division, employing about 1400 people, by

Dr Chakravorty its Director, creator of the Universal Spherical Wave; we rush from one laboratory to another, and soon he stops to explain, against the ear-splitting screech of an effluent pipe, their successful attempts to indigenize catalyst production; a fine mist drifting into our faces. He stops to wipe his eye and suggests we rub the mist from our own face, which is already beginning to sting, for it is a compound of "dilute nitric acid".

Finally we reach a small plant where "the Doctor" takes a bottle full of a sticky, jet-black substance and tries to shake its contents on to the ground. His two engineering assistants jump back in apparent alarm as some of it splatters out by our feet. Then gesticulating expansively he tells us that the black substance is an ammoniacal liquor concentrate which previously was dumped in a nearby pit, "on one occasion three buffalo mistook it for cooling mud and in that acid sludge they dissolved before our eyes" – I move gently back a pace or two from the man holding the black bottle, smile wanly and thank him for the tour. In his engineers he evokes an almost evangelical enthusiasm and I ply the Doctor with questions about pressure and temperature, progress and prospects.

We return to Sindri late at night after driving once more through the Dhanbad district, which is at the centre of the Jharia coalfields. Over-head conveyors move their loads silently in the dusk; and miners "homeward plod their weary way" with a pickaxe slung over their shoulder. How strangely these dark-skinned, small, emaciated men compare with their burly counterparts in Derbyshire and South Wales. The air is full of coal dust and slag, like a heavy evening mist, and after a lovely journey, the land seems to have been raped and left torn and filthy by the industrial revolution.

On arriving at Sindri we hear that one of the employees of the nearby cement factory has died. The story is a confused one; it seems that an old Muslim has driven a cow and its calf out of his garden since they were eating the vegetation there. A mob of Hindus quickly assemble, accuse him of wounding the animal, and beat the man up, he escapes, to return to his house late at night, where he is caught again and beaten to death. Cow is mother.

On Thursday morning we have our last conversation with this wonderful, spiky, volatile, enthusiastic, brilliant madman, Dr Chakravorty. It seems clear that some of his paranoia is wholly justified. He believes that the American private companies are trying to integrate new Indian companies into their production patterns of liquid ammonia and phosphoric acid. The idea is that they will have a guaranteed outlet for their own products and since they will be providing India with material (liquid ammonia and phosphoric acid) which only they can supply in sufficiently large quantities, once the proposed agreements have gone through, they will be able to force a very high price. He shows us a letter that substantially confirms all he says including that U.S.A.I.D and some members of the *Indian* Ministry of Finance are implicated. After lunch we leave, promising to do what we can to assist in the efficient indigenization of India fertiliser production and using what little influence David has in the Planning Commission.

On Friday, David and I spent most of our day with English and Indian executives of I.C.I – Imperial Chemical Industries, who intend setting up a plant at Kanpur in Uttar Pradesh to produce 200,000 metric tons of nitrogen per annum; it will be the largest fertiliser plant in Asia.

In the evening the four of us go for a long stroll through the streets of Calcutta. In the evening the harsh lights emphasize the grim and filthy atmosphere, the wretched poverty of so many of the people passing by, the children tugging at one's clothes for money and the young boys who scamper through the traffic like bats through a rock-strewn cave to hail a taxi for us. I tip the one I sent to get a taxi, but Margaret gives money to another, and they all chase after the taxi through the streets yelling, the boy who first got our taxi lashing out in fury and impotence at those who are trying to usurp him. None is older than 12.

We dine at Chung Wah's, a Chinese restaurant, and listen in our small cubicle (with its torn green curtain over the doorless doorway) to Lily Marlene played on a ukelele by an old sailor. A small cat peers through the wire netting over the window at sweet and sour pork, roast pigeon, pigeon and tomatoes, fried rice.

On Saturday I said good-bye to Paul. I was leaving for Orissa in a plane soon after midday. We talked briefly about the winds and rain of London in March, then of the theatre, cinema and pubs, and I felt he would like to be returning too. I wished him luck with the Singh family; I think that when he returns to London in 9 months he will probably bring Rani as his bride. How London will suit her, with its unfriendly weather, bustling populace, and how she will adjust to a life without domestic servants and without the intimacy and security of her family remains to be seen. Mair Jones, our Welsh friend, seems to think that she lacks that resilience of character to overcome the major problems of such a migration.

Puri is famous for two things: (i) it is the name of the

excellent pancake made out of wheat and oil and cooked so that it puffs up, almost into a globe. (ii) for its temple to Lord Jagganath, whom as you know is an incarnation of Lord Vishnu, one of the three great gods of the Hindus – Brahma the creator; Vishnu, the preserver; Shiva, the destroyer.

In June/July every year a great Car Festival is held at Puri when an image of Jagganath is brought out from the temple, accompanied by two lesser deities, carried on a giant chariot forty five feet high. Ropes are attached to the chariot and it is hauled by men through the town and down to the seashore where the assembled host bathe. It was believed that to die in the sight of the god ensured eternal happiness, and until the beginning of this century some pilgrims would throw themselves under the great wheels of the chariot to be crushed to death. This is how the term "Juggernaut" arose.

I did not visit the Jagganath temple since I was not allowed to. I remembered again how exclusive a religion Hinduism is. One is *born* a Hindu, one can never become one. Non-Hindus are excluded from many of the great centres of worship, and almost invariably from the inner sanctum of any temple, large or small. We peered down into the temple wards from a nearby vantage point, and our guide explained that although he had lived in Puri all his life he had never been inside the temple; like me, he was unclean, for he was of the sweeper caste, who are outcastes.

After having a shower in the delightful South East Railway Hotel, I walked to the beach which is about 200 hundred yards away and strolled quietly along the sand watching the sun setting, its orange and purple light luminescent on the sea. I imagined that you were holding my right hand swinging it gently, and looked to find you – but saw only the sea, the glimmering light and the blood-shot sun.

On Sunday I drove over to Konarak with an English couple I had met at dinner the previous evening. He is a mechanical engineer and works for the British Iron and Steel Research Association in Battersea (London) and came originally from Poland, arriving in England first in 1939. George and June Wistrich are their names, and I've promised to visit them in London in April.

The Black Pagoda, at Konarak in Orissa, was built in the 13th century by Narasimha in praise of the Sun-God, Surya. Konarak is an impressive sight from a distance because of its great height, and its impression of movement; at close hand it is fantastic. Into the faces of the temple are carved many thousands of figures, or groups of figures, most of them between 4" and 12" in height, but some as tall as eight feet. The outer temple, which was a dancing platform for the temple prostitutes who entertained visitors with their dancing, shows dancers in their different positions. Each figure is that of a girl with very full, bared breasts, bejewelled skirt, usually with large earrings, capturing one of the movements of the dance, often playing the mridanga (double-ended drum) or vina (lute) or pipe.

The main structure includes some figures of dancing girls, some images of Shiva, looking like Falstaff with an enormous belly and satyrical leer, and there are some friezes of battle scenes, including one with a giraffe.

However, the Black Pagoda devotes its sculpture over-whelmingly to the art of love. On every face, on every one of the great wheels, and high up on the vertical walls of the terraced pyramid, are men and women coupling eternally, sometimes a single man and woman, sometimes several women and a man, rarely two men, rarely two women, rarely several men and one woman.

Their desire is expressed in the most exotic manner and I can hardly think of any modality of intercourse between man and woman that is not carved into stone on this glorious pile of writhing, pulsating sandstone flesh. The single most recurrent theme is that of the mouth congress. Two figures I still remember with great clarity. One is set high in a niche of the wall of the Audience Chamber, it must stand 8'-10' high. The male faces outwards standing straight whilst the girl clings tightly round his neck, one foot placed either side of his waist, the sun gleaming on the muscles of her back and the sensual curve of her buttocks.

The other figure captures for me the beauty of Konarak. It is about 18" high, again of a man cut out of the stone, rampant, and the girl clings to him with one foot raised close to his right hip, her face bent upwards and seeming to melt into his in an eternal kiss.

Ah! my love, would that you were here to transmute these base stones into the fluid gold of our bodies.

I must have spent about 6 hours in all on four different occasions, and should have some excellent photographs, in particular of the dancing girls.

On Sunday afternoon I walked through a small fishing village on the shore, where the small, black-skinned men staggered like drunkards under the weight of their wooden canoes as they dragged them from the blue, blue, sea; women packed stinking fish into earthenware pots, scattering handfuls of coarse salt between each layer; small children waddled by, their bodies gleaming from a recent wash. The vile stench of rotting fish pervaded the whole area, but the people, although dirty and dishevelled, had a dignity in their bearing which is uncommon in the cities. I felt that if I had stayed here in the Oriyan countryside, in the fishing and farming villages and amongst the aboriginal tribal people of the forest, I could grow to love them.

On Monday afternoon I took the bus to Bhubaneshwar where I looked briefly at the major temple there – Lingaraj, literally Penis King – and caught the plane back to Calcutta.

Wednesday and Thursday were spent at Benares. I spent both mornings in a boat being rowed along the waterfront watching the pilgrims bathing on the ghats, long flights of steps that lead into the river. One ghat exercises special fascination, Manakarnika, the burning ghat. Here the bodies of the dead are brought, strapped to a bamboo stretcher, and placed on a heap of logs, with more wood piled on them. The fire blazes fiercely in the breeze from the river, their souls ascend to heaven with the blue smoke and their ashes are cast into the holy waters. How much more attractive a way of being disposed of than our fashion in Europe of burying the corpse to moulder and decay, to be signalled by a slab of marble covered in moss.

I was rather foolish on Thursday morning, spending over 3 hours on the boat, the glare of the spring sun very strong off the water, with my shirt off basking like some strange white fish. On my way back to the hotel I felt rather groggy, with a mild sense of nausea, belching and diarrhoea, coupled with a feeling of exhaustion, my skin glowing like red-hot coke. Sunstroke. I spent the rest of the day in bed and seem to have shaken it off. But oh! how I needed my Alicia to "mimar" me , bring me tea, cool my brow and gently kiss my lips.

I have begun to divide the erotic images into three classes:

(i)   multiple partners, where there is at least two women engaged in some form of sexual intercourse, or at least two men, or both. From a didactic point of view, these do not attract me, for I'm a severe puritan where promiscuity is concerned.

(ii) the grotesque, i.e. those positions which do not please me aesthetically, these include two friezes for which Khajuraho is famous, of one partner standing on his (her) head, whist the other is supported on top of him (her) by two handmaidens!

(iii) the passionate and beautiful, comprehending the majority of man/woman sexual acts.

As you've probably gathered, honey, these magnificent temples are a very powerful aphrodisiac – I'm sure I can't be alone in finding this. What delicious scenes I've conjured up between you and I – but always in the mind's eye since I'm alone.

Now I am back again in Delhi, and feel in retrospect that these two weeks would have been improved in only one way – to have you share it all with me.

You have been constantly in my thoughts, and I have missed you desperately,

I love you.
Steve

New Delhi
27 February 1967

Darling Alicia,

How are you, sweetie? I miss you lots. Now I'm back in Delhi I can write to you more regularly, and more legibly, tho' the subject matter may not be as fascinating as the ancient cities and temples of Northern India.

I was browsing in a small bookshop at Konarak, after visiting that magnificent erotic temple, when I came across a book on technique that I've decided to give you when you come to London, which I want you to study in detail. I hesitated at first because it seemed rather presumptuous, but since this aspect of our relationship is absolutely fundamental to its success and since, from your letters, it appears that you are relatively inexperienced in these matters, I thought that this small book, with its large number of illustrations – most of them in colour! – would be useful to you. As you may have guessed, my own tastes are exotic, not to say omnivorous. With the right girl my own appetite is voracious, and I think that as time passes our needs will begin to coincide more fully. Please honey, don't be angry with me for stating so boldly my views on such a visceral matter.

The first hurdle is past in my efforts to join the Government Economic Service. I have been accepted for an interview in London on March 15th. I get back on the 10th and will take a few days holiday until the Wednesday, reading about the British economy and on Thursday and Friday I'll go flat hunting.

A small dark cloud has scudded onto the horizon of

our beautiful summer. If I am successful at the interview I've told them I'll take up my appointment on September 15th. LSE have taken the news of my impending departure fairly well, but are anxious that I finish my book with David before I leave them.

So I *must* finish it before mid-September. I hope to complete it by June – hopefully – but if it extends into July then our time for holiday will be reduced. In any event we should be able to enjoy say mid-July to mid-September together, if all goes well.

Honey, when you come – and please, please come soon, the very day you graduate – bring a couple of long-playing records with cumbia, tango, cha cha cha etc. on them, then you can teach me to dance them and we'll play them at any parties we go to.

I love you, I need you, body and soul,
Steve

PS. On re-reading my letter I notice I forgot to tell you the title of the book I bought for you, it is called *Mrs Balbir Singh's Indian Cookery*.

PPS. What! But Alicia my innocent what were you thinking?

—◈—

New Delhi
1 March 1967

Darling Alicia,
Do I want to go home to England? Yes, but with mixed

feelings. You, in the past few months since the appendix from my body was so untimely ripped, have seen as deep into my black and spotted soul as anyone, deeper in fact, and you must have realised that although it would be incorrect, strictly speaking, to say I have been happy here, yet it is such a great country in many ways, with such a markedly different culture from European countries like England and Argentina, with the majority of the people so close to the fundamentals of life – birth, disease, poverty, violence, hunger and glorious beauty – that inevitably one is drawn out of oneself and becomes involved with mankind, no longer an island, for each man's death diminishes me.

My desire to go back is founded on my dislike of being still in a world of servants and hotels, my wish to be able to work undisturbed on the book in the surroundings of scholarship and diligence with little to distract me, my fervent wish to see my friends like Peter Razzell and Oscar Braun, and finally, but most important, because I shall feel closer to the girl I love.

Why don't I phone you on Tuesday March 28th at 6 pm Greenwich Mean Time and you can tell me all about your hectic month and the prospects for the future. Good idea?

Yes, there are usually some snowfalls in London during the winter, when briefly everything is cloaked in white and sounds are muffled; unfortunately the traffic soon turns it to slush and it soaks into the feet, which freeze. However, I don't recall whether or not I've mentioned it before, but when I was at University I was a keen, if incompetent skier, so if we have enough money perhaps we'll go skiing in Scotland or Italy next winter or spring.

Do bring your otter fur coat, I'm sure you'll look very

glamorous in it and you can use it as a lever to persuade me to escort you to watch Rudolf Nureyev and Margot Fonteyn dancing together at Covent Garden. I feel eminently capable of becoming a balletomane – perhaps that would have been my true métier, who knows?

You seem to be a teenee weenee bit confused about "cockney." It is the dialect in London that is specially associated with the working class families of the East End, where you'll be living initially. It is above all an accent, but does have its own limited vocabulary of "rhyming slang" e.g. "tea-leaf" means "thief." "This Sporting Life" was set somewhere in the north, I don't remember where, and the accent will be of that county, Yorkshire, Lancashire, Durham or wherever it was. Axiom: *cockneys never play rugby*, but they do have (in London) three of the finest football clubs in the country, West Ham, Tottenham Hotspur and Chelsea. Would you like to go and see a match with me, baby? It'll have to be next September since the season ends in April.

I am starting to get engaged in various odd, time-wasting little tasks, ably assisted by the British High Commission. I need an income tax clearance certificate, my plane ticket, must send off some papers by unaccompanied air freight, and let people in England know of my change of address. By the way I suggest you write to me in London care of my LSE address, in case my flat hunting is successful the week after next (most unlikely!)

Will write again soon to answer the unanswered.
All my love,
Steve

Buenos Aires
2 March 1967

My adored Steve,

My love, how I miss you today! I feel mimosa and want to be with you very much. When will the day arrive! I love you so much, I miss you, I want to be at your side.

This morning Horacio and Haydée (H&H) left for Europe. Perhaps that's what made me sad; on the one hand I am going to miss them, on the other I envy them for being able to go – I still have to wait for a while! But today, at the airport, everybody said that I would be the next one to leave...certainly within two or three months!

How was your arrival in London? How did you feel? How did you find your parents? I imagine that you have so many friends to see, and such a desire to see them! And the city, and the country, after a year of absence! Amongst all your other activities, will you find time to write to me as often as before? I miss your letters, it is more than a week since the last one. The ones about your trip to Calcutta, Benares and other exotic places have not arrived yet.

Tell me about London – that is, how the people are. About the beatniks, the girls in mini-skirts, the University, and the economic problems, etc. Are you going to grow your hair long and wear gaudy shirts? (I hope not.) Someone told me once that when you arrived in Buenos Aires your hair was very long. Is that right?

I carry on studying, as ever. I have changed my plans somewhat, regarding the order in which I'll take the subjects, but these are unimportant details in my general plan to graduate as soon as possible.

I like the idea that your letters will arrive more quickly from England.

My love, Happy Landing! I send you lots of kisses.

I love you,
    Alicia.

—∿∿—

Buenos Aires
6 March 1967

My sweet, darling, beloved Steve:

This morning I spent an hour-and-a-half reading and re-reading your adventures in India. You have an incredible capacity to pull my heartstrings, to make me feel deeply what you are feeling, through the things you say and write. I noticed it when you were still in Buenos Aires (without fully realising it), and you have it now, with these marvellous letters. I read – and through these descriptions and your comments I feel transported through time and space, and I feel as if I'd have been with you in all these places. During your journey I spent the days thinking about the beautiful things that you would be seeing, and following day by day your itinerary. Their names spin in my mind with such strange and beautiful sounds – Lord Jagganath, Konarak, the strange Dr. Chakravorty...

Sometimes I stand looking blankly into space, far away, imagining myself with you, walking in the twilight on the beach at Puri, seated in a train taking you who knows where, or, more than anything, being with you in Konarak contemplating the Black Pagoda with its marvellous friezes, the passion of mankind, the art of love, the Sun God, us really being the alchemists of love transmuting stone into our flesh and blood. Never has anyone made me feel that way…

While I'm writing I am listening to a beautiful Bach concerto, the Concerto for two violins, strings and continuum in D Minor, BWV-1043. The music suits my wandering mind. I have an exam in a few days' time, I ought to be studying Statistics, but I can't, I have to write to you.

Yesterday I spent so much time thinking about you! We were studying in my house and suddenly it began to rain. Through the open window, at dusk, one could feel the freshness of the rain refreshing the hot afternoon, and the delicious smell of wet earth. We switched on the radio, and they were broadcasting Concerto No. 1 of Beethoven, with Claudio Arrau on the piano. It never seemed to me so lovely as yesterday!

My darling, when shall I be with you? It seems to me that it's still such a long time to go, and sometimes I despair. Someone lent me a record called "This is Jazz", recorded by various musicians and singers, and amongst the songs is "Fine and Mellow" by Billie Holiday. Every time I hear it, I think about you yet again.

In Argentina things go on "così, così". We have a new Law of Civil Defence, which states that any citizen older than 14 can be called up to join the defence forces at any time – it's compulsory, and subject to military law. The new Law of Tax Reform increases various taxes. The University Law is still in President Onganía's hands and the Trades Union Congress is deliberating on whether or not to continue the Plan of Strife. Apart from staff dismissals, etc. four more lecturers in Sociology are going to resign in the next few days.

Well, my love, since it is already 12.50 am. I am going to bed. I ought to read "Biserial Correlation" or at least carry on reading the second volume of Burgin, but I am afraid that I won't do anything except cast another eye over your letter.

I have exams (if nothing weird happens at the University in the next days) on the 10th and 11th of March. So I may not write to you again until Sunday, unless I manage to scribble a few lines in a spare moment so that you don't have a whole week without letters.

Good-bye, my love, and good night. I miss you so much. I adore you.

Alicia
PS. How is London treating you?

———

New Delhi
7 March 1967

Good morning, darling,

Today I was up very early – 7am – had a shower, and have been reading your last half-dozen letters. How much I want to have you here with me now, to pull you under the sheets and savour the spices of your body! But we must wait, wait, wait.

I received the letter from your father; he seems, naturally enough I suppose, to have still a keen sense of regret at the way his life was put out of joint by the Russian Revolution, and he is clearly a man of great resource to have established himself in Argentina after arriving in such complete poverty. I am delighted that he and Ester are both coming to Europe in 1967/8, as I am anxious to meet him and try to understand why his influence on you is as powerful as it seems to be. Whether it be sympathy or antipathy I'm sure the relation between he and I will be a vital one and if, by chance, you and I *do* marry then the time to do it will be while he's in England so that he can give you away.

One thing I did want to discuss with you is your first few months in England. From your descriptions of life in Buenos Aires it is clear that you live in a delightful neighbourhood, in a comfortable house with the window of your bedroom overlooking a large garden and that the house is full of friends from the Faculty and your relations, with lots of parties, family dinners etc. Living at 32, Mayville Road will be very different, even if you set up an immediate and warm friendship with my parents. For Leytonstone, like a dozen other suburbs of London, is strikingly ugly with its high street choked with traffic and its long rows of terrace houses and their minute "backyards".

In addition, as I mentioned I believe in my letter of December 12th, my mother and father do not have many friends – in fact, looking back on it, my memories of that home in my childhood are the quiet and loneliness of the place, a kind of stagnation. In addition, since it's such a long way from the centre of London it'll be a long way for our friends to come when we want to invite them for dinner or to spend the evening with us. Of course, by the time you arrive I'll have a flat and we can use that as a base for operations. So if your Dad *does* make you some kind of grant then I think it will be much better if you regard Leytonstone as a temporary address and after settling in for the first few weeks that you start looking for a flat of your own – preferably near mine! – or a girl to share with. I have thought this all along but now feel I should make it explicit. Not that you'll be lonely in England when you first arrive, I'll not leave your side except at night (shame!), but you'll integrate with this terrible giant city more easily, much more easily, if, instead of living in a single room in someone's house in the suburbs, you can share a flat say with an LSE student nearer the centre. We mustn't underestimate the cultural shock you'll face on arriving; it'll be fascinating to see how you'll adapt, like a social experiment – you must take notes.

It is interesting that your contact with your parents and family is so close and mine so limited. One could relate it I suppose to factors such as that you are female and I male, that you are Latin American & Jewish and I am Anglo-Saxon, that you are an undergraduate and I have finished University, that you are more gregarious than I, and finally that you probably have a much wider range of interests in common with your parents than I with mine. But I'm very happy that you'll be staying with my parents for the first month or more because you'll have an opportunity of getting to know my parents well, and they you; you'll find my father very kind, and my mother very affectionate – especially so – since inevitably she'll regard you as a source of future grand-children, and next door live my uncle and aunt, George and Lily, who are really wonderful people. Vamos a ver *(we'll see)* – there's no point in anticipating ad infinitum.

I read French with facility, though have forgotten how to speak it, and understand little; my German, which once was excellent, when I was at school, has now decayed almost to putrefaction. [A metaphor I must have derived from the dead dog I saw by one of the major sewage pipes on the Ganga at Benares.]

I'll cut this letter short and post it and write again tomorrow.

Te adoro,
Steve

PS. I feel in a strange and rather happy limbo these days, neither in India nor in England, neither with you nor without you. I loathe waiting! Te amo, te beso, S.

―♒―

(Postcard)
March 1967

I LOVE YOU I LOVE YOU I LOVE YOU I LOVE YOU
(and I miss you very much)

Hi sweetie! I'm studying very, very hard and have no time to write long letters. Got your letters of Feb 27 & March 1, that did me a lot of good. Lots of things to tell you about, just wait a couple of days.

It's raining outside, and I love hearing the rain in bed while I am drifting into sleep.

Lots of love, Alicia
PS. Good luck in the interview on the 15th!

New Delhi
9 March 1967

Darling Alicia,

This is the last letter I shall be writing to you from India. Tomorrow morning I take BOAC Flight 781 to London, arriving in London at local time late in the afternoon.

The last month has been an excellent valedictory to India, for not only have I seen Calcutta, Konarak, Benares and Khajuraho, I have also attended a superb set of concerts with the very greatest Indian musicians, including Nikhil Banerjee on sitar, Bismillah Khan on shahnai, Ustad Vilayat Khan on sitar, Misra Bandhu vocalist, Devendra Murdeshwar on flute and Ustad Ali Akbar Khan on sarod. The concert lasted from approximately 6.45pm until 2 am, so I spent about 30 hours over the course of 4 days cross-legged on the floor, sometimes swaying like a cobra to the divine shahnai of Bismillah Khan or shaking my head in emotion at the glissandos of Ali Akbar Khan. I have long-playing records of several of these artists, and know some of them come to London each year, so you'll have the opportunity of hearing them.

David Rubin is a New Yorker, born Roman Catholic, but part-Jewish, although now an agnostic, who has lived here at the Centre for the past 8 months and whom I have come to know well and admire greatly. He is primarily a novelist, and has to date published the first two novels of a trilogy on India – he is writing a third now.

Well honey, I'll go out now to post this letter, and do the 1001 last minute tasks that I have neglected.

I love you very much,
Steve

———✦———

London
11 March 1967

Darling Alicia,

My journey back was fairly uneventful; the entire journey lasted only $13^{1}/_{2}$ hours, with brief stops at Bahrain and Cairo. Suddenly as we crossed the French coast at about 35,000 feet and I peered into the distance looking for the English coast I began to feel excited. The cloud formations were quite magnificent, as if a heavy fall of snow had covered the lush jungles of Kerala, with the anvils of cumulo-nimbus seeming to flow up from a boiling cauldron of vapours. England looked so green, the fields so large and distinctive. Then the great mass of the capital began to appear, with its neat rows of slate roofs in grey or red, hundreds of green football pitches, speeding motor-cars, towering blocks of flats, and the sun gleamed on the runways, wet from a recent shower, as we landed, and I knew I was home in my own country.

My mother and my Aunt Lily met me and after clearing customs we drove back along the North Circular to Leytonstone. I've been wandering round ever since with my eyes wide at the great city and its people; how unattractive are their skins, blotchy purple, mauve, white and red; how quickly they walk; how deeply swaddled in clothes and hunched up the middle-aged seem to be; how tall and graceful the buildings; how new the cars; how frequent the Negros; how strange to see a lady in Punjabi salwar – obviously a Sikh – giving some small change to a beggar at the Underground station; how polite and gay people seem; how incredibly short the skirts are and how attractive they look on a girl with nice legs; how good it felt to have to carry my own suitcase the whole 15 minute walk to the underground, without sweepers chasing me in horror at my willingness to carry out a manual task.

The house seems so tiny with the accumulation of my possessions over the years, and my mother fussing around that I'm very anxious to get that flat. By the way my mother says you can sleep in my (tiny) bedroom and have our best "front-room" as a lounge/dining room/reading room, which will be quite nice for you – she's even tried to make my room "more feminine" with the wall-paper and bed cover, so you'll like it more. Wasn't that nice? There's an electric blanket to keep you warm at night and an electric "blower" in the day. It's quite "nippy" just now, but the cold has a kind of energizing effect on me, and the sun kept breaking through the bunched white clouds so that the wet streets look most picturesque.

Only two things remain to make life excellent; you and you. Also a nice roomy flat near a park would be nice.

With all my love, I miss you constantly, my darling.
Steve

PS. Do you prefer 1. double bed or 2. single beds ?

Buenos Aires
12 March 1967

My dear, dearest Steve,

What a trickster you are! I fell like a trusting and incautious bird in the trap that you set for me in the letter of February 27th. After having read the first page I was really anxious thinking that I was going to have to quickly learn the Kama Sutra to acquaint me with certain exotic subtleties…

Good news: I have passed my first exam, Statistical Methodology II, with Distinction, and yesterday afternoon I sat the written exam of the seminar course, it went well, in my view, but I have the oral exam next Tuesday or Wednesday. The main difference between ordinary exams (where you have attended classes for a term) and 'free' exams, is that in the first case it is only an oral exam, and in the second case you first sit a written exam, then if you pass it they let you sit the oral. I'm really happy!

Of course I sent the birthday card to your father without waiting for your opinion, as you already know. What was their reaction? Tell me the gossip of the House of Merrett.

Yesterday and today I had an attack of 'dancing madness', that is, wanting to dance. Yesterday I did so at a farewell party for a University friend, Jorge Schnitman, who is going to Oslo for four months to work in the Peace Research Institute as a research assistant. We danced like lunatics until four in the morning, and afterwards there was an improvised session of jazz with piano, drums, clarinet and trumpet, and then we played something called 'the free association game' which was really entertaining and lasted until six in the morning!

Re – my LSE application, perhaps if you can speak with Dr. Sutti de Ortiz, in the Department of Anthropology, and ask her how my admission application is proceeding, and also tell me something about anthropology studies there.

I'd very much like to talk about our very different experiences as children and adolescents, attitudes to our parents, friends, life in general. To leave your country, to live alone, seems entirely natural to you; for me and the Argentines of my generation it is a very complicated question.

I am happy to accept the invitation to ski in Italy or Scotland, although I have never been skiing so I will have to learn. I also love the idea of going to a football match, and even more the opportunity to go to Covent Garden to see a ballet (I love ballet). I hope our summer holidays don't get cut too short, but it is not really that important.

Telephone call: the 28th of March isn't a good day, because I may have to be in the Faculty sitting an exam. It would be best if you could call me one Sunday morning, between 8 and 11 Argentine time, when I'll certainly be at home.

How unpleasant getting sunstroke in Benares! If I had been there, not only would I have cared for you, but even better, I would have foreseen the danger of your spending so much time in the sun by the river! But I'll be delighted to pamper you, when you are well and when you are not well.

How's the flat-hunting going? Keep me up-to-date and when you get a flat please tell me: (1) where it is; (2) what it's like; (3) send me a room layout; (4) and tell me how you feel inside it.

How did the photos of Konarak come out? Will you send me one? And I am longing to hear about the miniskirts. What I'd like to know is how many centimetres above the knee are the skirts of your female friends, for example Sonia. There are many sorts, shapes and lengths of mini-skirts, but I want to know how are they worn amongst the people I'll be with, the LSE students etc.

So you think that Paul will take Rani to London with him? It will be lovely to meet her. I hope she has no great problems with immigration – I hope that I don't either! What do you think about my ability to adapt? I feel confident, but you never know what can happen! We'll see…

Well, my love, I hope that you are enjoying London, the theatres, the cinemas, the pubs, all your friends and your work. I am completely immersed in the business of studying, trying to move forward as best and as rapidly as I can so as to be with you soon. My sweet love, I miss you a lot. What a pity you were not there yesterday to dance with me. Today I continue with the dance rhythm, instead of walking I went dancing right through the house, and I followed the rhythm of the music whilst I was studying.

I love you very, very, very much.
    Alicia

—⁓—

Buenos Aires
15 March 1967

My adored Steve,
    I still have no idea when I am going to sit my oral exam

in Agrarian Legislation. The Industrial Sociology exam should have taken place yesterday, but it was postponed until today. So today I arrived at the Faculty at 8.30 am and learnt that it has been postponed again, until tomorrow! And who knows what will happen tomorrow? So far I'm trying to stay calm and take it rather philosophically – not easy, as every trip to the Faculty takes nearly an hour. But there are other students who are on the verge of a nervous breakdown, particularly those who work and have to ask for time off to take the exam, and this can go on for several days.

There is so much that we shall do together in London! Shall we make a list? (!) (I'm an inveterate list-maker). The cinemas, the theatre, pubs, trips around London, to Oxford and other places, reading Shakespeare and poetry in English and Spanish, listening to music, watching football, ballet, etc.; reading our letters, talking about millions of things; and all that aside the time that we shall spend simply kissing, embracing, caressing each other, pampering each other and making love.

I have thought about what I shall do while you are at work, and before I start my studies. I want to read lots of Social Anthropology in preparation for the course, as well as other books; and I'll spend whole days walking along the city streets, to find my way round it, enjoying travelling by tube (I love the subway, metro, tube), seeing museums, taking photos, and even going shopping!

Currency devaluation here is increasing, so the price in pesos of my trip to Europe is increasing too. So, last week my father booked my ticket to England! What do you think?! I'll be flying, at a date to be settled once I have finished all my exams – I hope that will be in early May!

The problem is that since booking the flight, my father has been looking edgy and lonely – I think that he is now much more alarmed about my journey than I am!

Everything you tell me about the differences between my life in Buenos Aires and in Leytonstone is absolutely right, and it's what I'd expect. I have thought about it many times, and I remember you were telling me about the difficulties of adaptation that Rani could have, accustomed to the security of her family, etc., I thought that something similar could happen with me. It will be an interesting experience...

I don't know yet how much money my father will give me, and if it would be possible for me to live in a more central location, sharing a flat with one or two other girls. I wouldn't like to live completely on my own. I think it would be to add too much to the initial cultural shock. I have lived for short periods with other girls, so that would be better.

I have noticed how we both anticipate each other's thoughts in our letters. Sometimes you reply to a question before it has had time to reach you! For example: I wrote recently about the differences in our relationships with our parents, differences in education etc. and said that will be very interesting to compare our experiences. You said very similar things in your letter of the 7th, which you wrote before reading my letter!

The CGT's Plan of Strife failed completely, through government reprisals, and the trade unions' organization decided to suspend the strikes announced for the 21st and 22nd of this month, and to return to negotiations with the government. Defeat all down the line! There were several resignations amongst the CGT leaders, and the trade union bureaucracy is really wobbly.

I agree that your relationship with my father, when you finally meet, is going to be vital, and I am sure that you'll both like each other. It's a good idea that, if we marry, he should be in London.

Will I sit the exam tomorrow or not? It is as much a game of chance as to toss a coin in the air and guess what side will be uppermost (and I would almost say that for them to set the exam the coin should land on its edge!). Or you could take a daisy and pull off its petals, saying with each Yes, No, Yes, No, Yes, to see what will happen; or to make bets: who will bet yes – we'll sit the exam? – and who will bet no?

Well, my love, it seems I'll consult my pillow about the matter – as I do not have you here to consult! I hope your first letter from London will arrive soon.

I love you very, very much.
Alicia

Unit for Economic and Statistical Studies on Higher Education
The London School of Economics
16 March 1967

Darling Alicia,
Yesterday I received a very warm letter from H&H who asked me to get tickets for the National Theatre. I telephoned Mara and Enrico the other day and had a long chat with Mara in Spanish; she sounds delightful. They will probably spend the weekend of the 21st/23rd of April

with Horacio and Haydée. I said I would go round and have dinner with them next week and Mara said to bring my wife if I have one, so she's obviously not too clearly in the picture. It'll be a nice chance to practise my Spanish a little more.

The interview went *very* badly indeed, probably the worst I've ever given. It was at 10 am (ugh!) and there was not one single fucking question on my work since I left Oxford; but to be fair I was also very slow-witted and entirely ignorant of contemporary Britain, so I'm sure to have failed. Enough said.

I weighed myself two or three days ago, thinking I must have put on a good deal more weight in the last few weeks – which is almost certainly true! I weighed 8 stone 7 lbs! So whilst I was in India, at the worst period, I must have lost a stone in weight.

Everybody has been commenting on how thin I look; I'm glad you didn't fly in last week; you'd have taken one look at the thin hulk awaiting you and caught the next plane out.

In the last few days I've spent many hours tramping the streets of London looking for a flat, but to no avail, so I've decided to turn the matter over to an Accommodation Bureau. I was immediately offered a little bed-sitting room in Richmond, very close to our magnificent Kew Gardens, but turned it down since there was no kitchenette, so my honey wouldn't be able to cook me curry and curd, or papas fritas y un bife de chorizo.

Will write soon,

Can't wait till you arrive,
Love, love, love
    Steve

PS. This evening I received a pithy little note from the Civil Service Commissioners:

"I am glad to be able to tell you that the Selection Board which met on 14th March 1967 recommended that you should be offered appointment if the results of the Commissioners' enquiries into health and other points are satisfactory. We shall be writing to you again shortly on this matter."

So I got the job!

——∿——

Buenos Aires
19 March 1967

My dearest Steve,

The exam in Industrial Sociology was postponed until tomorrow. But on Saturday, at 8.30 pm (what a time to sit an exam!), I sat the oral in Agrarian Legislation, and I got 7/10. One less to go before graduation! I also sat the written exam in Argentine Sociology.

I suppose that you will need a few days to settle down in London before feeling at home in the city once again. I feel that whenever one returns from a journey, the house seems smaller, and things a little different from how you remembered them.

I'm really charmed by your mother's preoccupation with my future comforts in her home! I think that we'll have a really friendly relationship, and that I'll be very comfortable there. How long is the journey from Leytonstone to the centre of town? Can you travel by underground? I am used to travel a long way to get to the centre of town; from my home in Belgrano, to any place that's more or less in the town centre, it's a minimum of 30 minutes, and generally more.

I prefer a double bed, it's much friendlier and comfortable, don't you agree?

Don't feel low, there are many wonderful things in life apart from me; and when we are together, everything will seem superb. I miss you very much, lots of kisses,

Alicia

PS. I love you.

———~~~———

Monday, 20th March

Darling Alicia,

After 4 or 5 days of almost suicidal depression, when I found it impossible to write even though it meant my barring my griefs, I feel much more cheerful today. And so I should be for so many objective factors are encouraging: I have the promise of a very highly paid job with the government doing a kind of economics which I believe I'll enjoy; I am on the scent of a place to live, it's only a bed-sitter (i.e. single room), but I won't tell you any more until I'm sure I have it; I am eating well and have put on 3 lbs in my first week home; I am sleeping well; and the girl I love is coming to me in a matter of weeks.

Why was I so terribly depressed? I don't know. Partly a sense of isolation at LSE and in London; it can be a bloody lonely city even for an ex-Londoner. I even began to doubt the probability of our relationship's success, fearing that I could never make you happy in this grey city far from the sun and your swarming friends and relations. In the middle of the depression came your letter describing how gaily you had danced all night in Buenos Aires, and jealousy was added to my emotions, a jealousy and resentment so strong that I could not re-read your letter for 4 days.

But today all that is past; I have started talking to people, making small jokes, and last night my friends Mark and Cat gave a curry dinner for 18 people, where I began to relax again and begin to feel the pleasure of conversation.

Yet, perhaps no man could ever be the same after spending a year in India; whether the under-swell of emotion will be melancholia or detachment I cannot say. By the time you arrive I hope the latter attitude will have asserted itself as well as my pristine cheerfulness.

Surprise! Surprise! When I came home I found a letter waiting for me from Adriana, Mariella's sister, and now Mariella herself has written to my parents wishing them a happy Easter. Isn't that strange?

When shall I phone? Not on Sunday 26th because I'll be in Willie's flat in Belgium which has no phone; not the following Sunday because I'll be heaven knows where in Sussex. How about Tuesday, 4th April at 6 pm G.M.T? O.K.?

Last Friday I met Willie for the first time in over a year. He looked absolutely the same. I am to fly from Southend to Ostend on Thursday and come back on Easter Sunday.

It'll be wonderful to see them again. I told him how much I would have liked to have brought you, but he said anyway we'll meet in October next when he returns from Brazil. Then you can ask him about *his* globetrotting – he says "it's a poison".

The mini-skirt really is incredible. I had forgotten that English girls, however less beautiful they may be than the daughters of the haute bourgeoisie in India, really can be tremendously attractive, and have very ripe figures. Skirts worn by young women vary from the middle of the knee to the edge of their most chaste of treasures. Do you remember Laertes to Ophelia?

"Do not open your chaste treasure
To his unmastered importunity."

The shortest I've seen, and strictly on your account I have been conducting a very careful study, go some 9-12 *inches* above the knee. But 8 *cms,* your upper limit, would be very fashionable, not too demure. It all comes down to one's thighs I suppose, and girls seem to adjust them as far up the leg as is consistent with their own sex-appeal. You can give me a very private showing and I'll tell you what suits you best.

Alicia: "Is that fine?"
Steve: "Little bit higher"
Alicia: "Fine?"
Steve: "A wee bit more"
Alicia: "Now??"
Steve: "Just a little bit more, honey."
Alicia: "But, Steve querido, you can almost see…

"And now, viewers, we must draw a discreet curtain over the conclusion of this charming scene between such a delightful couple, and we return you, unfortunately, to the studio."

Oh! Alicia darling, how badly I've needed you in this past week, even though I feared your coming. I do want you so badly!

Come May,
Come the Spring's end
To begin
The Summer's heat.

TE AMO COMO SIEMPRE
Steve

—⁓—

Buenos Aires
21 March 1967

My dearest Steve,

Congratulations on your new job! I hope that the medical will be straightforward. So your feelings about the interview going badly were unfounded…..that's good!

I've also got some good news: at last I sat the exam in Industrial Sociology, with very good marks. I was very pleased because it was a difficult subject, and on the day I was quite nervous, while in earlier exams I felt quite calm.

As you say, Mara and Enrico knew nothing about us. He is a friend of Horacio's and I knew him because they used to study together in our house; but I've never met Mara. She's expecting a baby. Perla and my father visited them last September-October when they were in London. I'm glad that H&H have written to you and that you will go to the theatre together. They've written from Italy and they sound very happy. They must have arrived in Israel by now.

May I correct your Spanish? You don't say 'Cómo te vas', but 'Cómo te va', without the last 's'.

You have lost weight, while I have put on a couple of kilos instead, which I'm not pleased with! I overeat when I am studying… On the other hand I've been told that recently I've been looking rather pale and poorly. I do really feel quite tired and stressed by the exams. I have to last out just one more month, and then I can go and rest in England… what d'you think? I am sure that I'll feel much better once I am by your side, and that you'll look after me…

I agree that you should look for a flat with a kitchenette, so that I can cook. But I don't have the slightest idea of how to cook curry with curd. Would your mother teach me? Is she a good cook? And would she like to teach me? I'm a diligent student.

My love, I'm very tired, and tomorrow I have to get up at 6.30 am to go to the Faculty to see whether or not my oral exam on the Regional Leader seminar will be on. If I sit it and pass, I'll have only four subjects left to finish my degree! Half the plan completed, and already so close to the end! Well, good night my love, I miss you, I want to be with you as soon as possible. I love you very, very much.

Alicia

London
22 March 1967

Darling and beloved Alicia,

Lots and lots and lots of news. First, I have talked to the Immigration Department of the Home Office and I'll try to summarize the information. First, it seems to be an axiom of present policy that if it is at all possible to exclude a foreigner from making a permanent home in this country, then the Home Office will do it.

There are three ways in which you can enter this country: (i) as a tourist (ii) as a student (iii) as a worker.

Now then, after looking at all these possibilities, I feel strongly that it is best for you to enter as a *student*. In that case we need that you have, by early May, a place at the University of London – whatever the college. I am assured by LSE Graduate School that once your two references have arrived, they will be able to make up their minds, one way or the other, *within two weeks*. Dr Ortiz confirms this. So I feel you *must* expedite immediately the arrival of these two references.

Let me tell you now something about the student action at the LSE. Background: the LSE since the days of Laski has a radical reputation, which is not justified by the attitudes of many departments' academic staff; the LSE is very over-crowded and probably has the poorest facilities and amenities for students of our national universities; the LSE has about 1/3 of its students who are graduates, by far the highest proportion in the country; about 1/3 of the LSE's students are non-British, many hundreds of them are coloured.

About last September the Board of Governors decided,

after fruitless approaches to a number of other men, to appoint Dr Walter Adams as Director, previously the Vice Chancellor of the University of Salisbury in Southern Rhodesia. At the same time the Student's Union elected as representatives students who were much more politicised than had been the case in the past. The two events exploded on contact, for the students began a strident opposition to Adams appointment on the grounds that he was an incompetent administrator, had compromised towards the racist policies of the Southern Rhodesian government, and hinted that he might himself be a racist.

The conflict between leading members of the Administrative Staff and the students continued for several months and culminated in the suspension from the School for 3 months of David Adelstein, the President of the Students' Union, and Marshall Bloom, the President of the Graduate Students' Association. The students replied with a week-long sit-in, and boycott of classes, which ended only a couple of days ago when Easter began and is threatened to commence next term.

The dispute has been so vehement not solely because of the doubtful choice of Adams as director of a multi-racial school with a world wide reputation, but also because of the lack of sympathy on the part of the chief administrators for the student body; the poor facilities available to students; the almost complete lack of machinery for consulting student opinion in University decision-making; the major interest of staff in research and not in teaching.

The academic staff have been bitterly divided, with a particularly powerful pro-student group amongst the lawyers (!) and sociologists. You'll be able to see the development of the plot in May – only eight weeks.

Life seems very much better in London these days, tho'
I am purposively not going to all the films and shows available so we can enjoy them together. There is a constant
under-current of joy running through my life now, the
thought that soon we shall be in each other's arms.

I love you dearly
    Steve

———~~~———

Ostend
24 March 1967

Darling Alicia,

Let me tell you a little about my life in Oxford, where
I went after graduating from Bristol in Philosophy and
Economics.

Initially I was miserably unhappy, I suppose because in
the past I had always been able to match the best intellects
in any group I came into contact with, whereas at Nuffield
College, which manages usually to attract very brilliant
graduates I felt a fool and an idiot for the first few months.
I did like very much the great comfort of Nuffield, I had
my own little flat with a large study room, a separate
bedroom and a toilet, centrally heated and with lots of light.
I also made some very good friends, some of whom I hope
you'll meet in the next few months, but with two I was particularly close: Tony Rayner and Peter Razzell, the former
an econometrician and the youngest Research Fellow at the
college; the other a sociologist-cum-demographer. We all
loved to drink heavily, and some of the best times at Oxford

were our walks to and from the Trout, a superb pub on the Thames about 40 minutes walk from our college.

The other important feature of my life at Oxford is that I became politicised. At school, because I was in an essentially middle-class ambiente (*environment*) yet was of working-class parentage, I asserted on occasions an unsophisticated attachment to the Labour Party and antipathy to the Conservatives; but this disappeared in a strange kind of patriotism and belief in the "never had it so good" era when I was about 17 or 18. In the Air Force and at Bristol I was fundamentally apolitical. At Oxford, in my college, we had a couple of communists but the rest were almost all socialists or social democrats of some kind, and since Nuffield is composed only of social scientists, the majority of students and staff had a keen and excited interest in politics, and within a few months I began to regard myself as a socialist.

Well honey, Willie and I are going to arrive to Gent now so I'll have to leave you.

Con todo mi amor,
   Steve

—⁓—

Buenos Aires
28 March 1967

My adored Steve,
   Today I received two of your letters – one from London and one from Belgium. For you to get to Ostend, so close but in another country, is as easy as it is for me to go to Mar del Plata in my own country! It seems

incredible to me that countries can be so near each other; Buenos Aires is thousands of kilometres from any other country (except Uruguay), and getting there is extremely expensive (and I must add that the Argentines are certainly less keen on foreign travel than the British).

Your letter from London – it continues to fascinate me how we coincide in our thoughts, ideas and even spells of depression. I am coming out of a depression that lasted for the whole of Easter week and stopped me writing to you for some days! It wasn't a 'suicidal depression', but it left me exhausted because of its accompanying headaches. I asked myself if it really made any sense to try so hard to graduate, I thought that it would be very hard to be accepted in an English University, that my knowledge was insufficient; I asked myself whether our relationship would be a success or a failure, and whether my planned journey is nothing more than an absurd dream… I had no real reasons for being depressed: I was studying 10 hours a day, I went out with my friends from time to time, I was with my family, etc. etc. Normal life. However, I had an acute, internal sense of loneliness and of physical loneliness too. In spite of all the people around me and close to me, what I needed (and continue needing) is your arms to hold me, your mouth to kiss me.

Today I am better – and I hope that tomorrow I shall be better still.

I have already done the utmost for letters of recommendation from the University staff here to be sent to the LSE as soon as possible, but I don't know when they will be sent. I'll see one staff member on Friday during my fifth exam of the month, and I'll ask him if he sent it.

I wasn't very well pleased to hear that you have received letters from Adriana and Mariella! They make me jealous. Mariella once said that although her relationship with you had ended she might one day make a trip to England, as a tourist, given that she wanted to visit London, and that she had an invitation from your mother to stay at her house in Leytonstone (is that offer still open? I hope NOT. I am very selfish!). Next week, I'll pop in to the Di Tella Institute to see if I can find out something without arising suspicions. And how did Adriana find out that you had returned to London?

Do go to theatres and cinemas, but keep a few special things to go with me when I get there. What I'd really like is to be already there, but....

Eating out in London: I prefer Italian or French cuisine to Chinese; I suppose that there will be nice places to eat pizza and other delicious dishes, say in Soho? Are they expensive?

Thank you for your thorough research into mini-skirts. I suppose that I shall leave my skirts as they are and change their length in London if need be. Now another request: what kind are the stockings they use with the mini-skirt? made of nylon or wool? in flesh colours? or white, or in other colours? stretch? smooth? patterned? thick or thin? I hope you will not complain about such detailed requests, as it cannot be too disagreeable a task to research women's legs...(but make sure it is done from a distance – look but don't touch!)

In spite of feeling low and fearful about the journey, our forthcoming meeting brings to mind what Celia said in As You Like It: 'O wonderful, wonderful, and most wonderful! And yet again wonderful, and after that, out of all whooping!'

Not long to go! I love you very much,
    Alicia

Brighton
30 March 1967

Darling Alicia,

I'm really moving around aren't I? My four days in Belgium were very pleasant, though fairly quiet. I'd forgotten how taciturn Willy and Nicky are. It was fun sometimes to watch their children and begin to understand when crying, for instance, was a tactic and when it was a response to pain or shock.

Willy and I drove to Gent one day, and to Bruges, Holland and Knocke another. I ate like a pig – I'm fattening up a little just for you when you come – and talked about you a great deal. They are both going to Brazil, as I told you on May 1st, and returning provisionally in October. Willy is hoping to organize a conference in Gent next November on the Argentine economy at which he wants me to give a paper. Then they would like us both to go over around Xmas for a long weekend at Ostend, and Willy will throw a big party in the flat, which is very spacious and overlooks the North Sea from the 12th floor. Interested?

I have spoken to the deceitful Demon who regulates the weather here and he has complied with my every wish and, moreover, has promised that the forthcoming summer will be the most glorious for two decades.

I love you so much,
Steve

Buenos Aires
31 March 1967

My dearest Steve,

Hooray! My March plan has been met to the letter: today I passed with distinction my fifth subject of the month, called: 'Special Social History: Social and Economic Aspects of the Evolution of Argentina from 1880 to 1914'.

My friends congratulated me on my efforts and the achievements of having successfully passed these five subjects, and that made me very happy. Of the group that's been studying together over the last year, four of them have already completed their degree, two more graduate tomorrow, and three or four more of us will do so at the end of April or the beginning of May. There'll be a surfeit of sociologists! Most of them are planning to go away to the USA or Europe, either straight away or later, because they know that there are no decent jobs to be had in this country, which is really sad. So you'll probably get to meet some of them as they may come through London over the next year or two.

Today I spoke to Professor Pla, who holds the Chair of Social History, and he told me that he had sent a letter to the LSE last week, so I hope that it arrives soon.

Because of the exchange rates (how complicated they are!) my flight to England will not be with BUA but with Swissair. I hope to be able to tell you the date, time and flight number very soon.

My love, my depression has almost lifted, I am happy

and pleased with my 'mission accomplished' and I feel closer and closer to you. There is a tickle of joy in my tummy. I miss you and love you. Ever yours,

Alicia

———ᴧᴧᴧ———

Buenos Aires
2 April 1967

My dearest Steve,

Today was one of those days of intense rain and hurricane-strength winds that make you stay snugly at home, watching the rain, listening to music and eating delicious morsels of food. Which is exactly what Ester and I did. A well-deserved rest after twenty exhausting days with five exams passed. How lovely it would have been to have you with me!

Your stories about your days in Oxford, and about your friendship with Tony and Peter, are fascinating. It helps me understand the phenomenon of male friendship, which until now I haven't really understood. They are very different from female friendships. Male friendships seem to be deeper, more truthful, more sharing, and there's greater intellectual communication.

To achieve the remaining number of 'research hours' necessary to obtain the Licentiate in Sociology, tomorrow I begin work as research assistant in the analysis of data obtained in the research into prejudice for which I did some interviews in January. The work will continue for about 20-25 days, but I will work only about two hours a day. I am not particularly interested in the subject matter, but it is quite difficult at present to get a job within a research team, given that there's little research under way – the University's Institute of Sociology is still closed. And I need to do this as soon as possible.

The scene you described of the 'private show' on the length of my skirts could really happen – with one difference: I plan to talk in English, not in Spanish.

Have you read anything in the London newspapers about the Bolivian guerrillas? It seems it's quite a massacre. Guerrilla groups are springing up in many Latin American places, and they seem quite well organized. Many see the hand of Che Guevara behind it all. governments get into a panic and bomb the jungle from planes. The Red Phantom gets closer!

Your trips to Brighton and Ostend make me very envious – I wish I could have been with you!

I also envy H&H who soon will be with you. I miss you. I love you.

Alicia

London
3 April 1967

Darling, darling Alicia,

The walk from our home to Leytonstone underground station is about 12 minutes and the trip to Tottenham Court Road, next to Soho, is only twenty minutes.

How extraordinary that in times of stress your appetite

increases, I find the very reverse, I don't eat and soon look like a ghost.

My mother is an excellent cook, but her range is very limited, mainly I suppose because for most of her life she has had an occupation. But she'll certainly be able to teach you how to prepare roast beef, baked potatoes, Yorkshire pudding and Brussels sprouts, which I *adore* for Sunday lunch. But as far as curd and curry go, she'd be at a loss, so *you'll* have to experiment on my intestinal tract to get it right. I'm very easy to please.

Finally, honey, my very warmest congratulations on your passes in Agrarian Legislation and Industrial Sociology, especially your excellent performance in the latter.

I'll write again soon, not long now!

Billions of kisses,
    Steve

—⁓—

Buenos Aires
4 April 1967

Dearest Steve!

What joy it was to hear your voice on the telephone yesterday! Your 'I love you' had such a marvellous ring! Moreover, our roles were reversed: I, the great expert in telephone conversation, got so nervous and excited that I did not know what to say to you at first; and you, the one who has so many problems with the telephone, talked in a calm way, ordered, methodical. Well, I believe that certainly comes from the difference between the Saxon and the Latin character. I am often unable to control my emotions. Your voice was exactly as I remembered it; I don't know why you say your voice is 'such a croak', to me it seems sweet and enchanting! And I admire your prowess in Spanish, you spoke the language so well.

The sound came in waves; mostly I could hear you fine, occasionally the volume dropped, and then I heard very little. Three minutes seem short and long at the same time!

I was told that the call was going to be at 12.45 Argentine time, about two hours in advance, just when I was about to leave for the Di Tella Institute. I still call there in search of gossip. Here's the story:

Chacho: What! What are you doing here? I thought you were in England!

Alicia: No, I'll be going in May, I have to graduate first, and I have still three subjects to sit.

Chacho: Ah, then I got it wrong, as Steve wrote to me that you were going to London....

The rest of the conversation included a commentary by Chacho on the personality of the English in general: 'And...they're odd, they're different from us. You shouldn't forget that they are not Latins...but you can get along fine with them, look at me, I lived for a year with the Gringo (that's you!) and we got on fantastically well...'

On the first floor I met Teresa. I told her that I've got three exams to sit, and that afterwards I'm thinking of going abroad 'to study' and 'to some place in Europe, preferably London.' She says: 'If you go to London, for sure you are going to see Steve! I think they told me that he's already back there...Does he write to you?' I told her yes, that you had written to me. 'Where did he write to you from, from India or England?'. Me: 'Well...from India *and* from England...' Reply: a big 'Ahhhhh'.

In the secretaries' passage I bumped into Dr. Almada. Straight off he asks me: 'When are you going to London?' I replied in May, after graduating, and I asked him how he knew. Reply: 'Ah! I had the news from abroad!' (NB: Mariella was very close listening to the conversation).

Afterwards, Dr. Guadagni: 'And, Alicia, when are you leaving?' (As you see, rumours spread like wildfire!). But Dr. Guadagni has his personal theories. And he tells me: 'What's Steve got to do with your trip, Alicia? Because I think it has a *lot* to do with it...'. (Note: no one was listening). I told him that truly there was *some* link – but that obviously I wanted to study in London. (Note: I don't know whether he believed me.)

Mariella didn't ask absolutely anything. We exchanged a few words, but she seemed to me to be well and happy, and she told me that if she gets a loan she wants to buy a little flat and live near the Institute, closer to town. It seemed an excellent idea to me, and I told her so.

The next big problem (apart from sitting exams) to deal with is luggage. I have to keep it down as much as possible, and I find that quite difficult. However, it is lovely to have this kind of problem and not more serious ones! My father makes jokes about my 'metaphysical and existential problems', and full of laughter, he forecasts that from now until I leave I'll drive him crazy talking about the trip, you, luggage, the University, visas, etc. (I think I am becoming rather mono-thematic).

Yesterday, because of my work on the research into prejudice, I was looking at how IBM machines work, perforating and classifying cards. These machines thrill me; I could watch them in operation for hours at a time.

Today I thought of Robert Browning's words:

'Oh, to be in England,
Now that April's there!'

Well, my love, I am going to sleep, as tomorrow is another hard-studying day – I want to make haste, and get to London as soon as possible, so we can, as you say, 'begin our relationship seriously'.

I am very happy! I miss you so much. All my love,

Alicia

PS. When I arrive in London I'll certainly be so nervous and emotional that I'll not know what to say – but I'll make up for it with embraces!

———

London
4 April 1967

Darling Alicia,

How short a time is three minutes! When he disconnected us it seemed as if only 20 seconds had passed.

Wasn't I brave to speak in Spanish? In fact I was so nervous, my hands especially trembling and sweating, that my Spanish was much poorer than when I spoke to Mara and Enrico a week ago. But wasn't it good to hear each other's voices after a separation of 16 months! Soon you'll be here and our relationship can start "en serio". I LOVE YOU! Your voice seemed much deeper than I expected! I'm sure you'd forgotten how flat and bass mine is.

As I said in the conversation, LSE has still not received your references: perhaps they'll arrive in the next few days; I'll check with them in a week's time.

How did Adriana know I was in London? I suppose because my mother wrote Mariella a short letter in January (in reply to a card of hers) in which she said I'd be here in February. Mariella probably knows about us already because I've written and told both Chacho and Miguel about it.

Yes, there are lots of Italian and French restaurants in London, but the latter tend to be very expensive; I still believe I can convert you to Chinese at "The New Friend" (!) off West India Dock Road.

Stockings. Not very interesting. Most girls seem to be wearing colourless stockings, and those with mini-skirts, I'm told, have tights on. In winter, the thicker, more colourful stockings are more in evidence, because it's so cold.

Congratulations on the last two exams! 5 down and three to go. It looks as if *you'll* be the intellectual in the couple. I hope to God (figurative) that they don't close the Faculty during the month. You really have worked very hard, controlled your fears and impatience with great strength and I'm very proud to have such a wonderful girlfriend.

Last night I had a very curious dream of which I can only remember a little. I'm sure we were climbing a hill or mountain together, which is what happened in the only other (very brief) dream I have had about you before. Does that symbolize anything?

Anyway, we were together at some kind of social event, perhaps a party, and I became very jealous of your friendship with a young man and left in a great huff. You chased after me and caught me as I was closing the gates of a lift, saying (you were very hurt and unhappy) that my jealousy was completely unfounded – which I think I knew. Anyway we got into the lift together, and we kissed. Those kisses! It was as if I were eating a delicious watermelon, soaked in the sweet liquor of your mouth. Fantastically sensual. Then you said (rather as Zeus did to Hera) that you couldn't wait until we returned to the flat, and wanted to make love immediately. I agreed and we lay down on the floor of the lift. But before we had achieved our desire, I felt the lift decelerate and saw we had reached the basement where a porter was sitting reading a paper with his back to us. For some reason I can't understand, you had only to re-arrange your clothes whilst I had to put a long bath-towel round my waist. The porter looked at us and I could see from his expression that he knew what we had been trying to do. Then instead of it being at night-time, which we had thought all along, it was bright daylight and we were together travelling (I think) up in a lift – a more modern one – along with a crowd of people, possibly revellers.

I can remember nothing more save that when I woke in the morning I felt very lonely that you were not at my side. How strange!

Soon we'll be together,
I love you very much
        STEVE

PS. Do you know me well enough to have realised that I mentioned Mariella and Adriana's correspondence *just* to make you jealous, in revenge for my own pangs?

Te amo,
    S.

———

Buenos Aires
7 April 1967

My adored Steve,
    Hello, my darling! How are you? I love you very much. Today I felt very proud when, leafing through the work of Zalduendo on 'British economic imperialism and the 19th century railways', I came across a paragraph that said: 'Finally, the author thanks for the comments they made on the first draft Alberto Fracchia, and Steve Merrett, who drew my attention to the book by Balogh'. You're getting famous, my love.
    Willie's idea of having us round for a Christmas party sounds very good. Also the conference in Ghent in

November – I'd love to see Ghent and Bruges, I've heard they are the most beautiful places.

I have no intention of depriving you of your paranoia, because: (1) I like it; (2) If you want to shake it off, that's your business. I like kisses that chill the marrow. Will love a twenty minutes underground trip, not so much a 12 minutes walk, if it is cold and raining. I love yoghurt, curry not so much, I don't know what Yorkshire pudding is, and I am not desperately keen on Brussel sprouts. I prefer roast chicken, potato omelette, spinach pie, corn on the cob, artichokes, baked cheese pasta, and grilled lamb chops. Will I be able to cook that kind of food in London?

Lots, lots, lots of love. Trillions of kisses,
    Alicia

PS. Horacio and Haydée must be about to arrive in London, they are due sometime between 17th and 19th; are you in regular contact with Mara and Enrico?

—∿∿—

Buenos Aires
11 April 1967

Dear Steve,

I feel overwhelmed by paperwork – requests for references, certificates of hours of research, letters to write, etc. It is a very complicated business to graduate from one University and register at another! Papers everywhere. Now that classes have begun again in the Faculty and (some) lecturers can be found, I am running from one place to another asking them to sign my certificates for the research work that I have done during the course of five years of study; asking them to write letters to one or other college of the University of London, and trying to find out at what stage is my request for special exams.

As a result of all this running around, I found out that the special exam in Political Science will be held almost certainly next week, around April 20th. So I'm off to study lots!

I have decided to write in the next days to Mr. and Mrs. Merrett to tell them they should expect me in May. Is that O.K?

Nureyev and Fonteyn are in Buenos Aires and this week they dance in the Theatre Colon, but I'll wait to see them at Covent Garden with you. O.K?

How's your search for a flat going? I hope it has adequate space to cook steaks and roast chicken, curry and Indian food. As far as visits to restaurants go, I'll make the following proposal: once a month we'll go to those expensive French restaurants, and the rest of the time half in Chinese and half in Italian places. Agreed? And a question, out of curiosity: why do you say that you feel alienated at home? I can imagine your mother 'fussing around' but I don't see the link. How many hours a day are you at home on average? And another question: what are your working hours at the LSE? And yet another: which telephone did you use to ring me on April 4th?

I went to a party at Jorge Jasminoy's. It was a good party, but I wasn't in the right mood so I hardly danced…Perhaps I felt a bit guilty for the jealousy that I caused you with my story about a previous party…and now, with this strange dream you had!... it seems to me very symbolic. I'll make some comments about it when we are together.

Stockings and miniskirts: from what you tell me, not all the girls wear miniskirts. What proportion would you say do wear them? And what age girls? What about girls amongst the LSE students – more minis or more normal skirts?

It is strange that you say that I am going to be the intellectual one of the couple just at a time when I am becoming aware of how little I know and how much I need to study and learn, and I feel little confidence in the solidity of my knowledge. But it makes me feel very happy that in spite of everything you are proud of me.

I had not forgotten your voice, it is just as I remembered it. For me people's voices are very important and yours always pleased me very much. When you came to talk to Joan in the Di Tella Institute, as it wouldn't look good to be watching you a lot of the time, I concentrated instead in listening to your voice, and found it very appealing. It is not simply a question of the voice's timbre, it is also the expressiveness and the way of saying things.

Well, my dearest, it is already 1 am on the 12th of April. And today I had decided to start reading about 'Political Ideologies'; I was thinking of reading tonight something about Liberalism. We'll see if I can manage to read at least a few pages.

I hope that the kisses in your dream become reality soon. As for the rest, it has never before occurred to me to make love in a lift! I'll think about it.

I love you, I love you, I love you,
Lots, lots, lots and even more.
The days seem so long for me.
I kiss you hard,
    Alicia

PS. H&H are about to arrive!

———〰———

London
12 April 1967

Darling Honey,

First, one reference has been received by the LSE, from Prof. Pla, but not yet (at least on Monday) from your other referee.

Second, I have replied to H&H letting them know what night we shall go to the theatre, and also saying we (my parents and I) would like to have them to dinner one evening.

It's curious that you should ask me about the English coverage of the guerrilla movement in Bolivia; until yesterday it had been fairly generally ignored, I'd say. But then "The Times" splashed the story all over the front page, from their own reporter who says that with the Bolivian army he discovered a guerrilla encampment, big enough to hold at least 100 people, deep in the jungle "thicker than in Vietnam." On a rubbish dump (the guerrillas had left about 3 days before) they found a photo of – el "Che."

David Ovens returned from India, with his wife, about

2 weeks ago, and is now settling in at the Unit. I cannot say the work is going well because on the one hand there is such a large quantity of material, on the other the fact that we want to finish our work by mid-July – the first draft – before David returns to India.

Baby, what a pity you weren't here on Monday. I had lunch with an old friend from school – Derek Jacobi – who is now acting with the Old Vic, that is, the National Theatre Company. He suddenly said that he had two spare tickets for the public Dress Rehearsal of "Rosencrantz and Guildenstern are Dead," a new play – first play! – by a young English playwright called Tom Stoppard. Did I want to go? Did I want to go! The Dress Rehearsal is essentially the first run-through of a new play, as it will be performed on opening night, to get the feel of the audience's reactions. No tickets are sold, but given to friends in the theatre world, friends of the cast etc. etc. Peter Razzell came with me, and we both enjoyed it immensely. It is a magnificent piece of theatre because of the sparkling wit of the lines, and the superb opportunities for mime on the part of the "players." It concerns the role of Rosencrantz and Guildenstern in the tragedy of Hamlet, shows what ciphers they are, how totally marginal to the events they are caught up in, and the philosophy of the author is clearly whether life is like the players' performances in which each event is pre-determined or whether the possibility of free choice exists. The critics have given it very high praise indeed, for it opened with its London premiere on Tuesday night. I was very glad to have Peter with me, because he is an extremely sensitive and intelligent man with a real love of theatre – especially

Pirandello/Becket/Pinter – and we had a furious and immensely enjoyable conversation during the intervals about the meaning of the play. *This* was what I missed so much in Argentina and India!

I have two new friends: their names are Mara and Enrico Stefani. About two weeks ago I went round to see them at their home, and we chatted mostly about the USA, and ourselves – at least our careers. Last night I took them out to see "Chimes at Midnight", Welles' unsuccessful attempt to bring the great Sir John Falstaff to the screen and afterwards took them to Kwality's, an Indian restaurant off Warren Street where we had an excellent meal, talked at length about adultery, Bolivia, English and Spanish, and our work.

Enrico, it is very clear, wishes to stay quasi-permanently in London, mainly I believe because of the political changes in the University of Buenos Aires and because he is working very well and, I suspect, securing himself an excellent reputation at the University of London. Mara, however, obviously feels confined and restricted by life here, mainly because of Marcela, her daughter with another well on the way (she said, very funnily, that she hoped the Indian curry was not too hot otherwise she might give birth on the spot!), and partly because to get to know Londoners and London requires a fairly determined and conscious effort and they obviously haven't yet made it. Last night was the first night they'd really been out, without Marcela, since they arrived. I like them both very much and believe we shall be good friends. You and I must offer to baby-sit for them when you come!

That's all for now, Folks!

I love you and hate waiting so long,
Love and love and love and more love,
    Steve

—⁓—

Buenos Aires
18 April 1967

My dearest, sweet Steve,

I am very happy with your replies to my multiple questions. 'Better late than never', as the saying goes.

I am glad you liked Mara and Enrico. When my parents returned from London last year, they also commented on their lack of adaptation, particularly because of Marcela; I'm happy that Enrico is doing so well at work. I'll be happy to baby-sit, I'd had already thought about it (serendipity again!).

Have you heard further from the government Economic Service? And have you continued looking for a flat? Do make sure it has a nice kitchen, I've been hearing terrible things about the effect of English food on the Argentine palate!

As well as coinciding in much of our thinking, I'm happy to see we also coincide in our activities. On Monday 10th you went to see the dress rehearsal of 'Rosencrantz and Guildenstern are Dead' (will you go again to see it with me?), and on Saturday 8th I went to see the dress rehearsal of 'The Sunday Stroll' by George Michels, at the Instituto di Tella theatre. The director's sister gave me a free ticket. Unfortunately here the coincidence stops. The play I saw was not very good; it had some interesting scenes, but it turned out to be too long –

it was a gentle critique of the bourgeoisie.

I quite understand your being homesick in India and Argentina; I'd also be upset if I had no-one with whom to discuss the news, the local scene, the significance of events, plays, films, books you read, etc. – i.e., life. I believe that the value of things grows when you share them with someone who is spiritually close. (And physically also, of course – the spiritual is not enough!)

Well, my love, as always I am writing to you at night and it is time to go to sleep. H&H wrote to me from Paris saying that they understood from Mara that you got tickets for various shows. How are you getting on with them? Pretty well I hope (don't pay too much attention to Horacio's funny ways, you have to get to know him better).

Contracted, diminished
This story has finished.

I love you and I am tired of waiting for so long, I am not counting the weeks because I still don't know the date of travel. I love you, I adore you, je t'aime Amor.

Mountains of kisses,
Alicia

———

London
18 April 1967

Darling Alicia,
My phone call came from my room at LSE. I usually

arrive at about 8.30 am, read "The Times" and leave some time between 6/6.30 pm. I am at home in the evening from about 7.15 and usually go to bed at 11/11.30. I suppose I am at home for about 4 days in every 7 tho' I've never counted and naturally these days so soon after coming home are rather unusual.

Thanks very much, honey, for the very nice letter you sent to my parents. I think my mother is going to reply in a couple of days' time; I'm sure she's looking forward to seeing you.

I am opposed to eating one very expensive meal per month (which would equal about £3 per head). I'd rather go to the theatre three times instead. Of course if there is somewhere special you want to go, then we can do so, but I am not so interested in eating that I enjoy spending a lot of money doing it.

As a rough guess I'd say 1 in 2 girls at LSE wear mini-skirts, and perhaps 1 in 4 of the female population of London between 18 and 30; though trouser suits with bell-bottoms are also very attractive and not uncommon. I'm also told that you *mustn't* buy any clothes in Argentina, but *must* wait till you get to England, since women's clothes, according to Sonia, are fantastically cheap and very very fashionable.

I'm feeling rather uninspired tonight – partly because I was competing with the television – so I'll sign off and write again soon,

All my love,
Steve
xxxxxxxxxxxxx

8 Worsley Road,
Hampstead,
London N.W.3!
Tel. 01 794 4663
20 April 1967

Darling Alicia,

I am in the very best of humour. As you can see I have a new address, found through the University of London Lodgings Bureau. It is a house within a minute's walk of Hampstead Heath, which I can see at the end of the road, within 38 minutes by bus and foot of LSE, 4 minutes walk from Hampstead tube on the Northern Line, 2 minutes walk from Hampstead Heath diesel line which is one way of getting to Leytonstone.

The house is owned by 4 young men, one of whom has gone to the USA until Xmas, and whom I'm replacing for the next 8 months. One is still a student (23?) architect, two are young (25?) architects (including the guy in the USA) and one a man of about 33 who is in the Prison After-Care Service. They seem fairly withdrawn but quite nice. The student architect, who speaks with a beautiful upper middle class accent is ethnically Japanese, I should say, and is called Bill Tam.

The house has three floors, and my bedroom is on the ground floor, looking out onto Worsley Road, a quiet street running off Hampstead High Street downhill to the west-side of Hampstead Heath. I think you're going to like it. The cooking facilities in the kitchen – 4 gas rings, 1 fridge – seem very good for those delicious bifes and papas fritas that you said you would make for me. Apparently Hampstead has a lot to offer such as coffee bars, pubs, stately homes, shops. But that I'll only discover in the next few weeks.

So I'm all ready for you, honey; I think my mother is now looking forward to you taking over 32 Mayville Road.

Today I had tea (in a dreadful tea shop in Baker Street called "the Regent") with Haydée and Horacio. She is really very much more attractive than appears in her photo, a real honey in fact, and would look even better were she in London "gear", such as a pink trouser suit, say. Horacio was smaller, less thickset than I had expected from the photo, and with very fair hair, which came as a surprise. They gave me your two presents for which I thank you very much, especially the Guillén poems, which I've decided to read through completely without the dictionary before you arrive and then we can go through it with you explaining what I can't understand. OK?

Haydée I found voluble, speaks excellent English, enthusiastic, perhaps a bit "proper" (from the rather disconcerted way she reacted when the waiter brought tea in cups rather than in a pot), obviously very fond of Horacio, good-natured. Horacio I found reserved, with an amusing dry humour, direct, frank (he asked me at the very beginning of our conversation what was my salary to be in the Civil Service, which I told him quite happily, whilst Haydée cast him a sidelong glance as if to say "one doesn't ask such things so quickly", which of course one doesn't – not that I minded in the least), composed and self assured. I like them both very much and regret we shall see so little of each other.

Well, honey, it's getting very late.

Oh! one last piece of news, Teubal's reference has not yet been received; at this rate you'll *never* get into *any* London college, unless, as the English put it, your referees pull their fingers out.

Lovelovelovelovelove,
Steve

———∿∿∿———

London
22 April 1967

Darling Alicia,

As you say, echoing as we so often do each other's thoughts, as each day passes we are a little nearer each other. At present I subtract the day of the month from 30 and add 15, today giving 23 days! Anyway, it is sure to be in May.

Monday morning. Yesterday I went for a stroll on Hampstead Heath for the first time in my life! You see how parochial we East Londoners can be. It's rather wild, and looks very natural; in the middle one cannot see any houses and you can only guess you are in London because of the distant sound of the traffic. There were lots of kids playing and shouting, men working on their miniature remote-controlled motor boats on one of the numerous ponds, dogs running, ducks floating, daffodils shaking in the rather cool breeze. I even saw a film star, in which Hampstead apparently abounds – Susannah York who you probably remember in "Tom Jones." Hugh Barr, the prisoner after-care chap who shares the house with me, was kind enough to offer to walk round with me and point out different places of interest. It really is a very pretty part of London just here.

My dad received your card, and liked it, thanks. My mother's birthday is on the 21st of November. And your father's?

Please find enclosed a photograph, though I think it must be 2 years old now, but is still a good likeness save that my face is more lined (with all the heartache and uncertainties a certain young lady has been causing me).

I love you very much,
    Steve

PS. I want to make love with you very much [even on a Monday morning!]

———

Buenos Aires
23 April 1967

My dearest Steve,

This week I have received no letters from you, and I feel sad. I hope to get one on Monday morning.

I'll sit the Political Science exam next Friday 28th; I spent the whole of this week going to the Faculty every day to find out when it would take place, and every time they told me to come back the next day, which wasted a lot of time and really annoyed me. Only two days ago did they definitively fix the date. All this has left me a bit depressed because it delays the other exams until about May 20th, and that in its turn delays my travel to London. It seems the moment will never come! I miss you so much, my love!

I have been informed that *the only way* they can give me the degree certificate quickly is if I present a document which states that I need it urgently for reasons of work, scholarship, registration in a foreign University, or something equally important. So, could you possibly ask London University to send me a letter, explaining they need proof of my graduation in order to consider my registration in the University of London?

Questions for today: What do you think of the reappearance of 'Che' Guevara, and of the political situation in Cuba? Can I send you records by post? What does British Customs think about a tourist who brings in with her objects for personal use such as: (1) a tape recorder; (2) an electric flash for a camera; (3) a fur coat in the Spring-Summer season (well, I don't think that's so bad; you could assume that I'll go from England to Scandinavia, Russia, Siberia or the North Pole).

Well, my love, I am going to sleep, it's late again, and tomorrow I have to get up early to work on my research on prejudice (which has kept me busy these last few days). It is not as interesting as research on migration, but methodologically the work is of better quality, and I'm learning a lot of important things.

I hope to hear from you soon. I'll do my best to speed up the bureaucracy, I want to be with you soon. Next Sunday I'll have up-to-date news from H&H, how nice!

Millions of kisses,
Billions,

Trillions,
Quatrillions, etc.
I love you so much,
    Alicia

———

Buenos Aires
26 April 1967

My dearest Steve,

Congratulations for 8, Worsley Road, Hampstead! What makes me most enthusiastic is the bay window and thinking that from your description it must be a house just like the one that appears in 'The Knack'. Are you also going to paint it white, like the guy in the movie?

The other day I complained that I had not received any letters from you for a week and by way of compensation two letters arrived immediately afterwards. And today another one from Horacio and Haydée with the description of their meeting with you. I think that Horacio must have embellished things a bit.... But it seems that they liked you a lot (mutual feelings, I believe). Horacio describes you as 'a guy with brown hair, medium height, slim, with glasses, with a tie and without long hair' and he adds 'as a person he gives the impression of intelligence, and not too crazy'. And he tells me: 'Final conclusion, in Buenos Aires'; so I am waiting anxiously for his arrival on Sunday. Haydée says 'We had a lovely talk, and as a first meeting it was very good', and she also tells me that in Buenos Aires she'll give me more details as at that moment she was short of time.

I had great fun with your description of them, it's absolutely right. What I call the 'loony side' of Horacio is precisely his doing things like asking a person who he's only just met what his salary is. He has a great capacity to ask searching questions and at the same time to avoid answering any, so he gets to know others in depth, without telling them anything about himself. Did that happen with you?

I am happy that your parents liked my letter; I hope that you'll tell me too of their reaction to their dinner with H&H. With respect to my father, I'm worried by the fact that my departure for London is affecting him a good deal; it shows itself in his concern about what my sister will do when I go, how she will manage by herself to run the house, etc.; how I shall adapt to London; and many other small symptoms. Of course his attitude affects me too, and I think it's clear that when I go there will have to be some changes in the home arrangements, other people will have to do what I've been doing so far – I have had sad experiences in that respect, as you well know, and it is not easy. So I would very much like you to write another letter to my father, telling him about your new activities in London and your work plans etc.; he's always asking me about it and today he listened with great attention when I read to him Horacio's letter in which he describes his meeting with you.

I have decided that instead of going once a month to a French restaurant in London, we should go once every century. £3 per head for a meal! That isn't expensive, it's absurd. Never in my life have I spent such a sum on a meal, nor ever thought of doing so. For me the word expensive suggests a sum of £1, and that's a lot. I think I'll have to take up cooking. I'll take a good cookbook of

Argentine recipes. Do you think that's a good idea?

Today's question is: How do Londoners dress, generally speaking? What is the proportion of men with long hair and flowery shirts? I require statistics of the same degree of accuracy as the last ones you sent me on mini-skirts.

I'll continue writing to you at the LSE, unless you specifically tell me to send them to Hampstead. O.K? I hope to finish once and for all these exams, and be able to go to London (I'm fed up with studying); even if only because my typewriter appears to be tired of writing letters and is working badly just lately. I send you little kisses with sugar and honey.

Amor sweetie my love honey darling je t'aime te quiero.
Alicia

———

London
27 April 1967

Darling Alicia,

I'll be writing this letter during the next few days, and will hand it over to Horacio and Haydée on Saturday and they in turn can pass it on to you on Sunday, so you'll be right up to date.

The work is going more smoothly; we had a rather horrible problem with our sample of fertiliser industry employees, since we knew we had covered 100% of some groups, but other groups by a much smaller %. This meant that if we gave the results without "weighting" for the varying sampling fraction, the data on those represented 100% would have biased our results. We now think we can solve it by adding extra cards in those groups which we know to be under-represented or by punching on the computer cards a weighting index. I'll tell you more about it when you come.

COME!

On Monday evening Horacio and Haydée came to dinner at Mayville Road. It was a very pleasant evening; my mother cooked a hot and appetizing English meal of Roast (Argentine) Beef, Yorkshire Pudding, Greens, Baked Potatoes, followed by a rich Christmas Pudding with custard. We talked about you, about Europe, about India, WWII, about Argentina, and then I showed them the colour slides I took in India, some of which are excellent.

On Tuesday evening the three of us went to see "The Promise" of Alexei Arbuzov, the story of the love between three Russian adolescents during the siege of Leningrad, the effects on them of the war, and how they had changed 13 years later. We all thought it to be a dreadful play; I found it banal, clumsy and lifeless. The first act is good, but the second is uninspired and the third just plain glum. Such a shame, because there is so much that's good in the UK now.

On Monday a season of Satyajit Ray begins at the local cinema, the Everyman. It will last 4 weeks so perhaps we'll go *together* to see the last two weeks.

PLEASE COME SOON!

Yes, you can send me the parcels of books by post, but they should be second-hand.

Some good news: LSE have now received your second reference; your application was therefore forwarded to the department, and I'm told they'll make up their minds within about 1 week, so I guess you can expect to hear from them say on about May 15th by which time I am hoping you'll be in London. Write to them as soon as you know your date of departure. Fingers crossed!

Saturday morning. I'm off to see Horacio and Haydée in an hour so will close this letter, as ever sending my love and telling you I need you very much very soon.

Yours,
Steve

———— ∿ ————

Buenos Aires
28 April 1967

My most adored Steve,

Today I spent most of my time looking at your photo. I'm delighted! If I look fixedly at it for a few minutes it gives me the sensation that you too are looking at me with wicked eyes, between sweet and devilish, ready to jump on me at any moment; and I have a strong urge to put my hands in that tousled hair of yours, which makes you look more like an orchestra conductor than like an economist.

From what you tell me it seems that I'll love Hampstead Heath; I remember Susannah York very well, she is so pretty. How is she in real life? A short while back I saw her in the movie 'Un aventurero en Montecarlo' (I think it is called 'Kaleidoscope' in English).

What does 'prisoner after-care' mean?

My father's birthday is 11th of August by our calendar, but July 29th by the calendar of the Russian Orthodox Church. He always celebrates it in August.

What's wrong with making love on a Monday morning? It is as good a time as any, if you are in the right mood – don't you agree?

My father has spent these last two days in bed with a slight fever; it seems he ate something that didn't agree with him and his stomach has been very upset. I feel a bit guilty that he may be internalizing (something that happens frequently with him) his anguish over my journey – so his illness is psychosomatic. Economically things are not going bad, but not brilliant, so that he has told me he can give me no more than £50 per month; that's not much but it equals more or less the £12 per week that according to you, would suffice to live in London as a student. But I won't have much extra cash to spend on trips, clothes etc.; we'll see.

I await the promised letter to speed up the bureaucracy. I am anxiously awaiting the arrival of Horacio and Haydée on Sunday, the day after tomorrow! with their stories of their meetings with you.

Until next time. Kisses, kisses, kisses, embraces, millions, mountains, kilometres, I want to be in your arms, I adore you.

Alicia Alicia Alicia Alicia Alicia Alicia

Buenos Aires
1 May 1967

My most adored Steve,
   Today I have worn the necklace that you sent me, for the whole day, and the little heart-shaped box is in a place of honour, on my desk, by the head of my bed. And since last night it seems to exercise powers of love: I dreamt that we were in the same city (possibly Buenos Aires) and we saw each other frequently; both of us felt that an invisible current united us, but we couldn't come too close together, everything was limited to formal conversations; but once, I was sitting at my desk studying, with a friend (probably Raúl Mandrini, the boy who is studying Political Science with me), and I felt that you were coming close behind me; I didn't turn round but nevertheless I could see you. You came closer and you put your hands on my shoulders; I took your hand in my left hand and squeezed it hard, and you did the same, you bent over, closer, and I pressed your hand against my breast and you rested your cheek against mine, you were gently kissing me close to my neck; then I turned my head, I saw you very, very close and bringing our lips closer we sealed them in a kiss – long, infinite, sweet, profound, which was interrupted only by my slow awakening with an immense sensation of happiness.
   University of London: I'm happy that everything is in order at the LSE and that soon they will be able to give their decision on whether they accept me or not.
   I received your letter to speed up the bureaucracy. It looks like an ultimatum! I laughed a lot seeing your signature on it. I hope that it provides the desired effect on

the bureaucrats of the University of Buenos Aires!

Some other small questions: how much do you pay for your house in Hampstead? How much could a bed-sit with a kitchenette (vital!) cost me, sharing the house with other girls, preferably in Hampstead close to your house?

University of Buenos Aires:* Last Friday there was a lot of trouble in the different Faculties; the most aggressive were, of course, The Science Faculty, and Philosophy and Letters, where the police came in to break up the meetings. They used tear gas and arrested about 45 students, the majority of whom have now been released. My exam in Political Science was therefore postponed for next Saturday 6th of May at 10 am. Tomorrow afternoon I hope to find out when I will sit Latin American Rural Sociology.

There's something I need to clarify: from the little that Horacio and Haydée said, and from your letter (Oh, Satyajit Ray! Here they have not shown his films for ages!) I can see that you are cheerfully thinking that I am going to arrive around May 15th. That, my love, is completely impossible. My sweet, I am as impatient as you to meet, and you can be certain that I am not going to stay in Buenos Aires one single day more than is absolutely necessary, but I'm asking you to understand the difficulties specific to an under-developed country and my need to

---

*The military President, Juan Carlos Onganía, ordered a police attack on the Science Faculty of the University of Buenos Aires that signalled the violation of the long-respected University autonomy. The police stood in two lines outside the Faculty building, each man armed with a club, truncheon or rifle. As the students and staff ran through the lines, they were battered and struck from both sides. It became known as "La Noche de los Bastones Largos" – The Night of the Truncheons.

leave things in order before going away for such a long time – afterwards I cannot come back just any time, if something needs sorting out! I want you to help me, I get terribly edgy in feeling my impotence in speeding things up, and this nervousness and impatience makes things difficult for me because it affects my ability to concentrate on studying. My love, I have an overwhelming desire to see you, embrace you, love you, I too need to be with you very soon, and I'm doing everything possible to graduate a good few months before what's normal! But I beg you to be patient and for you to help me to be patient and do everything at speed but calmly.

Good night my love, I am going to sleep as tomorrow at 8 am. I have to start studying. Your heart (in the shape of a box) will sleep with me. I love you, I love you I love you, I love you, I love you very, very much.

ANYHOW, I SHALL COME VERY SOON!
Alicia

———✺———

London
2 May 1967

Darling Alicia,

Lots of quickies today. Yes, please bring a cookery book. That will make a change from the exotic tastes which Mrs Balbir Singh recommends to you. At the moment Bill Tam's mother is staying in London – she lives in Hong Kong – until September. She is said to be a superb cook of Chinese food (Canton style) so I'm going to ask her to give you a few tips, OK?

When I walked to Mara's the other day it took me 30 minutes; I think I could do it in 20/25 now I know the way. Pretty close eh? Oh, and by the way, I explained to my mother that perhaps once a week we would be baby-sitting for Mara and Enrico, and that if they come back so late that it's too late for you to go back to Leytonstone you'll stay the night with them. The plan (*my* plan) is that whether you baby-sit or not, you certainly shouldn't stay in West Bere overnight but in Worsley Road (much nicer!) I really want to sleep with you *all* night, just to have your arms around me, see your eyes heavy with sleep and loving in the morning, feel your leg hooked over my thigh, your mouth against mine. All night long.

What did you mean about "Che" reappearing? There's been nothing about it in the newspapers here, save that they still get rumours that he is here, there and everywhere.

Yes, you can certainly bring in a fur coat and a flash for your camera, but a tape recorder would make them very suspicious I think. If it's just a question of a letter from LSE saying you've been accepted plus a letter from your father or me saying you had a guaranteed maintenance allowance, why don't you come as a student and send everything you want to bring in a boat? You might pick it up in London about 6 weeks later.

Let me tell you about the gas cooker in our kitchen. It's large, lights by simply turning on the gas and – like me – doesn't need a match, has four rings for pots and frying pans, a grill enough to take one large, if elongated, steak and a pretty big oven. Will that suit you?

I still find I enjoy washing up (after a year of idleness in India), and don't mind cleaning out the kitchen once a week as my part of our joint (i.e. Worsley Road lads) household chores, but I don't like cooking myself a meal when I get back from work in the evening.

Of course I'll write to your father – within the next two weeks.

As you can perhaps tell I feel very frustrated today. First, sexually frustrated because I want to make love very much but my love is half a world away; secondly, emotionally because for several weeks now I've been counting on May 15th as a best estimate of the great day, and now I feel very disappointed because it won't be until June probably – or July? It seems that as every week drags past the date of your arrival is delayed by yet another week. But I know, honey, it must be an embittering experience for you too, to study so hard and have people constantly procrastinating.

Hampstead, England, and your love are waiting,
    Steve

———

Buenos Aires
2 May 1967

My dearest Steve,

Today I spent a whole hour with Horacio and Haydée talking about London and about you and me. They told me that your parents are very nice and affectionate people, and that they liked you very much and were sorry not to have had more time to get to know you better. We spoke particularly about the difficulties that I shall find in London; for me it was just a confirmation of what I have thought before. I have decided to tell you all I have thought about and ask your opinion about it.

1) The material difficulties. They consist fundamentally in having to manage to live with little money in a city where everything is very expensive, starting with the necessities such as housing, food, transport.
2) The general difficulties of adaptation: to be able to settle in, I should ideally share a flat with other girls, and consider Leytonstone as a temporary home when I first arrive; it is rather far from the centre of town and from Hampstead (where other friends also live), a sort of barrier to which I am not used to; the problem of getting back home at night on my own, etc.
3) Language problems: I could have them initially but I'm convinced that in one or two months at most I'll speak English fluently.
4) Problems of communication and personal relationships: The English are Saxons, and their character is inevitably different from the Latin one; it could mean I will feel a bit lonely. But in spite of these forecasts I hope to be able to establish a friendly relationship with English people I come across. I plan to make a big effort!
5) Problems with you: there could be some related to 4). Probably I am much more 'cuddly' than you and to feel comfortable and more or less protected I need physical demonstrations of affection. In any case I think that I know you well enough to know what to expect, and we should be able to get over the problems that may come up with a bit of give-and-take on both parts; we have to find that out in practice.

Those are broadly my thoughts. I am not really worried about it all – I am just conscious of it.

Will continue in a few days. Now's time to go to bed. I love you very much and want very much to be with you soon.

Alicia

———ᴠᴠᴠ———

Buenos Aires
7 May 1967
2 pm of a lovely sunny day

My dearest Steve,

Hooray! I passed Political Science! Only two subjects to go! I got a 'Distinguished'. It was a pleasant exam: I could choose what theme to speak about (so I chose my favourite, Michels and the iron law of the oligarchy). Each exam approved means there is less time to go until my graduation and my journey to London!

A couple of days ago I received the letter from your mother, very friendly and affectionate. I too very much want to meet her.

Amongst other things, Haydée told me that you get along very well with children – like Julián and Marcela, and that the day that you took the letter to bring to BA for me, you were playing with them a lot, and they had great fun, so that she could pack their bags in peace. I think we'll make a great pair of baby-sitters, don't you?

Well my love, in spite of this lovely sun and the pleasant temperature outside I am going to study for my next exam, which is next Friday 12th; and after that there'll only be one left! I don't know when it will be, but very soon. I love you lots and miss you.

Alicia

PS. Horacio and Haydée told me that they took several photos of you, but they have not finished the roll yet, so it cannot be developed. I so much want to see the photos! I'm quite annoyed that they are still inside the camera.

—⁓—

London
8 May 1967

Darling Honey,

My very warmest congratulations to you on your being accepted by LSE. I went up to the Admissions Office today and made quite a fuss running from one office to the next enquiring about your case. It's wonderful news. The last barrier, the last external barrier falls. They tell me – I am assuming you have already received a letter from them – that admission is conditional on your getting good grades in your final examinations.

Immediately on hearing of your triumph I went round to the Immigration Office to find out how you can come to the UK as a student. It is remarkably simple. On arriving at the Immigration counter at London Airport you must possess 3 things:

1. A valid Argentine passport.

2. A letter from LSE saying you have been accepted. The letter you have already received (or are about to receive) will be fine, I think.
3. A letter from your father saying he will be sending to you £50 per month for your maintenance.

I suggest you send off your trunk(s) with all your books, records etc. etc. fairly soon so that they arrive in London about the time you do.

Now some quickies. "Prisoner after care", a generic term referring to social work carried out on behalf of men and women who have recently left prison; designed to help them adjust to their 'new' environment. Flowery shirts are still very rare amongst men, tho' many girls wear dresses like this and gay plastic mackintoshes. My share of the house is very reasonable and comes to £5.10.0 a week. One girl in a bed-sitter, say sharing kitchen and toilet with friends, would expect to pay at least £4 but no more than, say, £5.10.0.

Recently I had dinner with David Ovens and his wife Margaret, who invited a Colombian girl along to make up a four. It was a delightful evening, even though the girl was strikingly ugly. But she was gay and charming nevertheless. After she went home David suggested I stay the night in a spare room they have. It was amusing to see how they have prepared for any chance guests with a small box containing aspirins, alka-seltzer, cotton & needle, sticking plaster and a packet of sheath contraceptives. [By the way the latter are known – because of their brand name – throughout the UK as DUREX – so take care when you want to ask for sticky tape.] I promised we would occasionally baby-sit for them, which they'd be pleased to have and they said we'd be most welcome to stay overnight if they return late; the spare room has an excellent large double bed. O.K.?

I also had a meal the following evening with George and June Wistrich, whom I met in Konarak, and who invited an Australian girl to make up the four. The evening was quiet but pleasant in spite of the fact that *she* is strikingly ugly. Anyway the upshot is that I've invited David and Margaret and George and June to a steak dinner at Worsley Road cooked by no other than ANK. ¿¿¿De acuerdo??? We must have a party here too, once you've arrived.

I read your account of your dream this morning and suddenly found I was short-breathed and dry in the mouth with desire to slip my hand on to your breast, under your dress, and run my thumb against your nipple until it hardened with desire.

Oh! darling Alicia, I want you in so many ways; walking on the Heath, listening to Lady Day, watching Satyajit Ray, drinking wine, making love the whole night long. The waiting is too distressing – you see how my hand shakes!

I love you,
    Steve

—⁂—

Buenos Aires
8 May 1967

My dearest Steve,

Yesterday I wanted to go back to studying after writing to you, but it was such a beautiful day that I decided to first go for a stroll through Belgrano for half-an-hour; it was lovely. How is the Satyajit Ray season going? How I'd love to see it! It's an age since I went to the cinema or the theatre.

State of the bureaucracy here: next week I hope to know: (1) the date of my Social Psychology exam; (2) what's happened to my request for the urgent issue of my degree certificate. This Wednesday I'll go to renew my passport; and in a few days I'll arrange to get the International Driving Licence and a smallpox vaccination certificate.

My typewriter is behaving worse by the minute; I ought to send it to be fixed but I cannot because I use it continually; when I leave they'll have to send it to be reconditioned.

I have made a retrospective study of my eating pattern while I study, and this is it: breakfast (some time between 7.30 to 9.30 am) At 11.30: coffee and biscuits. At 1.15: lunch. At 3.30: coffee. At 5.15: a delicious tea, with little cakes and sandwiches. At 8.30: dinner. At 10: coffee. At 3 am: little biscuits, because I am always hungry at that time (when I stay up late studying or writing letters). Conclusion: weight two kilos more than I should. I hope to put my schedules in better order as soon as I have finished my exams.

Well my love, I'm off to read 'The Sociology of Rural Life' by T. Lynn Smith. I am expecting a letter from you tomorrow! I send you big kisses heaped up in mountains. I want to see you soon. I love you.

Alicia

PS. I want so much to make love with you (especially on a Monday night as lovely as this).

—⁓—

Buenos Aires
9 May 1967

My dearest, adored, sweet, darling, beloved Steve!!!!!!!
THE LSE HAS ACCEPTED ME!!!! Had you heard?
Don't you think it's stupendous?

The letter that I received today says: The Graduate
School Committee has now considered your application
and recommends your admission to the School as a can-
didate for the DIPLOMA IN ANTHROPOLOGY. This
offer of admission is subject to your obtaining the
Licenciatura en Sociología with a satisfactory result, etc.
etc. The rest is not so important (except that I have to pay
a £250 sessional tuition fee).

I am so happy that ever since I received the letter I have
been jumping for joy. And they made up their minds so
quickly! I wasn't expecting the letter so soon! I am going
to send my acceptance document to the LSE straight away.

So now I should have no luggage problems, since I can
bring unaccompanied baggage. I have been checking out
the student visa and I think that having the LSE letter and
another one from my father saying that he will finance my
studies will be sufficient.

I think the cooking facilities at Worsley Road are excellent. I'll be delighted to learn how to cook Chinese food if
Mrs. Tam will be kind enough to teach me. I have discovered that I know more about cooking than I thought I did
– perhaps it is because I am now fulfilling home duties here.

I think that the spatial dimension of the Londoners and
the Buenos Aires citizens is different. You tell me that to
get to Mara's takes you 20/25 minutes walking, and that
that is pretty close. It seems very far to me. I live 6 blocks

from Cabildo (6/7 minutes walk?) and that seems very far to me! I suppose that in London I'll get accustomed to walking, if that's what the locals do.

I think that your baby-sitting plans are great, as it involves staying overnight, so we can baby-sit once a week for Mara and Enrico, and once a week for Alicia and Peter (or more often?), because I think it is absolutely *fundamental* for us to sleep together from time to time. (BUT I am not going to tell my father anything about it while I am still in Buenos Aires.)

I told you about the re-appearance of Che because we heard here that during a speech in Cuba, Fidel had shown very recent photos of Che. Had you heard anything about it in London?

Another reason for which I am interested in studying in the LSE is because I understand that there are lots of foreign students of many colours and nationalities, and they will constitute ideal subjects for my planned anthropological case study.

My love, I am going to sleep because it is already 2 am and tomorrow I have to be up at 9 am in town to continue working on the Prejudice research; and then to study for the exam on Friday 12th. I still don't know the date of the last one.

My love, I am so happy with my acceptance by the LSE. That solves several problems, meets my wishes and fills me with joy and satisfaction (as you have already noticed! As you see, my behaviour is more extrovert and noisy – Latin, in fact). I send you several trillion kisses and hugs. I love you more each day, and I miss you a lot.

Alicia (today, completely mad).

Buenos Aires
14 May 1967

Darling Steve,

I have so many things to tell you that I don't know where to start. To begin with the most unpleasant (and the only unpleasant one, apart from the fact that I miss you a lot), the exam in Latin American Rural Sociology has been postponed until Tuesday 16th, due to some unknown problem with the lecturers. I cannot stress enough how fed up I am with postponements of every kind. But I cannot do anything about it!

I shall try to send my trunks with books, records, heavy winter clothing (I suppose that I'll not need it in June in London?), etc. by boat as soon as possible, but I don't know whether I'll have time to choose everything prior to the last exam.

It will be a great pleasure to have David/Margaret and George/June for a steak dinner at Worsley Road. But: (1) Before inviting them I'll have to have a trial run (would you be my guinea-pig?) and (2) I hope that the girls that they invite to make up the four are strikingly ugly, if not I'll get very jealous. Baby-sitting: delighted, the place seems very comfortable. (PS.: I don't like Durex).

Today's 'curiosity' question: what is the usual temperature in London in June? I'd like you to tell me the average, maximum and minimum temperature. In degrees centigrade, please, as I don't understand Fahrenheit.

Dear Steve, let's think that each time there's less time to

go! The waiting is terrible, but inevitable; but yet we'll make up for the long wait! I love you.

Alicia

———∿∿∿———

Hampstead
15 May 1967

Darling Alicia,

Last week I went with Peter Ledward, the architect of Nº 8 to see "The Music Room" of Satyajit Ray. It gave me great pleasure, because simple camera techniques and occasional use of flash-back were used with great subtlety to tell of the decline and fall of one of the old land-owning families of Bengal as a result of the passionate love the scion of the house had for music, to the exclusion of all interest in his decaying feudal estate. "The Music Room" also contained many songs by really first class Bengali and North Indian classical singers, which were superb and brought back my nostalgia for the artistic delights of Calcutta, Benares and Allahabad.

On Saturday my friend from Bristol days, Keith Williams, and his wife Sheila, came up for the day, which we spent talking and walking round Hampstead Heath. I have promised that we'll go down and visit them soon after you arrive. We could travel down on the Friday evening nine days after you arrive and catch a train back on Monday morning. [3 more nights in bed together!] We plan, if the weather is good, to go to Arundel Castle, or to Brighton. I think you'll like them both. I'd never met Sheila before, since I was in India when they married, but she seems very friendly once she has overcome her initial shyness, which causes her to act in a rather distant way.

Yes, LSE is full of foreigners. Perhaps one person in three; many of them are black Africans, or Indians or North Americans.

I had a strange dream last night, and I woke up sweating and frightened. Suddenly I realised it had been a nightmare and immediately became angry with you, and hurt that you were not there to sprawl on my chest, wipe the sweat from my forehead, kiss me gently on the lips and tell me not to have fear.

Darling, I love you.
Steve.

—◦◦◦—

Buenos Aires
16 May 1967

My dearest Steve,

Today, good news and bad news. First: I passed another subject! – Latin American Rural Sociology, with a 'Distinguished' mark. There's now only one left! I also tried to find out what day they will set the exam in Social Psychology and had the following replies:

From Professor Brie (Director of the Department of Sociology): the exam will take place in the May round, but the precise date is not known. From Mr. Ramos (Faculty Secretary): Prof. Brie has not given us any instructions on preparing the exams, and if he continues delaying, we shall have to postpone by at least a week the May exams round. From Miss Vina (secretary in the Department of Sociology):

Prof. Brie designated the lecturers for the May exams a week ago, and we have sent the list to the Faculty; she could not understand how they can say they know nothing.

Result: a total blank. If everything goes well I shall get to take the exam next 23rd or 24th of May. If there are problems – who knows?

My sister Ester has just arrived bringing her first ceramic pieces: really lovely. This girl has an amazingly creative imagination. She made a duck-ashtray in white, orange and yellow that is really fabulous. I am thinking of taking with me to London one of her coloured mobiles to decorate my room.

My father received your letter today, and he's very happy with it. It really is a very friendly letter.

I hope to get some letters from you soon! I was very envious that my father received a letter and I didn't. I miss you a lot. I want to be with you *soon*. I am tired of waiting. Damned bureaucrats! Heaps of kisses.

Alicia

Hampstead
19 May 1967

Darling, darling Alicia,

How can you be so cruel to leave me alone so long? Must I wait till the leaves become russet, the evening air chill, the nights long? Please come, because I want to know you, to pierce your body; I want to know you, to listen to your words; I want to know you, to see your hand swinging in mine. How have I harmed you that you should wound me so, lady?

The average maximum June temperature in London is 20.8 C, and the minimum 11.9 C.

I don't like Durex either, but if our babysitting is not to be transformed into baby making we must use something. Do you prefer the pill, diaphragm or loop? Which reminds me, I am extremely jealous about all your past lovers (so much for free love after marriage!). The only way to exorcise this, I suppose, is soon after meeting to tell each other about our past affairs, accept it as water under the bridge, and discover our *own* kind of loving. ¿De acuerdo?

Since my income, after tax and saving for the future, is not much greater than yours, I think we should "go Dutch" in all things we do together, that is, expenses equally.

On Wednesday, Oscar, Peter and I had a little pub crawl of Fleet Street. Six pints each. We talked about Stalin and the Chinese Revolution, 'embourgeoisement' of the working classes, the economic history of England in the 18th century, and that strange dream of mine. Excellent evening.

Finally, I enclose a letter that is rather historic. First it comes to Worsley Road – my first; second it is the first letter ever addressed to both of us. It is from Bob and Susan Darnton, American friends who were at Oxford with me. As you can see, they hope to be in England together by about June 18th, for a week. We'll show them something of London (they know it well, anyway) and try to go to the theatre together or the ballet. D'accord?

Querida mía, te amo. The tide is at its flood.
One long, infinitely long kiss,
  Steve

Buenos Aires
21 May 1967

My examination in Social Psychology is not going to take place on the 23rd – no surprise! Professor Brie changed the dates, so that it will not now be before the 30th. Tomorrow I'll know the exact date. Last Thursday, when I learnt this, I threw my books to one side (given that now I have lots of time) and decided to have a good time for a little while, because I was fed up with studying.

Ah! How marvellous to have conversations like the one you had with Peter and Oscar! I listen, learn and from time to time timidly give my opinion, but more frequently I ask questions (in many gatherings, I prefer to chat with the boys and not the girls, whose conversations about dresses, domestic problems, dogs, cats and mothers-in-law bore me to death).

I'm sure I'll like Keith and Sheila a lot, and the trip to Bristol, Brighton and the castle, the name of which I don't quite catch, sound great.

A curious fact: Friday afternoon, while I was studying, I suddenly realized it's almost a week since I've had a letter from you, and I thought something must be happening to you. A crisis, I thought. Depressed? No, I did not think it was that. Annoyance with me, I thought. Yes, that rang truer. You are angry because my journey is ever more delayed. But it is not really anger; it is an ambivalence of feelings, it is needing me and hating me exactly because I am not with you and you need me. Well, I was anguished to think about it, as I can do nothing about it.

The only possible solution would be to catch the first plane for London, and that would be absurd, as I have only one exam to go, and some bureaucratic manoeuvres to get my degree. But the excessive delay is bad for our nerves, the tension increases, they can cause a crisis that has to be overcome. But I have to go at the right time, and not too early; in this journey I feel that my life is at stake (not my physical life, but my future life) and that I must be prepared as much for success as for failure; and that in any case my personal fulfilment, through studying, is terribly important for my internal balance and for how I relate to the world.

The next day I received your letter with the description of your nightmare and the reaction that you had when you awoke. (!)

My love, I don't think it is necessary to tell you again that we both need to be patient, to understand and to think that the time until we meet is always getting shorter. I can tell you that I want to be lying next to you, the whole night, feeling the warmth of your body, your arms around me, your mouth on mine, my heart close to yours.

I love you so much.
Alicia

London
22 May 1967

Darling Alicia,

I have just received your letter, which has bitterly disappointed me. Starting from 16th May there are three stages to your receiving the degree:

1. waiting for the last examinations;
2. waiting for finalization of the degree process;
3. waiting until they actually hand over the degree.

If each process takes 50% more time (optimistically) than your estimates this would mean:

1. 8 + 4
2. 20 + 10
3. 10 + 5

which equals 57 days, which would bring you well into July. Horrible! I have found a solution.

In order for you to take up your studies at the LSE (see pp. 30/33 of the LSE "Graduate School" booklet) you have to

1. receive final acceptance from the Graduate School Committee;
2. register with the University.

For (i) it will be sufficient for them to receive a letter from your professor (e.g. Teubal) saying you have passed all your examinations and will receive your diploma in due course when all the administrative details have been completed.
(ii) the same letter plus the acceptance of the Graduate School Committee will satisfy the registration authorities

So *all* you need to do as soon as you pass your last examination is to get Teubal (or some other professor) to write the necessary letter, and get all the necessary papers for you to conduct the rest of the paperwork from England, via the

Ministry of External Relations. It would seem the English are much less officious than the Argentines.

Please write and say whether you agree,
Lots of love,
    Steve.

———∿∿———

Buenos Aires
25 May 1967

My adored Steve,

How can you be so cruel to make me feel guilty for not being with you? I must wait till my exams are over, till the degree papers are ready, till the bureaucrats of the University of Buenos Aires say 'O.K.', till the cold comes to Buenos Aires and the summer goes to London. Please be patient, because I also want to know you, to feel your body; I also want to know you, to sense your kisses; I also want to know you, to go walking with you; I also want to know you, to talk with you. How have I harmed you that you should tell me such things, sir?

My choice is the diaphragm. I'll take care of that. All said. Please don't get jealous. And with respect to that I have discovered two things: (1) That I too am jealous of your former lovers; (2) That I am pleased that you are jealous about me!

D'accord in going Dutch. In Argentina it's called 'to go English' (isn't that funny?). Nevertheless, I hope that from time to time, and if only to recall my Buenos Aires customs, you invite me 'a la latina' for the cinema or theatre. O.K?

How is the book on the work in India progressing? When will it be ready? An aside: have you had more news from the Government Economic Service? And do you know yet what Ministry you'll be working in?

My exam in Social Psychology is next Monday 29th of May. Or at least it starts that day. I don't know when it will finish, since it is a subject that has not been examined for a long time (the entire staff resigned last year, and everybody there now is new), and therefore there are a few hundred students who have to sit the exam. We'll see!

In addition, I have been really nervous these last days. I am going through a difficult time. On the one hand, the final exam is always a source of worry; on the other hand, my imminent departure makes me feel the pain of farewells (independently of my desire to leave). Also, I don't much like the subject that I'm studying, so I find it difficult to concentrate. To complete the picture, Ester went off to Mar del Plata with some friends, and my Dad also went off on a trip for the weekend to try out his new car. So that I am alone in the house (which is quite big and lonely), something that doesn't please me too much, and even less in the state of pre-exam nerves that I'm in.

I spent several days sleeping badly, because I found it very difficult to fall asleep (I was tossing in my bed for two hours), and I also felt very tense; one day I dreamt of you, a strange dream, very ambivalent; there were moments when we held each other close and other moments when we pushed each other away. But I woke up happy because at the end of the dream you came close to me, embraced me and took me to a bed. Then I woke up! What frustration! Now I'm sleeping better, but for a change have no appetite. I hope to cure my anxiety in London!

A curious fact: yesterday, when your most recent letter arrived, after reading it I went to the kitchen to make my breakfast. Whilst I was preparing it in a mechanical way, my thoughts were still submerged in the letter and on the things you were saying in it. I came out of reverie, startled, when a plate nearly fell from my hand; and then I noticed that I was preparing breakfast for *two* people!

I will write next week replying to your unanswered questions, after the exam. Tell the tide to wait a few days more. I love you so much.

Alicia

Hampstead
27 May 1967

My beloved Alicia,

What a sensitive creature you are, you seem to be able to read my very soul. Your letter of the 16th came as a bitter blow and my need for you did indeed generate anger and hatred for you, emotions already revealed by my reaction on awakening from that strange dream. I wanted to wound you for causing me all this agony, although my rational personality could see that you were not at fault. My paranoia flourished like a malignant growth. But now your letter of the 21st comes to calm me, and reassure me that I still have your affection, friendship and passionate love.

The sun is shining through my bay-window, birds are chirruping, the 3rd suite for Cello of Bach is playing on my stereo, I've just done a little shopping in Hampstead High

Street and smiled at the eccentricities of the ladies' clothes there, saw a Rolls Royce pull over to the right hand side of the road thus blocking off the traffic while the driver chatted with a friend on the pavement, then slid on as a police car drew up to them. I feel relaxed, and my bitterness of the past week seems to have melted like an icicle in the weak afternoon sunshine of this May day.

In spite of everything else, I did manage to see some good things last week: on Monday I saw "Shakespeare Wallah", on Wednesday "The Dance of Death" by Strindberg, and last night "A Man for All Seasons."

All the people who have come to see my new place have commented on the line of pictures of you on the mantelpiece and asked in surprise if they were all of the same girl. The latest photo you have sent me is very attractive: I keep it in the right hand drawer of my desk at work so I can see you whenever I want.

I love you very much,
    Steve

PS. In India I sold my typewriter, so send over your own when it's mended.

———

Buenos Aires
28 May 1967

Well my love, please don't get so upset! Those 57 days are, of course, a frightening calculation but we'll solve it.

I assure you that Argentine bureaucracy makes me sick, I hope that the English, as you have said, are much less officious than the Argentines.

It's overwhelming. To request my degree title, I should go and speak with Mr Gutiérrez, head of the titles section, to check that the record of my last exams has been placed in my file. Well, since this usually takes a couple of weeks, it usually happens like this: as soon as a request for title arrives, Mr Gutiérrez looks at the personal file; as it is *never* the case that everything has been recorded, a letter is sent to the student to present him/herself at the Faculty to clarify the issue. Then the student says: 'I passed such-and-such subjects on such-and-such days", and then Mr Gutiérrez burrows in his files and exam regulations, confirms that what the student says is right, and writes everything down.

It's enough to make you feel seasick, don't you think?

I still don't know the date of travel to London, and probably will not know it until the last moment. I have even thought that if I do not manage to send you a letter letting you know the date, hour and flight of my arrival, I'll send you a telegram. According to the telegraphic address of the LSE, I'll send it to: Merrett-Poleconics-London WC2. Is that correct?

You can be sure that I am doing everything in my power to sort out problems and get to London as soon as possible, and I hope you'll write me sweet and tender letters giving me strength, and not letters that are furious and disillusioned. Don't forget that I am now in a period of transition – farewell from Buenos Aires, at the end of a University degree, but not yet integrated into my new life – and that I feel, as Yves Montand sings, 'Partir, est mourir un peu'. It is not only finishing my exams and flying off. I have to leave a family in a state of adaptation within itself, so that my absence pains them a little less.

Moving on to another theme: what do you think about

the crisis in the Middle East? I didn't give it much importance in the beginning, seeing it from the point of view of a "Holy War". But now that the political and economic motivations are much clearer to me, and the closure of navigation and the threat to cut the supply of petrol to the West has been placed centre-stage, I have begun to get quite concerned. As always, the Argentine newspapers are very superficial and only describe the diplomatic fuss at an anecdotal level. The possibility of a generalized armed conflict scares me much more than a limited one, of course.

Well, good night, my love, don't be afraid, stay calm, I shall be with you as soon as possible, and that is very soon.

Alicia

———

Hampstead
30 May 1967

Darling Alicia,

This evening I visited Mara in hospital. We chatted about you, and her pregnancy. Later Enrico came in for 20 minutes and then, poor guy, went off to cook Marcella a meal and to wash her clothes. Mara seems very cheerful, and tells me she will have her baby sometime between tomorrow and one month's time. There seems to be every chance it will be born fit and well. She is obviously very eager to get out of hospital – tho' thanks to our National Health Service it's all free and she has her own room – and get back home. She was explaining to Enrico some details (in Spanish) of the child's progress in her womb. Even in English I don't think I could have understood, I'm really very ignorant about these matters. It's a pity you're not here because she would have liked to talk to someone straight from home, an Argentine, a girl, I'm very sure. I'll go to see her again next week, after phoning Enrico to make sure she's still there.

I was very touched by your breakfast-for-two day-dreaming and the whole letter was very sweet and affectionate. Your dreams seem less complex and less powerful than mine, don't you think? Or perhaps it's just that you remember them less well. Peter Razzell was saying the other night, after we saw a "Man for All Seasons", that his own self-psychoanalysis, using analysis of dreams and free association for instance, has revealed to him a great deal about his own psyche which he never knew. He is certainly the most incisive questioner about my own dreams – I feel he has a real talent for psychoanalytic examination. He said my dream about the lift was very optimistic and he envied me for having it.

On Thursday I'm going to Bloom's in Aldgate East for a kosher meal. A friend of mine – with whom I went to see "The Dance of Death", his name's Paul Alper and he is an American and a Jew – has invited me and a third guy – all of us from the LSE Research Unit – Marc Nuizière, a small and rather nice Frenchman. He (Paul) says the stuffed intestines are very good; I've promised not to ask for pork chops with yoghourt.

Nothing more for now, save that I love you and need you with me,

Steve

Buenos Aires
30 May 1967

Happy Birthday!
Have bought you a 12-song Yupanqui,
To be listened to at Worsley Road,
Preferably in the company of A.N.K.

I love you,
Alicia

—◦◦◦—

I AM NOW A LICENTIATE IN SOCIOLOGY!!!

Buenos Aires, May 31st, 1967, 3 am.

MY DEAREST, MOST ADORED, DARLING STEVE:
I HAVE GRADUATED! Yesterday, Tuesday May 30th of 1967, at 17.30 hours Argentine time. I passed my last exam, Social Psychology, with OUTSTANDING (10 points – the highest mark possible!). I talked about the theories of socialization of George Mead, about alienation and anomie. After the exam, I was congratulated on my graduation by Prof. Brie (he took the exam) and by Prof. Plá. On leaving the examination I found my friends Graciela Genijovich, Juan Carlos Garavaglia, José Luis Fernández, Benjamín Hadis and Claudio Armengol all waiting outside for me, and the six of us went to the corner bar to celebrate the triumph with coffee and coca-cola. The

whiskies were served in the evening in my house, and all my uncles, cousins and a good few friends, as well as those already mentioned came to congratulate me.

The outstanding events of the night: a discussion about the situation in the Middle East between Mario Neumann (a doctor friend of the family, who is pro-Israel) and José Luis Fernández (Haydée's brother, who is pro-Arab); and a chat about Russian cinema between José Luis, Juan Carlos and my Dad.

You cannot deny, my love, that in spite of a few days' delay, I fulfilled my original plan, which was to graduate in the month of May. Today I initiated the procedures for the degree and the provisional certificates, but I cannot forecast the time that this will take. You'll have to arm yourself with patience and expect that the date of my journey will be settled at the last moment.

How wonderful to think that tomorrow I won't have to study! Lots of kisses and hugs. I love you very much,

Alicia

———✺———

3 June 1967

My adored Steve,

My daily rhythm is completely turned upside-down. As I always study much better at night than in the morning, I got used to going to sleep at about 3 am and getting up at 10.30 am; and now, although I would like to change the cycle, I find it impossible. I go to bed at 1 am, and I'm not sleepy, and I can never fall asleep without tossing around in my bed for a couple of hours. I hope that once I got used to being a Licentiate (or Licentious, as some say) I'll also adapt to more normal hours.

'A Man for All Seasons' has not yet been shown in Buenos Aires nor do I think that they'll show it very soon, so I'll have to see it in London, maybe on an afternoon, while you are at work.

Now, the state of affairs concerning my degree. Today they informed me that the Dean of the Faculty officially approved my request for the urgent issue of my degree, and Gutiérrez, the key person responsible in the Degrees section, has already been ordered to carry this out rapidly. I spoke to him myself and I have to meet him again on Monday at 2.30 pm to check my file with him and put everything in order.

Therefore during the coming week I hope to be able to fix, if only provisionally, a date for my journey. From my point of view, I could travel within 10 or 12 days, which would be sufficient time to put in order all my personal affairs. But as the most important part of the business does not depend on me but on these cold bureaucrats, I am very much afraid that I'll be delayed a little more. I do take into account that the LSE will not ask for the degree document before January 1968 – or maybe never. But it is important also for me to make sure that I am leaving everything prepared before departing so that I shall get it sometime – and that it is not lost en route to London, or that I have to come back to Buenos Aires to get it. O.K., Mr. Paranoiac? (PS.: I'm glad you're getting more rational now).

Your description of the sun entering in through your bay window, so enchantingly poetic, contradicts all my theories about foggy London. So you do have sunny days sometimes? I AM SO PLEASED TO HEAR!!!!!!

It is very cold in Buenos Aires, and I have already begun to wear heavy clothing, gloves and boots, and to shiver in the street. Fortunately my house has excellent heating. How are the chimney-places of London? Will they keep my feet – always frozen – warm?

It is now 4 am, and I am finally feeling sleepy. Good night my love, I loved getting your letter today and knowing that you felt calmer, and that in spite of the distance I have been able to communicate my affection.

I send you millions of kisses. I love you very much.
Alicia

—∿∿—

Hampstead
4 June 1967

Darling Alicia,

My initial reaction to the present Middle East crisis was one of great sympathy for the Jews, an industrious, cultured and tenacious people, who have made the deserts blossom, surrounded on all sides by a much larger population threatening them with a Holy War. However, my opinion has changed a good deal during this last week. So in terms of moral judgements I am to some degree ambivalent.

If I were an Israeli I think I would feel that the only way to prevent the destruction of my country would be, firstly, through diplomacy and the support of the USA, but secondly and almost inevitably through military conflict, in particular a land attack across the Sinai desert, preceded if possible by a surprise pre-emptive strike against the Syrian and Egyptian air forces. If I were an Arab I think I would say Israel now exists as a State, let us accept it and live in peace with them, and fight the war of hunger not of tanks. But if my brother Ali were to say that the dynamism of the Jewish people in Israel is so great that one day they will need to extend their boundaries (especially if the USSR allows, one day, its Jewish population to emigrate), then this would disturb me.

I think there will be a war of great cruelty, sometime during the next five years, and that the Israelis would do best to wait until after the Vietnam conflict is finally decided before forcing its initiation.

Floods of Kisses,
    Your own S.

—⁓—

Buenos Aires
5 June 1967

My dearest Steve,

Today's theme is, necessarily, the war in the Middle East. When you receive this letter, perhaps the situation will have been clarified a little; but today, the first day of hostilities, everything seems confused, uncertain and terrible. I am most preoccupied, for various reasons: (1) I am a pacifist and the idea of a war, partial or total (Horror!) shocks me; (2) I have my stepbrother, aunt, uncles and cousins in Israel, and evidently the situation is not easy for them; (3) I fear that the USSR and the eastern countries will feel involved in the conflict and therefore the struggle will spread. Today my attitude is a bit irrational, of panic and desire that the conflict comes to a quick end, so that I cannot make a rational analysis of the problem; I await your comment, and we'll discuss it personally.

I am happy that you have been to see Mara and have found her well; when you see her again give her my regards and my best wishes that everything works out well.

Today I got (great triumph!) a provisional certificate from the Faculty, which says that I have requested the title of Licentiate in Sociology and that the latter is under preparation. With respect to the Certificate of Subjects Passed, that will take a few days longer.

Other preparations: I'll be getting the smallpox jab, vital for travelling. I am sorting out books, papers, clothing, etc., to leave everything in order and to be able to physically fit them into my suitcases and trunks (the latter going as unaccompanied luggage). I can already see that, as always, I shall have an excessive amount of luggage, so that I'll have to carry in my arms (literally!) things such as fur coats, camera, umbrella, bag, purse, etc. It would be good if you can meet me at the airport by car.

Something else I have to do is to teach Ester how to run the house, given that she knows very little about it.

With respect to my dreams, I think that there are various aspects to be considered: on the one hand, it is possible that they are less complex than yours, and/or that I remember mine in less detail; but on the other hand, because I summarize them in my letters, I don't tell you all the details. The other day I had a very worrying one, I'll try to relate it in more detail.

We were at a concert, seated in the third or fourth row of

the stalls; you were on my right, having arrived in Buenos Aires the day before, and to my left was seated a male friend of mine. I was pretty nervous, I was looking at you from the corner of my eye, but you were very serious and hardly spoke to me; then I started to talk with that friend of mine, about various things to do with the Faculty. Now and then I looked at you and made an effort to bring you into the conversation, but you stayed silent, and I felt very inhibited, although on the other side I was chatting normally and vivaciously with my friend. I remember very clearly that at one moment I felt anguished and thought: the letters are useless, when I am with him I feel as shy as ever. To increase my anguish, at that moment a girl wrapped in a fur coat came to sit down in an empty seat next to you; it was Mariella.

You looked at her in a serious way and the two of you did not talk. The lights went down, and we were all silent whilst they played the first piece. As soon as the lights went on for the interval, my friend got up and left saying to me that in the second part he was to play the piano (the strange thing is that I do not have any friends that play the piano). The situation was tense. Mariella, without saying good-bye to anyone, got up and began to walk away along the gangway towards the exit. Before she had left, you got up and giving me a kiss on the cheek told me that you were going because you were tired and the concert did not interest you much. I felt that you were leaving with Mariella, but I did not want to force you to stay with me, and smiled saying, 'Shall we see each other tomorrow?' You replied: 'We'll see.' You left and at that moment various friends of mine came up to me and began to chat and ask me things, but I felt desperate, and a few seconds later I got away from all these people and ran out from the theatre.

I found myself in Corrientes Avenue, and looked in all directions for you, but I did not see you anywhere; I ran to a bar which was just a few metres away, thinking that perhaps you would be there, but you weren't; then I felt an enormous desperation thinking about the possibility of losing you and I began to run in search of you along Corrientes, at night, full of people who looked at me with surprise. Then I woke up, in terrible anguish.

I believe it is a dream that reveals mixed feelings: on the one hand, the insecurity and uncertainty about what would be my relationship with you when we meet; and on the other hand, jealousy and guilt. I link it with the fact that precisely the day before I had gone to a concert, but at the Theatre Colón (which is not on Corrientes). Well, I'll tell you about the concert: the Juilliard Quartet, which is very good, has a marvellous sonority and perfect technique. They were playing a Mozart Quartet, and one by Ginastera (extraordinary!) and one of Debussy.

How was the kosher food? Did you like it? If they do cheese beigalej I would like to go sometime and eat there, what do you think?

I would very much like to chat with Peter Razzell about psychoanalysis*. I know something about that, I have some experience of it from having undertaken group psychoanalysis (for a time – I've left it now), and I would like to compare our opinions and experiences, above all if, as you say, he has a special talent for psychoanalysis.

*Psychoanalysis has long held a prominent position in Argentine culture. Argentina has the highest number of psychoanalysts per capita in the world and psychoanalytic terms permeate the language. Among the Jewish middle classes in particular, it is common to attend psychoanalytical sessions, not for mental health problems, but for 'existential' reasons.

I know a bit about the development of a child from the joining of the egg and the sperm until it's born; I studied biology in the Faculty as an optional subject, in 1965. If you like I'd be very pleased to pass on to you all my knowledge on the subject.

Well, now I am off to sleep. When the copies of the provisional certificate are ready, I'll send one to the LSE.

I still do not know the date of my arrival in London; it will not be before the 17th; but please don't build your expectations that it will certainly be that day, as it is possible I'll be delayed a little longer. You already know that if I see there's no time for a letter to arrive, I'll send you a telegram.

My love, it's late; I am going to sleep. I miss you a lot. I'd like to be already with you and have you stroking my hair and you pressing me close and telling me not to be afraid of the war, that nothing serious will happen.

With all my love,
    Alicia

—◦◦◦—

Hampstead
9 June 1967

Darling Alicia,

First and above all things, my warmest felicitations, congratulations, compliments and accolades on graduating. You've worked long and hard and deserve it, and how nice to go out on an 'outstanding'! I'm very proud of you and send you a kiss of congratulations.

The verses of Yupanqui are very apposite to us, I suppose one always tends to interpret artistic creation in terms of one's own needs, desires and emotions but here the parallel was precise.

I am following your attempts to deal with the Argentine bureaucracy with keen interest: I have already told you what the situation is here in London and so have no further advice to give.

Oh! I forgot, I'm going round to see Mara on Sunday, who is now at home and still expecting.

If you go to my old place of work before leaving, please follow-up all the latest gossip, and if you see Ernesto or Miguel tell them they are both *hijos de puta* and owe me a letter each.

The English are a masochistic people; that is why we have not already all emigrated from these rain- and wind-swept shores, eat muck and call it food, and install extremely inefficient heating systems in our houses so that one side of the body is roasted raw and the other numb with frost-bite. A curious people.

My birthday was full of event. At 11.30 I played a game of squash with one of the chaps in the Unit and beat him hollow. In the afternoon I bought some cakes and took them to tea in the Unit library, which pleased everyone – it's a rather nice Unit custom this one. At 6.10 I played another game of squash, this time with Paul Alper, and played extremely well (for me) but still didn't win a game. Today I played him again and won 2 games out of 5 in our best match yet.

Thank you, honey, for my birthday card, which was very amusing and original, and my promised Yupanqui.

After my game of squash this evening I returned to the flat feeling full of vigour, in such a mood that if you'd been here I'd have pulled off all your clothes, dragged you on to the bed and bit deep into your hip, just to see what you'd do. [Bite me back, I hope.]

Un beso dulce y calentito sobre tu boca,
    Steve

—⁓—

Buenos Aires
11 June 1967

My dearest Steve,

Finally, the roll of film that Horacio and Haydée had taken in England, and that was finished in Buenos Aires on the day I graduated, has arrived. So now I have TWO PHOTOS OF YOU IN COLOUR. One is taken from a bit of a distance, and you cannot be seen well, but the other, in which you are all stiff, with your arms crossed, looking at the camera, seems to me MAGNIFICENT. Just as you say, your face is a bit more 'lined up' than before; it is the most 'real' image of you that I have since December 1965. Your hypnotic blue eyes seem to look fixedly at me, and I continue having the permanent temptation to thrust my hands into the thicket of your hair. After looking at the photo for a while I thought of a way to project it against the window of my bedroom that gives on to the garden, so that you seemed to be in the garden, looking at me through the window. Rather hallucinating, don't you think?

The journey issue makes me feel quite out of sorts recently; I go through periods of euphoria, and then get in a bad mood, sometimes happy, and sometimes scared; every conversation on this subject with my father leaves me feeling bad, and he for his part has psychosomatic symptoms, mostly a bad stomach, and I note this with anguish. Ester apparently remains on the sidelines.

Degree business: it's going very well, 'the wind is in our sails' as they say in Buenos Aires. I went to the University and my request had already arrived there; on Wednesday I have to return, and probably sign the papers that day or the day after. Then there's an 8-day delay for the Diploma to arrive at the Faculty, already signed by the Rector of the University. Then we need Ramos to keep his promise to conduct a 'private swearing.' If there were some kind of delay (I hope not) I would try to travel on the 30th or on July the 4th, so that I would arrive on the 1st or the 5th of July. O.K? (Yes, I know there's a delay, and that you must be impatient to see me, and that if your paranoia returns you'll really hate me, but.....I've already said enough on this subject).

The conflict in the Middle East now seems calmer; we hope that it stays that way a long time. I can tell you that my own position on it has wobbled a bit because of the Israeli wishes to keep substantial Arab territory (apart from Jerusalem), and because of the enormous number of Arab refugees, especially Jordanians.*

It's very cold in Buenos Aires. I think that Argentine women are poorly prepared to resist the cold; our clothing is hardly adequate for shiverers like me. I need thicker stockings, heavier pullovers, lined gloves (the only ones I

*Alicia's father was deeply concerned about the consequences of the Six-Day War in the Middle East and the possibility of the conflict extending to Europe. Having himself lived through great hardship during the Russian Civil War and the aftermath of the First World War in Europe, he did not want his daughter to travel until the situation was resolved.

have are Italian, because here you cannot get them), rubber-soled shoes (which are rare here) and high boots (same). I hope to be able to stock up well on those items in London. My hair, on the other hand, is so long that the wind continually blows it in my face, so that I never go out without covering it with a scarf.

Well, my love, it'll be Good Night for now; I send you a special kiss behind your ear and lots more. I love you very much,

Alicia

—◁ᴠᴠ▷—

London
13 June 1967

Darling Alicia,

On the Middle East question our views are very, very different, and if you were here – which as always you're not – we could have had a fine verbal battle. Here's a subject we could *really* have fought about, and may do yet. I mentioned it (The War) to Enrico on Sunday and he almost leapt down my throat with a passionate defence of the Arab cause, and a furious invective against imperialism, and the support of the USA for Israel. It was only at the end of his harangue that I managed to get a word in edgeways and tell him I agreed with everything he said. Mara is in excellent health, and we three + Peter and Alicia + all 3 children + one unborn infant spent the afternoon strolling round Regent's Park. I may see them next Sunday too.

Of course I'll meet you at the airport in a car, tho' I'll be so very, very nervous I'm sure I'll drive it abysmally.

No more news from the Government Economic Service.

Your dream was really an expression of the most severe anxiety, wasn't it? The only way to bring this to an end, of course, is for us to meet. Today I took your 'certificado provisorio' into the Graduate School and they told me it will be perfectly sufficient for your admission. So you don't need any more documents. In fact they seemed ever so slightly amused that we should be trying so hard to prove you have graduated. I tried to justify your fears in terms of the Argentine method of doing things. Their reply was devastating in its simplicity: "I suppose here we just tend to trust the students."

Don't wait any more honey,
Yours,
    Steve

—⁓—

Buenos Aires
15 June 1967

My adored Steve,

The colour slide that Haydée took of you in April is causing a sensation in Buenos Aires. Everyone who has seen it, whether they know you or not, say that you look very handsome in the photo and/or that you look like a very interesting person. What is your opinion? (I refer to the original, not the photo).

The English may be masochists but the Latins are not,

especially me. So that between July and September I hope to develop, with your help, an effective method of complete body protection against the cold. I'm really happy to be arriving in England in the summer, to have time to adapt to my new environment before having to contend with the cold winter. I am developing a theory on How to Feel Less Cold in Winter, and after deep thought and participant-observation I have proved that there are two important ways of diminishing the cold felt in the street: (1) To be well wrapped up; (2) To walk quickly (now I understand why the English do that!).

Today, as it is actually very cold here, I was strolling through Buenos Aires going from one place to another, and with very few stops, from 8.30 am until 9.30 pm, and as a result I feel completely exhausted, and typing makes my bones sore and hurts my shoulders. I spent the whole morning (as well as a part of yesterday) running back and forth from the University to the Faculty, because of one accursed paper that was missing, but luckily everything is now in place and I have signed all the papers and they have returned my University Folder with a stamp that says 'Graduated' and a document that will allow me to get my Diploma within approximately ten days.

The game of squash is puzzling me. My dictionary translates the word squash in a rather confusing way – please explain. And you spend half the day playing instead of working! Is that a good thing? (The controlling super-ego is speaking.)

Tomorrow I'll go to the Centro de Investigaciones Económicas *(the Di Tella Institute)* and try to carry out your requests.

Well, my love, although it is only midnight (early for

me!), I feel very tired and sleepy, so I'm going to bed and I hope to have lovely dreams about you.

I love you very, very much.
Alicia

PS. Not only will I bite you back, I'll sink my sharp nails into you.

———~~~———

Hampstead,
15 June 1967

Darling Alicia,

I decided a few days ago to check my bank accounts, which I usually do once a month but had neglected for about six weeks. I added up all my own personal spending since I arrived back from India and then calculated how much I had been spending per week – £35!!! I checked again, but the figure would not diminish. The period included some very large figures, especially £77 on my stereo, £53 on rent up to June 25th, £40 to North Vietnam, but still I had obviously been living much too lavishly. So I made the following calculation:

monthly income = £85 [after tax]
   less rent   = £22
   less gifts   = £8.10.0 [I give away 10% of my income]
   less savings = £20.0.0

THEREFORE permitted weekly expenditure = £9. The

great "CAN'T AFFORD" has entered my post-University life at last, after the luxuries of Buenos Aires (£2,700 p.a.) and my expense account living in India. Still £9 a week's not too bad (*after* rent) especially since I don't smoke, drink relatively little, and don't escort expensive dolls, in fact I don't escort any dolls. Tho' there is *one* whom I'd like to sweep off her feet with fish and chips in paper and a pint of Red Barrel, but she's playing *very* hard to get.

I received a little note from the Ministry of Technology the other day saying it's likely I'll be transferred to them, but not certain, and would I come and have a chat about the kind of work they do, so I'm going next Thursday.

Friday June 16th. 10pm.

I've just come back from the Heath where there are a couple of traditional Jazz groups playing, and several hundred people sitting around listening attentively as the evening light fades, and a Vickers V.C.10 roars overhead East from London airport, its fuselage and twin engine nacelles burnished by the setting sun. One fashion which I've noticed more recently lately is a trouser suit made of silk or very shiny artificial fibre, and gloriously coloured and patterned, very tight over the bottom and flared at the ankles, like a very exotic pair of pyjamas.

When I got back I put on my Billie Holiday and one of the tracks, one of the greatest she ever made, is exactly suited to my present mood. It's called Love Me Or Leave Me.

Saturday 17th. 15.15

No letter from you since last Tuesday. Miserable.

At lunchtime Bill and I went down in his car to shop in Camden market. It was most attractive because jostling each other amongst the stalls glowing with fruit were English, Indians, Cypriots and West Indians, they were mostly working-class people but there was a liberal sprinkling of the swinging professional classes from Hampstead and Highgate and Belsize Park and Swiss Cottage. The place had a wonderful cosmopolitan atmosphere.

Today is cloudy and cold so I've switched on my electric blower to warm my room.

Monday morning.
Still no letter. What's happened?

    All my love,
      Steve

—✑—

Buenos Aires
17 June 1967

My dearest Steve,
First, the business of getting my degree certificate is going well. On Monday I have to telephone to find out when it will be signed by the Rector. In any case I have provisionally reserved a seat on the plane for Tuesday 4th of July, arriving in London on Wednesday 5th, via Geneva, on Flight 810 of Swissair. O.K? I hope that I don't have to change it; I'll confirm next week! Arrival time to London is 10.35 am GMT.
Second, the Middle East crisis. We may argue over the

issue, but I hope we won't really fight over it. At the heart of the whole question there's an affective-subjective tendency that inevitably draws me towards wanting the Israelis to win any armed conflict. A violent solution seems to me absurd and useless, I don't believe in solutions imposed by force; I prefer the diplomatic route, although it promises to be long and messy.

Ester has become a bit of a hardened dealer, so that when I asked her to make an additional mobile for you, she said 'I'll think about it' or something like that. But she's soft-hearted, so she probably will.

They are about to screen Paul Scofield's picture, here translated as 'Un hombre de dos reinos'. So perhaps I'll see it in Buenos Aires and not in London.

Lots of kisses and see you soon. I love you heaps.
Alicia

———

Hampstead
21 June 1967

Darling Honey,

Yesterday I received your letter of the 11th (it took 9 days in coming!) and today that of the 15th so now I feel far more cheerful.

Your description of the wind catching your hair and blowing it across your face conjures up an untamed spirit, full of joy.

Your technique for avoiding the cold in the streets of England seems profound and well-reasoned. May I suggest one for the evenings, which can be very bitter? Take one mouthful of Scotch whiskey, get into a large double bed with 7 blankets, place one Stephen Richard Merrett on top of you and his arms around you, and pause for 15 minutes. Money back guarantee if you do not break out into a very passionate sweat and the perspiration bead your brow within the allotted time.

Incidentally, I am growing my nails a little longer and a little sharper. Purely as a weapon of self-defence you understand.

The Middle East question has now lost some of its news value. In England the news that 20 British soldiers were killed yesterday in Aden has dominated the headlines. My own feelings are that Israel should be allowed to retain only the Gaza strip and the Syrian hills just North-East of their border. The West Bank of the Jordan and Jerusalem should remain in the hands of the Jordanians – they have almost nothing of value. However, I'd be much less ambivalent about the Middle East question if one had not seen the dummies of Jews being garrotted in the main streets of Cairo, or heard the call for a Holy War by the Muslims.

In a lighter vein – Peter, Wendy, Steve, Alicia are all going, it is planned, to SCOTLAND for a week to 10 days, starting about July 14th and driving up to Fort William in 2 days, camping whenever the weather is pleasant (Wendy hasn't much money), walking and driving around the West coast for six days, then returning possibly via the Lake District. Should be magnificent, don't you think? If you have a sleeping bag in Argentina, bring it with you.

Leytonstone, 22 June

Came home this evening just to fulfil my filial duties. The interview with John Boreham at the Ministry of Technology was interesting. Their offices are in John Islip Street, parallel to Millbank which lies on the Thames, not a stone's throw from the Tate Gallery and 5 minutes walk from the House of Commons. Almost certainly, when the security checks are finished, I'll be asked to join the government Service, in which case I'll hand in my notice to LSE, and three months later will be free to join the Civil Service.

Love, kisses, embraces,
Your very own,
Steve

—◦◦◦—

Buenos Aires
23 June 1967

My dearest Steve,

I am going to make a formal protest to the Post Office Head. For three weeks or more they have been playing the same dirty trick: they deliver two or three of your letters at the same time, and then they leave me for eight days without a single one. So I've had no letters since last week! I protest!

I have spent the whole week drifting around: I sleep until 10 or 11 in the morning, I have few things to do and I do them slowly, I spend my time wandering about, going to the cinema, meeting friends, etc. And every day, of course, ringing the University to find out what's happening with my degree title.

Amongst the multiple reasons for this current delay, is the fact that my father, under various (subconscious?) pretexts is trying to delay my departure; for example, he says he has no cash in hand, and he won't have enough of it before 10th-15th of July. I have told him that just a few pounds will suffice (and then he can send the rest), but he insists that he will not allow me to leave Buenos Aires without enough dollars. And I assure you that it is very difficult for me to face up to this and tell him that as soon as I have the degree title I am leaving without waiting for anything else. My staying in Buenos Aires a little longer means a lot to him just now. But I do know that a further delay means a lot to you too. And for me, it means prolonging this tension with which I am living, the sleepless nights, the half-empty days. I am tired of waiting. Leaving is a trauma, but having made my choice, I want to leave once and for all! The waiting is unbearable. I fantasize about how our first meeting will be (it's absurd, but I cannot avoid it) and I have the feeling that it will take me two or three days after arrival to feel normal again, to speak to you properly, to be myself, just as you know me through these letters.

Today I lack inspiration, I'm sad and I want to leave here and meet you soon, and I cannot, and I'm starting to feel very low, although I know there is such a short time to go.

Well my love, I hope to receive a letter from you tomorrow, so my sadness will lift. It is 11 o'clock in the evening, and I hope that today I'll fall asleep easily, and not have such a bad night like last night.

I recently received two letters from the LSE: one, good, in which they say they have received my provisional certificate, that I must present my Diploma in September, and confirming their offer of admission. The other, bad, in which they say that I have not been awarded the Leverhulme Studentship.

Good night, until soon, I send you all my love.
Alicia

—◦◦◦—

Buenos Aires
26 June 1967

My adored Steve,

The Rector of the University is ill. For a week the Rector has signed nothing. The Rector has half the University paralyzed. The Rector is a son of a bitch. I Have Spoken.

Every day they tell me to phone the next day to see if he has signed. I have given him up to Friday the 30th. If he does not sign, I'll kick him. And when I get angry…you'd better run!

I have set the date of my flight for the 11th, Tuesday. So I should arrive on Wednesday 12th, again via Geneva, Flight 810 of Swissair, at 10.35 GMT. I hope that this will be the last postponement!!!

I was very moved by the words of the song by Billie Holiday that you copied out for me. And I very much want to listen to her singing it.

I really wanted to be with you in your visit to Camden Market, at the dinner in the 'Sardar', at the Jazz concert on Hampstead Heath and seeing Marat/Sade! That makes me even more angry with the Rector, as well as increase my annoyance about the other reasons that still keep me in Buenos Aires. How strange that you saw Marat/Sade a couple of days after I saw 'The Lord of the Flies', also directed by Peter Brooks.

Have you recently given further thought to a possible trip to the USSR, visiting Moscow and Odessa (I have an uncle and aunt there, whom I never met) and preferably Leningrad too. No doubt my father will pay for the journey, because he is very keen for me to go there. If we choose somewhere else (like Poland, Czechoslovakia, Hungary) I don't think my father will give me any extra money, but I probably can save some myself, and pay at least for part of it.

I was very amused with your calculations on your weekly spending. If I spend as much as you do, £9 per week, that's about £40 per month. My father says that he'll send me about £50 per month for the first three months, which means that if I don't have to pay either rent or University fees over the summer period, I'll have more than enough to go travelling etc. From October my father will increase my allowance to £70, to cover University fees. If University costs come to about £21 per month, and it costs me £40 to eat, travel, go to the cinema and other small expenses, only £9 are left for rent, which is insufficient (given that the minimum possible is £4 per week, according to what you said). Well, that's as far as I've got. I don't know how I will cover the deficit. And £9 a week's not too bad, especially since I don't drink, smoke relatively little, and don't escort expensive guys, in fact I don't intend to do so, on the contrary I expect to be escorted by a certain guy who tells me things I don't understand about chips in paper and Red Barrel and who forgets to compute invitations to the theatre, etc. in his weekly expenditure.

Well, my darling, I've got to wash my hair – it is so long that it takes an age to dry. And a woman in rollers is a very depressing sight, don't you think? So one of the first things I shall buy in London will be a good hair dryer.

Good night, I send you a mountain of kisses and hope that there will be no more postponements (if the Rector behaves well) so that I see you, touch you, embrace you, etc. (!) very soon. I love you very much.

Alicia

PS. Next week I'll send you confirmation of the date.

—⁓—

Hampstead
26 June 1967

Darling and most beloved Alicia,

Last night I dreamt about you, but I've forgotten the dream almost entirely. I know there was some kind of civil war on, in Ireland. The conflict had been going on for some time and Oscar, who had already met you, came to see me. He explained that you were the kind of girl a man looked at very hard for a second time. Then you appeared, very diminutive and wearing a skirt of a very light fawn canvas sort of material. I remember how long it seemed for it seemed to go as far as your knees. We met and you kissed me on the cheek, which I received with a keen pang of disappointment. Then a few moments or hours later we were together again in a place which looked very much like an airport lounge. You were very pale in the face, and so small I could easily put my arm around your shoulders, and shyly you kissed me on the lips – what a delicious kiss that was.

This will be my last letter before you arrive, as I'll post it off tomorrow when I've seen whether or not I get another letter from you during the day.

Until I hear any differently I'll expect you on Swissair Flight 810 on 5th July at 10.35am GMT.

I forgot to mention, I think, that I (you) can get from LSE to the building off Millbank where I'll be working in about 20 minutes walking and Tube, and my beloved 24 bus will take me from Hampstead to Parliament Square in about 25 minutes, from where it's only a 10 minute walk.

Saturday evening was very good. I went with Bob and Susan Darnton and a very nice guy called Mark Leyton and his girlfriend and her brother to the best Chinese restaurant in London, located in the East End and called "The New Friends." I was in one of my gayest moods, full of witticisms and bonhomie. Bob and Susan went off to Paris yesterday: there is vague plan we 4 should meet up in late August or early September in Budapest or Yugoslavia on those magnificent beaches.

Tuesday 27th July. No letter today. The last one I received, that of June 17th arrived yesterday, so it took 9 days. Nothing more to say, save that when the day comes to leave you'll probably feel very frightened, everyone will show their anguish at losing you, and their tears will flow as thick and fast as those of a woman making onion soup. Don't be too scared, for I'll be at London Airport waiting to take you in my arms, kiss you on the mouth and say "I love you, Welcome to England."

My beautiful girl, until very soon,
Yours,
    Steve

—∿∿—

Buenos Aires
28 June 1967

My adored Steve,

CONFIRMED!!!! I arrive on Wednesday 12th of July, Flight 810 of Swissair, London Airport, at 10.35 am G.M.T., via Geneva. It seems that the Rector was shocked by all the things I said about him, and he recovered speedily, signed my Diploma, which has already arrived at the Faculty, and my (private) oath-swearing ceremony will be on Friday at 11 am. So I could *almost* travel on the 4th, but the main reason for not doing that is that next Saturday 8th of July my aunt and uncle, Elena and León Liebeschutz, arrive in Buenos Aires from Israel. I haven't seen them for three years, and I don't want to miss them. Aunt Elena is my mother's sister and has been my favourite aunt from birth to 18, and I really want to see her. And she would never forgive me if I left four days before her arrival in Buenos Aires.

Various other aunts have been gossiping about how can I spend *only* two days with my aunt, and say I should stay longer. But I have STRONGLY REFUSED to listen to them, telling them that we are due to leave for Scotland on July 14th and that cannot be possibly postponed; and I confirmed my seat on the plane for the 11th. My father promised to give me about £50 to take with me and he'll send the rest in a few days.

I don't have a sleeping bag, you'll have to get one for me, or I'll buy one when I arrive. When I have occasionally gone camping here, I borrowed Horacio's. In truth my wardrobe is meant for the city, not the countryside (I have had a very bourgeois life-style recently). But we'll look into it once in London and if I am missing something I'll have a few days to go shopping there. THE IDEA OF A TRIP TO SCOTLAND FASCINATES ME. Will we also go to the Island of Man to visit your friend?

The Ministry of Technology sounds wonderful and I hope that you really can work in Millbank. I have looked at a map of the centre of London and calculated that if you are five minutes' walk from the Houses of Parliament, you cannot be more than 15 minutes walk from the LSE. Is my calculation correct?

It seems to me an excellent idea to use a stove Model S.R.M. in the evenings; however I do not agree with a mouthful of Scotch whisky, because I don't like whisky; but I would swap it for a cup of tea. In fact I dislike most alcoholic drinks, with the exception of a little white wine, light beer or champagne, depending on the occasion. My favourite drinks are (in order of preference): water, tea, coffee, soda water, coca-cola, banana milkshake, and hot chocolate – and orange juice. I am aware that in London you cannot get a decent cup of coffee, as the English do not know how to make coffee, but I hope to drink delicious tea.

I hope it stops raining soon so I can go out and send this letter by express post. I don't like going out in the rain in Buenos Aires, with its broken pavements and heaps of mud, although I suppose that in London I shall have to get used to the rain, as it will be more frequent than here.

I expect to be able to write a couple more letters before leaving, and I hope to receive another one from you between now and the 11th.

I am so happy thinking that I'll be with you so soon! I hope no new complications come up!

Lots of kisses and hugs.
Until Wednesday the 12th in the morning.
All my love.
    Alicia

———∿∿∿———

London
Undated

Darling Alicia,
    Hurry! Hurry! Hurry!
    All London is awaiting you. 10 million kisses
    Signed: Steve
    pp. the inhabitants of London

———∿∿∿———

Buenos Aires
2 July 1967

My adored, dear Steve,
    The letter I received yesterday moved me a great deal.
You say that it will be the last; as I had to postpone my
journey until the 11th, I still hope to receive one more.
    The degree ceremony has now taken place, I am in pos-
session of the degree document, of which I will take pho-
tocopies, which I will bring to England. I've been told that
I should really do other things, such as legalizing the
document, registering with the Ministry of Foreign
Affairs, etc.; but I don't think I'll do any of that, as the
LSE has not asked for it.
    I think that your dream also implies ambivalent feelings
about my arrival. I think you will find my skirts rather
long, although they are extremely short for Buenos Aires,
my father complains, and I get unpleasant male stares and
even crude comments in the street.
    I must send this letter now. I'll go on tomorrow.

    Kisses. I love you.
        Alicia

———

London
undated

Darling Alicia,
    Yesterday (3 July) I received your letter of the 28th
June. Today I received letters of March 2, June 23rd, June
26th. Imagine my feelings: anger, bitterness, despair. We've

been writing for too long. My doctor has put me on a ten-day course of sedatives (truthfully). No further delays acceptable, they're too damaging to me; see you on *12th*. I love you too much.

Your own Steve

———ᵕᵕ———

Buenos Aires
4 July 1967

My adored Steve,

Your postcard of today has been a delightful surprise, I didn't expect to receive news from you in these last days. And yesterday and today I was (and still am a bit) worried because I was afraid that you would not receive my letters in time telling you of my new arrival date of 12th July. If you were still expecting me on the 5th, and gone to the airport, that would have been a catastrophe!

All this week I've been terribly hyperactive. I have a thousand things to do, from visiting relations, saying good-bye to friends, etc. through to carrying out every kind of bureaucratic procedures with regard to the degree title, and in connection to the trunk I am sending by ship; early tomorrow I have to go to the British Consulate to collect a document accrediting me as a student, because the Argentine Customs requests before it agrees to send my books, etc. At 11 am I'll be meeting my friend Silvia Kuperschmidt who is in Buenos Aires for a few days (she now lives in Montevideo); afterwards I'll have lunch with Mario Bronfman; at 2.30 pm I'm going to the hairdresser's

(I hate them, I visit them rarely, but at present my hair is in an impossible state); at 5 pm, I'll visit a cousin of my mother's; then I'll come back home for dinner, and at 9.30 pm my father is taking me to say good-bye to the Epstein family (his partners at work). Every day has a similar sort of exhausting timetable.

In fact, I do not know whether this letter will arrive before I do, as the post has been so delayed recently! It is almost one in the morning and I am tired, and tomorrow I have to get up early, but I so much wanted to write to you.

Goodnight, my love
Until Wednesday 12th at 10.35 am G.M.T.
Flight 812 of Swissair, Geneva-London,
At London Airport (Heathrow),
With a huge hug, and
Millions of Kisses, and
A Mountain of Love,
    Alicia

Buenos Aires
9 July 1967

Darling Steve,
    Hurry, hurry, hurricane,
I'm coming, I'm coming;
Will it be really be true?
I can hardly believe it.
No more delays, I hope,
I don't want to damage you, my love,

I love you too much.
Will we meet to collide or to coalesce?
Will we ever meet? Yes!
Will the 12th ever come? Yes!
Will our love be true and real?
I hope it will.
I want to be with you and I will be, soon –

Your own,
     Alicia

EPILOGUE

On the 11th of July 1967, Alicia enjoyed a tearful send-off from dozens of friends and relatives at Buenos Aires airport. Fate, however, still had a couple of extra hurdles to put in her way. The first Swissair flight took her uneventfully to Geneva, but when she went to board the connecting plane to London, Alicia discovered she had been booked onto the wrong flight – one that departed two hours later. She begged and pleaded with airline officials and was finally allowed to board the earlier flight on which Steve was expecting her to arrive. (Sharp-eyed readers might have noticed a discrepancy in the flight numbers mentioned in her letters.) On arrival at Heathrow, she discovered her luggage had gone astray – it had been put on the other connecting flight. Sorting out the paperwork was predictably bureaucratic so she hovered about near the automatic door to the waiting area and managed to wave to a rather nervous Steve to reassure him that she had actually arrived.

When she finally emerged from the arrivals lounge, Steve and Alicia threw themselves into their first tingling embrace and continued kissing all the way during the long drive to Steve's parents' house in Leytonstone – driving rules were not so stringent in 1967! Steve's mother, Ada, greeted Alicia warmly and gave them lunch of baked beans on toast – a meal that Alicia had never come across before. Afterwards, Alicia and Steve set off to Hampstead to spend the afternoon together, Steve's mother waving them off with a knowing smile. In response to the Radio 4 Afternoon Play, one listener asked whether, after such erotic letters, they had managed to get out of the airport without making love. Alicia replied "Just about". They returned in the evening to meet Steve's father, also called Steve, and eat Ada's excellent spread of roast lamb, baked potatoes and greens.

The early years

The couple spent their first week in London taking trips to famous landmarks like the Tower of London, Westminster Abbey and Lord's Cricket Ground where Steve tried to introduce Alicia to the joys of cricket – a game that she still finds incomprehensible. They also met up with a number of Steve's friends, including Peter and Wendy. The four of them went on a memorable camping holiday in Scotland and later took that long planned trip to Eastern Europe, eventually choosing to go to Yugoslavia. Steve and Alicia visited Enrico and Mara in Hampstead, though they never actually babysat for their children. They also had dinner with David and Margaret Ovens – but unfortunately David never did complete the famous report on the Indian fertiliser industry.

In spite of it being a rather grey August, Alicia very much enjoyed her first summer in London. Steve had to work during the week so she was a carefree tourist, walking around the city and shopping in Oxford Street. Amongst her first purchases were two machines, a typewriter and a sewing machine. A vital thing for Alicia was the freedom enjoyed by people in England. In Buenos Aires, if you were caught in the street carrying a 'subversive' book, you could be arrested, so people tended to cover such books (including Sociology textbooks!) with brown paper dustcovers.

In the Autumn, Steve joined the Ministry of Technology and became the economic adviser to Tony Benn on the civil space programme, dealing with rockets and satellites. Alicia lived with Steve's parents in Leytonstone throughout the summer and then found a room to rent in Hampstead. But in spite of all their earlier rational plans, they spent most nights in Steve's bedsit in Worsley Road, so eventually decided to rent a flat together in the area. It was clear that Alicia was in London to stay the course – in spite of her two stepbrothers' gloomy forecast that it would all be a disaster and that she would be back in Buenos Aires within three months. However, her father later on told her that he always thought it would work out well with Steve, and that he fully expected her never to return to live in Argentina.

When they moved in together, Alicia cooked, and Steve washed up – a very satisfactory arrangement that continues to this day. But Alicia did not take to Indian food, so she never did use Mrs Balbir Singh's Indian Cookery Book. Instead, Steve learnt to cook Indian food, and for a short while enjoyed showing off his culinary skills at dinner parties. The outfits that Steve brought back from India had very different histories. Alicia loved the material of her sari but did not feel at home in it, and only wore it occasionally. Her sister Ester wore her salwar kameez once, for a party where all three of them wore their Indian outfits. Steve always loved his Indian suit, and remembers wearing it at the National Theatre when the ballet dancer, Rudolph Nureyev, strolled up and looked admiringly at it.

Alicia reveled in being at the LSE while swinging London was at its height. It was the year of student upheavals throughout Europe, there was full freedom of speech and she felt in her element. However she was not impressed by the LSE's Social Anthropology course, finding it very 'imperialistic'. She found it shocking that anthropology could be considered a tool for understanding the 'natives' and therefore for the British colonial administration to 'control' them better. So, for this and other reasons, she left the LSE at the end of the first year of the Diploma.

Steve and Alicia got married on July 13th 1968, at Hampstead Registry Office in Haverstock Hill. The ceremony was followed by a very successful dancing party in a central London hotel. Alicia's father, new stepmother, and sister came to London for the occasion. Alicia's father, unsuited to living on his own, had married another widow with grown-up children. Alicia felt more relaxed about staying in England now that her father had company and somebody who could run the house, and her sister had another stepmother with whom she got on well.

Working lives

It took about a year for Alicia to become really fluent in English, and particularly to be able to understand English being spoken at speed. In the autumn of 1968 she got a secretarial job at the Tavistock Institute of Human Resources. Steve became heavily engaged in opposition to the Vietnam War, and in 1969 he was dismissed from the Civil Service for publishing material exposing the UK's complicity in the war. By then Alicia had become an Assistant Librarian at the LSE Library, in charge of their

Latin American social sciences collection, with a good salary. Steve spent the next couple of years doing part-time and freelance work, and continuing his activities as an anti-Vietnam war campaigner. Over the years, they both joined in many of the anti-war and CND marches in London.

Steve joined University College London, and spent 20 good years teaching and researching British housing policy. He also published the definitive history of British council housing for which he was awarded a Doctorate of the University of London. Over the years Steve has written a large number of academic books and specialist articles. By 1981 Steve had joined the Labour Party, and Alicia soon followed. At one stage, Steve advised Clive Soley (now Lord Soley), then Shadow Minister, on housing policy, and political activities took a lot of their time and effort. They were also close to some of the South African exiles in London – Albie Sachs, now a High Court judge in Johannesburg, and his family, lived in the flat below theirs, and their children were close friends.

In the mid-nineties Steve left the University and since then he has worked as an international economic consult-ant on short-term contracts, particularly with respect to water resources policies, in places as far spread as India (again!), Latvia, Lesotho, Mexico, Peru, Russia. He resigned from the Labour Party over the invasion of Iraq.

In the mid-seventies Alicia studied photography very seriously, and specialised in portraiture and documentary photography – mostly in black and white, developing and printing film in her own darkroom at home. The death of her father, and the difficulties of obtaining childcare made her move on to other fields. With the children at school, she became active in the Parent-Teacher Association and later became a School Governor. All her life, Alicia has continued to make clothes, knit and carry out a variety of craft activities, as her mother had done. In the eighties she became aware that you could actually study such subjects in England, and after attending a number of courses, she took a City & Guilds course in Creative Toymaking. For the next 15 years, Alicia was a professional toymaker, teaching and writing several books on soft toys, teddy bears, cloth dollmaking, etc.

In the nineties, when the girls had left school and stopped playing with toys, Alicia decided to change craft fields. A trip to the USA and an exhibition in London made her decide to become a contemporary art quilter. She is now very successful in her chosen field, teaching and exhibiting widely, and is well known in an area of craft enjoyed and practised by hundreds of thousands of women in the UK and Europe, and by millions in the USA. Her work can be seen on her website, www.alicia-merrett.co.uk and is featured on the cover of this book.

Friends and Family
During her first two years in London, Alicia had many Argentine friends, as so many people had left the country because of the military government. Her friends slowly drifted back to Argentina or to other Spanish-speaking countries, and Alicia became more immersed in English culture, making many English friends through University, work and political activities. One of the Argentines they stayed friends with for quite some time was Oscar Braun, who came to live first in Britain and then in Holland. He and his family had to flee Argentina in the mid-seventies,

to escape certain death from the military junta, as he was considered a 'subversive' for having set up a University course in Marxist economics.

Steve and Alicia's first daughter, Selena, was born in 1971 and their second, Juley, in 1975, by which time they had moved to the Tufnell Park area in London. They first lived in a rented house, and then bought a couple of large houses with a group of like-minded friends, and converted them into flats.

Alicia made a couple of trips back to Argentina in the early seventies, one of them for Ester's wedding, but for over a decade afterwards she was unable to go back to her homeland. Oscar Braun had thanked Steve for his help in various books and, given the power of the Argentine Police, Steve and Alicia felt it was unsafe for them to travel whilst the military were still in power. In the mid-eighties, after the Falklands war, they finally returned, taking Selena and Juley to meet their cousins. Alicia's visits to Argentina have been few and far between – only five trips in over forty years with Steve accompanying her just twice. Alicia has perhaps become 'too English' and finds she no longer easily fits in to Argentine society. Alicia still keeps in close contact with her sister, Ester and step-brother, Horacio – by email now instead of by letter – and plans to pay a much overdue visit before too long.

Alicia's father and his third wife visited them in London quite regularly. Ester and her husband and daughters also came to see them, as did Horacio and Haydée. Alicia's father died in 1979 at the age of 75, and his third wife survived him by four years. Steve's mother, Ada, was a much-loved doting grandmother who has been greatly missed since her death in 1990. Around this time,

Alicia made a number of trips to Israel to visit her Aunt Elena, her mother's sister, by then in her eighties. She also re-established close friendships with her cousins and their children.

Alicia is as fascinated by machines as she has always been – she took to computers like a duck to water – while Steve continues to hate them as much as before! Their daughters inherited their father's technophobe tendencies, but thankfully some of the grandchildren seem to lean towards Alicia's technophilia. Steve's gift lies in his uncanny ability to relate to, and entertain, children – a quality inherited by Juley – and he has a very special relationship with his grandchildren.

Selena and Juley both have long-term partners and children, and live in the South West of England. At the end of 2008 Steve and Alicia left London after more than forty years in the city, and moved to Somerset to be nearer to their daughters and their five grandchildren Louis, Ella May, Sol, Sasha and Melody.

Alicia still keeps Steve's first present, the Indian heart-shaped trinket box, by the side of her bed.

APPENDIX I

Darling Alicia – The Radio Play

This book is dedicated to Gill Pulsford, a long time friend of Steve and Alicia, who first saw the potential for drama in their letters. Gill, then a BBC editor, introduced them to one of her producers, Vernee Samuel, who turned the hundreds of pages of letters into a 45 minute drama. On the 27 July 2006, Darling Alicia was broadcast as an Afternoon Play on Radio 4. It was repeated on 12 Oct 2007 and the credits run as follows:

Darling Alicia
Adapted by Vernee Samuel

Alicia: Celia Meiras
Steve: Carl Prekopp

With the real voices of Alicia and Steve Merrett.

Produced and Directed by Vernee Samuel and David Hunter

APPENDIX II

What happened to some of the people mentioned in the letters?

Family
Alicia's sister **Ester** married and had two daughters. She and her husband later divorced and she now has a new partner. The whole family still lives in Argentina, and one of her daughters has given Ester two grandsons. Ester became an artist and is now involved in fashion design and jewellery making.

Alicia's elder stepbrother **Carlos** was District Psychiatrist of Jerusalem and still lives in Israel. He married twice and has four daughters and many grandchildren and great-grandchildren.

Alicia's younger stepbrother **Horacio** is a neurologist. He and his wife **Haydée** still live in Buenos Aires. They have a son and twin daughters, and two grandchildren.

Alicia's **Aunt Elena,** her mother's sister, died at nearly 90, and Alicia stayed in close contact with two of her children, Alicia's cousins. The death of her eldest cousin, **Shula**, a fellow quilter, in 2007, was a sad blow.

Friends and colleagues
Oscar Braun, Steve's Argentine friend, was killed in a car

accident in Holland at the end of the seventies. His young son, who was sitting in the back, survived unscathed. Steve and Alicia still sorely miss Oscar. His son, Miguel Braun, grew up in Argentina, studied economics in Buenos Aires and Harvard, and, like his father, became a highly regarded academic.

Derek Jacobi, Steve's school friend, is a world-famous actor and they still meet up when they can.

Willie and Nicky Van Ryckeghem, close friends of Steve when he was in Argentina, returned to Belgium, where Steve and Alicia visited them once, but they soon lost contact.

Paul Matthews, Steve's friend and colleague in Delhi, married his Indian bride, Rani. The four of them met in London once but to Steve's very great regret, he lost touch with Paul at the end of the sixties.

Marc Nuizière, one of Steve's colleagues at the Unit in LSE, went back to France and was involved in the "May 68" events. He went to work in Chile when Salvador Allende was president. They still keep in touch and meet up now and then.

Sir Robert Rae C.B. returned to the Isle of Man but died in 1971 before he could meet Alicia. His obituary read "We have lost a faithful friend, counsellor and a highly esteemed elder. His presence radiated a gentleness and refinement."

David Rubin, another of Steve's friends in India, finished his novel, *Love in the Melon Season*, in which the character Michael Dowson is based on Steve. He died in 2008.

Stephka Peneva, Steve's Bulgarian scientist friend from India, returned eventually to Sofia and her husband, and they had two sons. Steve and Alicia visited them several times and they still keep in touch.

Peter and Wendy remained their good friends for a number of years, but eventually the two couples drifted apart. Peter and Wendy separated some years later, and Peter continued his academic career as a social scientist, most recently at Essex University.

Mara and Enrico left London after Enrico completed his Ph.D. Later, they separated, Mara re-marrying a famous Argentine poet, and Enrico becoming a highly regarded Professor in the University of California NanoSystems Institute.

Alicia's University friend **Graciela** studied in the USA for a year, married on her return to Argentina, and had two sons.

Alicia lost touch with most of her University friends as many of them had to leave Argentina for political reasons. Some prospered in other countries while others did not survive the culling of 'subversives' carried out by the military Junta of 1976, and count among the 'disappeared'.